Mutual Causality in Buddhism and General Systems Theory

SUNY Series in Buddhist Studies

Kenneth Inada, Editor

Mutual Causality in Buddhism and General Systems Theory

The Dharma of Natural Systems

Joanna Macy

State University of New York Press

Published by
State University of New York Press, Albany

For information, address State University of New York
Press, State University Plaza, Albany, N.Y., 12246

Production by M. R. Mulholland
Marketing by Theresa A. Swierzowski

Library of Congress Cataloging in Publication Data

Macy, Joanna, 1929–
    Mutual causality in Buddhism and general systems theory : the
dharma of natural systems / by Joanna Macy.
        p.   cm.—(SUNY series in Buddhist studies)
    Includes bibliographical references and index.
    ISBN 0–7914–0636–9 (CH : acid-free). — ISBN 0–7914–0637–7 (PB :
acid-free)
    1. Causation (Buddhism)   2. Pratītyasamutpāda.   I. Title.
II. Series.
BQ4240.M33   1991
294.3′422′011—dc20
                                                              90–39937
                                                              CIP

10 9 8 7 6 5 4 3 2 1

For my husband Fran

Contents

Preface

Encounters between modern Western thought and ancient Asian philosophies figure among the more fruitful features of the twentieth century. Buddhism, with its reliance on direct experience and its sophisticated, psychological analysis, offers particular rewards to Western inquiry. It reveals remarkable relevance to a major shift occurring in contemporary thought and science—the shift toward a dynamic, systemic, process view of reality.

In my own encounter with Buddhism, which started a quarter century ago among Tibetans in India and continued with doctoral studies in the West, the teachings which I first found most compelling point to the process nature of the self. They reveal the self as a changing, fluid construct created by the dynamics of mind. Through attention to these dynamics, without recourse to supernatural entities or absolutes, these teachings explain the suffering we create, the traps we fabricate through fear and greed, and the possibility of liberation from them. I apprehended this at first through the doctrine of *anattā* (no-self), aided by instruction in *Vipassanā* or insight meditation. Later, in my studies of the early texts, I realized the extent to which this perspective on the self arises within a more comprehensive view of reality.

The contingent nature of the self—and the consequent spaciousness and workability of experience—is, I soon learned, grounded in the radical interdependence of *all* phenomena, set forth in the Buddha's central doctrine of causality, *paṭicca samuppāda*, or dependent co-arising. In this doctrine, which the Buddha equated with the Dharma, or saving teaching itself, everything arises through mutual conditioning in reciprocal interaction. Indeed the very word *Dharma* conveys not a substance or essence, but orderly process itself—the way things work.

This fact was initially obscured to me because of the tendency, evident in all major religions of the last two and a half millennia, to posit metaphysical absolutes as source of value and goal of spiritual life. Even in Buddhism, at various points in its history and despite the original teaching of dependent co-arising, supraphenomenal levels of reality came to be postulated, with consequent value dis-

tinctions between the realms of mind and matter. Furthermore, perhaps because a hierarchical view of reality and its concomitant, a
one-way linear view of causation, is endemic to mainstream Western thought, it led many Western scholars, as I point out in Chapter
3, to ignore or distort the distinctive meaning of *paṭicca samuppāda*.

It took me a while, therefore, and some dogged study of early
texts, to realize that such a hierarchical view of reality was not true
of the early teachings of the Buddha. No aspect of reality, even
nibbāna, the cessation of suffering, is separate from dependent coarising. Not only suffering but liberation from suffering unfolds according to the Dharma of mutual causality, without the necessity of
supraphenomenal absolutes. I was struck by this radical departure
from the one-way causal notions that imbue much of both Western
thought and Hindu philosophy.

This recognition was aided by general systems theory, which I
encountered some eight years after meeting Buddhism. The systems view of reality as process, its perception of self-organizing patterns of physical and mental events, and the principles it discerned
in the dynamics of these natural systems struck me as remarkably
consonant with the Buddha's teachings. Like the doctrine of *paṭicca
samuppāda*, systems theory sees causality as reciprocal, arising from
interweaving circuits of contingency.

Furthermore, because general systems theory draws its data
from contemporary physical and life sciences, it reveals this kind of
causality at play throughout the observable universe. This helped
me discern in the early Buddhist scriptures the breadth and import
of *paṭicca samuppāda*. Systems theory cast light on the Buddha's distinctive teachings about the relation of mind to body, the relation of
past actions to present choices, and the relation of the self to society
and nature. Conversely, I also found Buddhist teachings illuminating the import of systems concepts.

I found myself engaged, therefore, in a mutual hermeneutic
between these two bodies of thought as I used each to interpret the
other. Despite the obvious contrasts in their origins and purposes,
each of them—early Buddhism and contemporary systems theory—
can clarify what the other is saying.

Through this reciprocal hermeneutic, intricate and overarching
patterns and principles of order emerge. They constitute a Dharma
of Natural Systems, which I perceive as a philosophic basis and
moral grounding for the ecological worldview emerging in our era.
This emerging dharma discloses moral values that do not stem from
divine commandments nor from human nobility alone but instead

inhere in the fundamental causal interconnectedness of all phenomena. This interdependence sets the limits and provides the scope for our conscious participation in reality.

I wrote this book out of religious and philosophic concerns made urgent by the global crisis of our time. The progressive destruction of our biosphere, the acceleration of human need and desperation, and the risks of deliberate or accidental use of nuclear weaponry are the context for this work. These developments overshadow all our lives. My own active engagement with these issues over the past three decades, as researcher and organizer in the U.S. and overseas, ran parallel to my scholarly work on this book and posed some of the questions I sought to clarify.

How is reality organized? I wanted to know, so as to allow effective action for the healing of our world. How are we connected with each other and all beings? Are the dynamics which can free us from egocentricity—and which I glimpsed in Buddhist practice—reflected in patterns of nature and society as well? What do these systemic patterns tell us about our power to act and our resilience in the face of severe political and economic dislocations?

My pursuit of these questions was shaped by certain moral and philosophic biases concerning the source of values and the locus of power. In a hierarchical view of reality, and in the linear, one-way view of causality to which it leads, both value and power are attributed to an absolute or entity or essence, unaffected by the play of phenomena. I describe this in Chapter 1 where I also show that even when belief in an absolute erodes, habits of thought bred by the one-way view persist in the assumption that power works from the top down. This notion becomes particularly dangerous in a time of increasing planetary disruptions and scarcities. It tempts people to assume that personal freedom is inimical to collective survival, and that order must be imposed from above. Indeed the political fanaticisms and religious fundamentalisms of our time give voice to the belief that common will and coordinated action require subservience to a particular leader or deity.

While exploring both Buddhism and general systems theory, I uncovered a radically different perspective on the source and nature of power. As both these bodies of thought make clear, order is not imposed from above, by mind exerting its will on dumb material forces; it is intrinsic to the self-organizing nature of the phenomenal world itself. When we recognize our participation in its co-arising patterns, we can claim our power to act. We can then, through our choices, give expression and efficacy to the coordination at play in all life-forms. The political implications of this view, in terms of the free flow of information and the welcoming of diversity, are elaborated in this book in both Buddhist and systems theoretical terms.

To act for the healing of our world, we must move beyond the fear and hatred of matter that we have inherited from hierarchical views of reality and the unidirectional causal paradigm. My own bias in this regard helped me discern how both Buddhism and general systems theory revalorize the material realm. Indeed, they present it no longer as a separate realm from mind, but as causally co-arising with mental events or inseparably correlative to them. The relief and spaciousness that this perspective allows to human consciousness is, I hope, conveyed in this book.

The dharma of living systems presented here focuses on its most distinctive feature: the mutual causality of all phenomena. It does this in scholarly terms, drawing from the two bodies of thought which most clearly articulate this causal paradigm. I take this academic approach for three reasons. I want to present the case for mutual causality in the broadest philosophical terms. I want to correct and enhance scholarly understanding of the Buddha's teaching of *paṭicca samuppāda*. And I want to show the philosophic and moral implications of general systems theory.

The focus on scholarly goals excludes discussion of the political and social activities that accompanied and encouraged my study of mutual causality. During the years that this book has been in preparation, I undertook work in the U.S. and overseas which let me see the dynamics of mutual causality in practical terms. The forms of this work have been described in three books, but I refer to them now to convey some of the wider contexts of my thought and experience and some particular applications of mutual causality.

In the late 1970s and early 1980s I studied and participated in a Buddhist-inspired community development movement in Sri Lanka called Sarvodaya Shramadana. With the support of a Ford Foundation grant I researched this movement's use of Buddhist teachings to motivate local villagers in self-help projects differing from the dominant Western model of centralized, mechanized, capital-intensive development. I took part in training programs for rural organizers, cut roads and dug latrines in Sarvodaya work camps, and sat in on countless meetings with villagers and local Sarvodaya monks and organizers. My findings from this rewarding experience are detailed in my book *Dharma and Development*.[1] As it describes, I found that the movement applied Buddhist teachings more pervasively and explicitly than I had expected. In particular, I saw how the Buddha's teachings of *paṭicca samuppāda* was conveyed in ways that empowered villagers to take charge of their lives.

The teaching of dependent co-arising is painted on the walls of Sarvodaya village centers, with the four Noble Truths portrayed as wheels of causation. These wheels illustrate the interdependence of phenomena. Interlinked factors of disease, illiteracy, poverty and conflict portray the co-arising causes of degeneration. On the positive side, causal wheels showing the mutual interaction of health workers, teachers, and cooperating groups of mothers, farmers, and youth reveal how they can mutually reinforce each other, and how the process of awakening can begin at any point. Sarvodaya's modes of organizing, through collaborative work camps and self-help projects, provide the practical, persuasive basis for this understanding. I repeatedly saw in action what the movement's president, A. T. Ariyaratne expressed in words: "A Sarvodaya workers learns to understand and to experience the interrelationship that exists between different manifestations of the living world."[2]

A quote from *Dharma and Development* conveys some of the terms they use: "Because reality is seen as dependently co-arising, or systemic in nature, each and every act is understood to have an effect on the larger web of life, and the process of development is perceived as multidimensional. One's personal awakening (*purushodaya*) is integral to the awakening of one's village (*gramodaya*) and both play integral roles in *deshodaya* and *vishvodaya*, the awakening of one's country and one's world. Being interdependent, these developments do not occur sequentially, in a linear fashion, but synchronously, each abetting and reinforcing the other through multiplicities of contacts and currents, each subtly altering the context in which other events occur."[3]

Tragedy has overtaken Sri Lanka since the years of my local participation in the Sarvodaya movement. Tragedy and civil war, fostered by extremists in the conflicting ethnic populations of Tamils and Sinhalese, and aggravated by external interventions and supplies of arms, rip the society apart. The fact that the Sarvodaya movement has survived as a major force for reconciliation and rehabilitation is in large part due, I believe, to its understanding and teaching of interdependence.

Work for social change in the West provided an equally instructive arena for perceiving and applying the dynamics of mutual causality. Alarmed by the health effects of nuclear power plants, I engaged over the years in efforts to organize fellow citizens to take action for a safe environment. In this process I became increasingly aware of the psychological factors which impede people from responding to the massive dangers of our time, even when they suffer from them in their own lives. Clearest among these are avoidance, denial, and psychic numbing.

Buddhist experience led me to understand these phenomena, and the powerlessness to which they give rise, in terms of dysfunctional notions of separate selfhood. Drawing from both Buddhist practice and the perspectives of general systems theory I developed an approach which took form in group processes and training and came to be known as "despair and empowerment work." This approach helps people to overcome denial by acknowledging their pain for the world, to experience this pain as healthy evidence of their interconnectedness in the web of life, and to recognize this systemic interdependence as the source of their power to take effective action. The theory and methods of this work are described in my book *Despair and Personal Power in the Nuclear Age.*[4]

That book sets forth "the psychological and spiritual work of dealing with our knowledge and feelings about the present planetary crisis in ways that release energy and vision for creative response. . . . This work helps us to increase our awareness of [this crisis] without feeling overwhelmed by the dread, grief, anger and sense of powerlessness that it arouses in us."[5]

"As our pain for the world is rooted in our interconnectedness with all life, so surely is our power. But the kind of power at work in the web of life, in and through open systems, is quite different from our customary notions of power."[6] To elaborate that kind of power, and to offer group methods for perceiving it, I draw directly from the considerations of mutual causality described in this present book.

Working with many thousands of individuals in hundreds of workshops in this and other countries, I learned a lot about our dependent co-arising. I saw how the acknowledgment of pain for our world, when understood as evidence of our interconnectedness, can shift people to an awareness of their profound mutual belonging, and how that awareness in turn helps them instigate creative, collaborative projects for social change.

The Norwegian philosopher Arne Naess coined the term *deep ecology* for this mutual belonging that extends beyond the individual or family or even species. I found this term to be an appropriate, secular referent for *dependent co-arising*—and it is easier to say. I began to use it increasingly in connection with the methods that I and my colleagues were developing to free people for constructive social action. These methods continue to draw from Buddhist practice and general systems theory, and they provide personal experience of deep ecology—in accordance with Naess's call for forms of community therapy appropriate to our planetary crisis. Deep ecology work, as it has come to be known, seeks to expand the notion of self beyond the confines of ego and personal history, and to extend concepts of self-interest to include the welfare of all beings.

A popular approach to this work, with group processes, is offered in the book I co-authored with Arne Naess and rainforest activists John Seed and Pat Fleming called *Thinking Like a Mountain: Toward a Council of all Beings.*[7] Since its publication, the methods this book describes have spread widely, especially among environmental activists in North America, Australasia, and the countries of Eastern and Western Europe.

"Once we have experienced the fierce joy of life that attends extending our identity into nature, once we realize that the nature within and the nature without are continuous, then we too may share in the exquisite beauty and effortless grace associated with the natural world."[8] These words of John Seed become more real for me each time I facilitate deep ecology work, and see the healing and empowerment that occur as people open to the dynamic interconnectedness that links them to each other and their world.

These three areas of action—Sarvodaya, despair and empowerment work, and deep ecology work—have provided me fresh perspectives on mutual causality. Yet, reflecting particular political and social concerns, they are tangential to the philosophic purposes of this book. My aim here is more fundamental: to explore the nature and causal implications of the systemic co-arising of phenomena. This dharma of natural systems is offered in the hope that it will serve not only systems theory and Buddhist scholarship, but also our common welfare.

Notes

1. Macy, *Dharma and Development.*

2. *Ibid.*, p. 33.

3. *Ibid.*, p. 33.

4. Macy, *Despair and Personal Power.*

5. *Ibid.*, p. xiii.

6. *Ibid.*, p. 30.

7. Seed, *et al.*, *Thinking Like a Mountain.*

8. *Ibid.*, p. 16.

Introduction

Causality, usually defined as the interrelation of cause and effect, is about how things happen, how change occurs, how events relate. The Buddhist term *Dharma* carries the same meaning. It also refers to the Buddha's teachings as a whole, stemming as they do from his central doctrine of causality; for the ways that life is understood and lived are rooted in causal assumptions.

A major shift is occurring in our time from notions of linear, unidirectional causality to perceptions of dynamic interdependence where phenomena affect each other in a reciprocal or mutual fashion. A mutual causal paradigm emerges, and the conceptual tools for understanding it can be found in general systems theory, an interdisciplinary approach arising from science. The systems view of causal process also reveals striking convergences with the Buddha's teaching of causality, called *paṭicca samuppāda*, or dependent co-arising. These convergences are illuminating, although they arise between bodies of thought that are distant from each other in time, culture, data, and methods.

The purpose of this book is to use these two bodies of thought—general systems theory and Buddhism—to illuminate the character of mutual causality and to let a Dharma of Natural Systems emerge. It examines the causal processes at work in a dynamically interdependent world; it studies their implications for our notion of the self and its experience; and it explores the ethical imperatives inherent in a world view where no absolute exists to constitute an ultimate locus of power and moral sanction.

Early Buddhist teachings and contemporary systems theory provide the basis for this book because I find that they yield the clearest and fullest articulations of mutual causal process that are available. In addition to providing complementary perspectives on mutual causality, one from the ancient East and one from the modern West, these two bodies of thought also offer tools for understanding and interpreting each other. Despite their differences in origins, methods and goals, a useful, reciprocal hermeneutic can function between them.

Systems concepts provide explanations and analogies which can illuminate Buddhist ideas that are less accessible from a linear causal point of view. Systems theory also offers a broad range of data showing the operation throughout the phenomenal universe of the causal principle the Buddha taught. For its part, Buddhism reveals the existential, religious, and ethical implications of the systems view of process. It allows us to see, in the arising and interaction of self-organizing systems, causes of suffering and of liberation from suffering.

For my examination of the Buddha's teaching of causality, I rely chiefly on the *Sutta* and *Vinaya Piṭakas* of the Pali Canon. Because these scriptures are generally agreed to represent pre-Abhidharmist thought, I call them "early Buddhist teachings." In the long, vast, multi-cultural Buddhist tradition, the texts are accepted as authoritative by all. I focus on them, furthermore, because their presentation of dependent co-arising differs from the Abhidharma in some subtle but significant ways, which, as I delineate in Chapter 3, have implications for our understanding of mutual causality. These differences are often overlooked since the Abhidharma has tended to influence later interpretations of the Pali texts as a whole, and *paṭicca samuppāda* in particular. While the later concept of emptiness (*śunyatā*) in Mahayana Buddhism renewed the emphasis on radical relativity found in the early teachings, such similarities fall outside the focus of this book.

Since I draw from the Pali texts, Buddhist terms are generally given in their Pali form. An exception is my usage of the words *dharma* and *karma*, whose later Sanskrit forms have become so prevalent in the West as to make their Pali forms (*dhamma* and *kamma*) seem unnecessarily specialized.

My exposition of general systems theory is based on the foundational works of its pioneering thinkers in the life sciences and systems cybernetics. For my discussion of the wider implications of its causal premises, I draw as well from a wide range of systems theorists in philosophy, psychology, and the social sciences. Mathematical formulations and graphs of systems properties and circuits are, perhaps fortunately for the general reader, beyond the purview of this book.

In the course of a paradigm shift, terminology can be awkward, for the words at our disposal are stamped by previous usage. This is particularly true in the case of *causality*, which carries connotations accumulated in the linear, unidirectional paradigm, where to a large extent, as I show in Chapter 2, causation is linear by definition. In this paradigm, causality excludes the notion that the cause of an effect could be influenced in turn by the effect itself. From such a perspective, mutual causality is a contradiction in terms. I retain, however, as do many systems theorists, the term *causality* in its widest sense to refer to the flow of influence between phenomena, how one thing affects another. I employ the terms *causality, causation, determinacy,* and *determination* synonymously. The expressions *mutual causality, reciprocal causality, dependent co-arising, interdependence,* and *interdetermination* are, for the purposes of this book, taken as roughly equivalent in meaning.

As to the term *general systems theory,* it is not a theory proper, in the sense of a single hypothesis about a given set of phenomena, so much as a coherent set of principles applying to all irreducible wholes. These wholes, be they molecule, cell, organism, personality, or social body, reveal common principles and properties that are amenable to understanding when we view them as self-organizing systems. What we have here is not a theory about a general system, but rather a general theory (or set of principles) about systems, which allows their dynamics and characteristics to become intelligible. While it has been popularly identified largely with its application in computer science and organizational management, its relevance is much broader, as seen in such fields as psychology, political science, ecology, and philosophy.

Some thinkers prefer the term *cybernetics* for the concepts and processes pertaining to self-regulating systems. When I use the term in this book, I broaden it to *systems-cybernetics* and use it interchangeably with *general systems theory,* which, deriving from the life sciences as well as information and computer science, is more inclusive.

The book is organized so as to permit the early Buddhist teaching of causality and the general systems view to emerge separately, in sequence, and then interact as their implications are explored. The initial chapter provides an overview of causal ideas, with emphasis on the origins and nature of the linear, one-way view of causality in the West. The main body of this work then falls into two sections. The first is devoted to expositions of mutual causality from the early Buddhist and systems perspectives.

The final portion of the book is concerned with implications of mutual causality for considerations of epistemology, ontology, and value. Here the Buddhist and systems views interact more directly as we consider in turn the image of the self, the nature of its knowing, the relation of mind and body, the self-organizing character of choice or karma, and, in the final three chapters, the social ethics implicit in mutual causality.

Part One

Background

1

Considering Causality

The clear bead at the center changes everything.

—Rumi[1]

Assumptions about causality are basic to the choices we make. Whether we are brushing our teeth or casting a vote, they impinge on our expectations and actions. Yet theories about the interrelationship of cause and effect rarely claim our attention outside the classroom or the philosopher's study. They seem too abstract to be relevant to the concrete situations in which we find ourselves, where our attention focuses on more pressing questions—like why and how something is to be done.

Stepping back, however, we recognize that the very questions of why and how are the substance of causal theories, which spring from the primordial human desire to understand why things are as they are and how they change. Just as these theories vary, so can a problem be approached in different ways. Once we shift the focal length of our thought to include these underlying assumptions, new possibilities emerge—both in the way we understand our world and in the way we respond to it. Then, like "the clear bead at the center" of which Rumi spoke, these possibilities "change everything."

Like the Air We Breathe

Presuppositions about cause and effect are as invisible and pervasive as the air we breathe. They are implicit in every world view, at work in every enterprise.

In science they influence the selection of empirical data and the tests to which the data are put. In medicine they inform the diagnoses of disorders and prescriptions for their cure. They imbue the goals of religious belief systems and the practices they enjoin. They shape a culture's perceptions of power as well as the means by which it is attained and exerted.

In our personal lives assumptions about cause and effect are no less telling. They provide the very ground for our sense of coherence—that is, the ways we find the world intelligible and the ways we posit our relationship to it. Do we see events as random, discontinuous, and beyond our control? Or do we see effective relationships that give leverage to our actions? These are essentially questions of causality and they shape our attitudes and behaviors. They are basic to our notions of responsibility and our attributions of blame and guilt. They color our encounters with conflict, guide our efforts to find solutions. Causal assumptions even affect the relative reality we ascribe to ourselves and our world. For the relationship we see between the mental and material realms of experience can lead us to ignore one or the other as a significant determinative factor.

In eras when a world view goes unchallenged, given notions about causality are taken for granted. Considered self-evident they are no less operative for being tacitly assumed, whether by voodoo priest, Zen monk, of IBM executive. These assumptions constitute a *paradigm*, to use the term widely adopted from the work of Thomas S. Kuhn, philosopher of science.[2] As a mindset about how things happen, a paradigm represents the mental context within which problems are perceived and endeavors mounted. These endeavors tend to justify the assumptions on which they are based until problems—queries and data which do not fit the paradigm—accrue to dramatize the inadequacy of the paradigm's assumptions. In periods of radical change, dissonance arises between previous assumptions and present experience; the paradigm is brought into question—and into consciousness.

This is happening. Words like *synergy, feedback, causal loops, symbiosis* have become current and useful. They suggest that events affect each other in a back-and-forth manner, creating circuits and networks of contingency where causes and effects interact reciprocally. They express a paradigm which challenges the assumptions about causation that have dominated Western culture for over two millenia.

What this new paradigm challenges is not the notion of causality itself, that events modify each other in objective and intelligible ways, but rather the manner in which causality has been perceived. It challenges the idea that causal action flows in one direction only, from cause to effect, from producer to produced, like a series of billiard balls or falling dominoes. To understand the momentous nature of this development that is taking place in our time, let us look at what it replaces: the linear unidirectional paradigm.

The Linear Unidirectional Causal Paradigm

As the words suggest, we refer here to a one-way flow of influence from the cause A to the effect B.

$$A \rightarrow B$$

The direction of causal efficacy is from the producer to the produced, from the action of the agent or actor to its results in the acted-upon. This causal model implies that there is no new behavior in the effect B which cannot be traced back to its cause A. Another way of putting this is that there is no less information in A than in B. A corollary of this assumption, operative in scientific research, is that distinctive features in the effect B must correspond to similar features in the cause A. Hence it is assumed that similar causes yield similar effects, and that different effects derive from different causes.

By the same logic causal chains arise, as B acts on C, and C in turn effects D and so on.

$$A \rightarrow B \rightarrow C \rightarrow D \rightarrow \ldots$$

The chains carry the causal impulse or efficacy onward in a series of effects, like a chain of command. By these chains of cause and effect, both explanations and predictions are made. Explanations are contrived by tracing the chain backward, to find out what started it all. Predictions are formulated by extrapolating it forward. The operative assumption is that from a complete knowledge of the present (hypothetical as that may be), the past and future can be inferred.

The unidirectional causal flow is also called "linear." In physics and mathematics the term *linear* denotes a uniform progression which, when its formula is graphed, yields a straight line. Put in informational terms, we can say that, in linear causality, inputs determine outputs in proportion to the information the inputs carry. An example is a simple machine like a typewriter whose printout is determined by which keys are struck—a one to one effect, in contrast to a computer whose printout is codetermined by its memory stores. As reflected in its popular usage, the term *linear* carries connotations of *predictable* and *mechanistic*.

One-Way Causality in the West

The linear paradigm owes its centrality in Western thought to the Greeks, and particularly to the fact that it was Parmenides and not Heraclitus whose views took hold of subsequent major thinkers.

The view of reality offered by Heraclitus was dynamic: He saw reality as an ever-changing river where *panta rhei*, "everything flows," all is in process, arising and passing and yielding novelty. In contrast to such an unsettling vision, Parmenides of Elea, influenced perhaps by the earlier views of Anaximander who saw the world in terms of substance and not process, declared that all was permanence, a fullness of Being so complete and eternal that change itself comes into question—and is, indeed, denied. "If anything changes, something which was not comes to be; since not-being is nonexistent, change is impossible."[3] *Ex nihilo nihil fit*, he said, "nothing comes from nothing," or, put another way, all that is must pre-exist in its cause.

The import is clear: What is really real does not change.

Plato subscribed to this equation of reality with changelessness and set it in terms that deeply influenced the history of Western thought. Reluctant to deny the experience of change, he subsumed it into permanence, positing eternal and immutable Ideal Forms from which the world of change is merely derivative. Possessed of an absolute, ultimate reality, these Ideas are unaffected by changing phenomena, whose shapes are but pale and imperfect copies of them. Whatever the degree of reality subsequently accorded to the world of change, unidirectional causality is grounded here, in the assumption that the effect pre-exists in the cause.

The principles of causation developed by Aristotle bore the Parmenidean imprint as well. Giving more attention to the empirical world of experience, Aristotle accorded reality to change. Things are as we see them, changing. Yet he still assumed that stability or permanence was primary and that, therefore, change must be accounted for as derivative from that stability—as caused by some external agent. Everything that moves must be moved by something else, for matter itself is passive and inert.

Aristotle's delineation of the forms of causation profoundly shaped categories of subsequent Western thought. He posited four determinants of phenomena:

- the material cause (the stuff of which a thing is made, say, the clay of a pot),
- the formal cause (the form a thing takes, the shape of the pot),
- the efficient cause (acting externally upon it, as potter to clay), and
- the final cause (the thing's purpose, or the goal the potter had in mind).

Of these four causes, only the efficient cause moves. The first two, material and formal, are motionless and incapable of change, and the fourth acts only by attraction, without itself moving. If change occurs, it must be pushed into existence (by the efficient cause) or pulled into being (by the final cause). On both their parts the action is unilateral and unidirectional. Given this unidirectionality Aristotle was, by his own logic, drawn into the postulation of an Unmoved Mover, as a final cause of phenomena. Sometimes, to explain how things become, he thought there must be a plurality of Unmoved Movers; sometimes he concluded there was only one— and in that way he saw God. This was a God whose unidirectionality of influence is so thorough and uncompromised that he is subject to no external action. This God cannot respond to lesser beings or even have a thought outside the divine self.[4]

In the third century C.E., Hellenistic philosopher Plotinus took one-way causality and cast it in imagery that strongly stamped subsequent thought. In seeking to understand the One toward which his soul and intellect yearned, this Neoplatonic mystic borrowed the image of the sun, which he saw shedding its effulgence without being affected in return. Plotinus viewed creation as a kind of "overflow of the One," and all things as emanations of this "eternally perfect, unmoved," and sun-like One.[5] As being radiates out from the One, like light from a light bulb, its power naturally and gradually lessens with distance, and entities become progressively multiple and impure, less conscious, less real, and less valuable. In this manner "what is eternally perfect produces something inferior to itself," without its own power and radiance being in any way lessened.[6] The Neoplatonic postulation of one single, unaffected source of being, along with its persuasive imagery of light, entered Christian theology through Augustine and others, and firmly anchored one-way causality in the Western mind.

A millenium later the monumental work of Thomas Aquinas carried forward the one-way notion of causality and in explicitly Christian terms. Thomas used the logical necessity of the Unmoved Mover as a proof of God's existence; continuing to assume a one-way causal flow, he argued that God was necessary to avoid the only other and untenable alternative, infinite regress. In this fashion the Hebrew God who interacted with his Chosen People, scolding and making covenants with them, as well as the God of the New Testament, who entered the world to suffer in human flesh, took on the Greek mantle of static perfection. From this fusion derives God's awesome features of omnipotence, immutability, and impassibility—for by logical necessity, God is incapable of being affected by his creation. Though considered to be all-powerful, he is yet unable to change and is above all emotion or response.

Mary and the saints filled the gap between divine aloofness and human need. They were moved by the prayers of the faithful and interceded on their behalf. But when the Protestant reformers evicted these mediators, their followers were left with an absolute Unmoved Mover. His omnipotence and omniscience made the doctrine of predestination reasonable and even believable.

To be aloof from the actions of others and unaffected by them became a sign of one's moral strength.

> Who, moving others are themselves as stone
> Unmoved, cold and to temptation slow:
> They rightly do inherit heaven's graces
> And husband nature's riches from expense.
>
> (Shakespeare, Sonnet 2)

Descartes' rationalism did not mitigate this one-way causality. In the radically dualistic move that separated mind from matter into two discontinuous realms, he accorded all efficacy to his idea of God, "infinite, eternal, immutable, independent, all-powerful, and by which I myself and everything else, if anything else does exist, have been created."[7] God's unilateral power extends to the very concepts the thinker can make about him; that is, as Descartes explained, he can derive the idea of himself from the idea of God, but not the idea of God from the idea of himself. Therefore, he concluded, the source of the idea of God must be God himself. By virtue of the Cartesian separation of mind from matter, the aloofness of this God now becomes emulated and mirrored in the aloofness of the human mind from the phenomenal world. Categorically distinct from this world of contingency and matter, mind can now imagine itself acting upon the world in a similarly impassive and unidirectional fashion.

The rise of modern science incorporated the unidirectional causal model, although Unmoved Movers and Ideal Forms, as well as Aristotle's formal and final causes, were rejected as both unnecessary and unempirical. Only material and efficient causes remained appropriate to scientific inquiry—and both, in their different ways, were assumed to have a one-way relation to the conditions they produced. Explanations were sought by reducing phenomena to their basic components, to building blocks that could be uncovered by dissection and analysis. Changes in their condition were assumed to derive from an efficient cause or external agent impinging upon them. With Newton's law of inertia, movement no longer appeared to be a secondary characteristic, less real than stability, but the notion persisted that an external force was needed to explain changes in velocity and direction.

Newton's Third Law of Motion, stating that every action produces an equal and opposite reaction, might seem to challenge the unidirectional causal paradigm. But Newton's religious beliefs remained firmly anchored in one-way causality. The God he described is so unilaterally powerful that he need not obey the very laws he created, and so unmovable that he cannot respond to prayers.[8]

The logic of the one-way paradigm led to determinism, as Pierre Laplace, the French astronomer, demonstrated. For if everything is moved by something else, how could it act otherwise than it does? Novelty, as Parmenides had asserted, is precluded. If we could conceivably detect all the external forces at work, then we could predict the movements of every star and every atom, claimed Laplace.

In contrast to such a view and in a radically empiricist move, philosopher David Hume denied causal necessity altogether. Events have no necessary and objective connection, he said, beyond our observation of the way they succeed each other in time. To escape from the determinism implicit in the unilateral causal paradigm,

Hume and his followers had to reject the objective nature of causality itself and retreat from any claim to know the external world.

Even with the later advent of dialectical and process philosophies, unidirectional causal assumptions held sway. Hegel's dialectical progression of thesis, antithesis, and synthesis seemed to allow the new and unprecedented to arise. But what unfolds in this process is the rational principle or idea that is aloof from the random and inert material stuff of the world, and shapes it unilaterally. Alfred North Whitehead's process thought of a century later strove to give scope to creativity and the emergence of novelty. Yet he posited a Platonic realm of God and 'eternal objects' endowed with a one-way causal connection with the phenomenal world. As systems philosopher Ervin Laszlo pointed out, "Whitehead's eternal objects can ingress in actuality and thus qualify its course, but actuality does not affect them."[9]

Process theologian Charles Hartshorne, writing a generation later, made these operative assumptions about causality quite explicit. "We shall assume . . . that a 'cause' in the widest meaning of the term is always independent of its particular effect, while this is always dependent on its cause."[10]

Linear causal notions have shaped the scientific method in various and telling ways. An area of research is chosen and circumscribed so that causal chains can by hypothesized and detected. The variables are reduced to those that can be empirically tested and controlled. Seeking the root cause or "active ingredient," variables are artificially separated and tested one at a time, in disregard or ignorance of their action on each other. As he proceeds, the scientist makes the caveat of "all other things being equal," although that assumption is empirically unverified.

This methodology has yielded powerful results. They seemed, at least until recently, to have served the goals of analysis, predictability, and control. But, as the tools and inquiries of scientists expand, it is increasingly evident that the universe does not always conform to expectations. When events interact and patterns are superimposed on each other, they yield novel, unpredictable, nonlinear results. As Ian Stewart, a mathematician working in chaos theory, states: "Linearity is a trap. The behavior of linear equations—like that of choirboys—is far from typical. But if you decide that only linear equations are worth thinking about, self-censorship sets in. Your textbooks fill with triumphs of linear analysis, its failures buried so deep that the graves go unmarked and the existence of the graves goes unremarked."[11]

One-Way Causality in Indian Thought

The notion that causal efficacy flows in one direction only is not exclusive to the West. We find it enshrined in the thought of ancient India as well, though its forms and the goals that it served are distinctive and indigenous. It arose as early as the Vedas, the earliest scriptures of the second and first millennia B.C.E.

In seeking to determine the ṛta, or order, underlying all phenomena, the postulation was made that change can be understood in terms of a potency inherent in these phenomena. It was termed svadhā, or own power,—that is, a power or property inherent in the cause to produce the effect. As such it stands in clear contrast to the Aristotelian, Thomist, and Newtonian notion that change requires an external agent. Yet, as in the West, this causation was seen as operating in a one-way fashion independent of other variables and unaltered by its own effects.

With the Upaniṣads and to an extent unparalleled in the West, the reality of change itself came into question. As with Parmenides, Plato, and the Neoplatonists, the equation was made between the real and the immutable: Ultimate reality does not change. Yet in India that equation was taken more seriously. For some schools of thought, the phenomenal world of change was māyā, illusion. For others it was partially real or, as with Sāṃkhyan philosophy, real enough but completely disjoined from the mind and its spiritual goals. But whatever the ontological status accorded to the things of this world, they were engendered or caused in a unidirectional fashion. In the Upaniṣads and Sāṃkhya, this causal relationship was termed satkāryavāda, the effect pre-existing in its cause. Whether these Indian views consider change to be real or illusory, they are essentially linear; potency and efficacy are presented as flowing in one direction and deriving ultimately from a source that is supraphenomenal.

In the intellectual ferment that characterized sixth century B.C.E. in India, these notions were debated. It came to appear to some that causality hinged on the existence of a supreme agent whose reality could not be experienced, and that it was deterministic, foreclosing the possibility of novelty. While some schools of thought defended determinism, others, such as the acausalists or accidentalists, challenged it, arguing the notion that all is random. In the next chapter, as I present the Buddhist teaching that challenged these views, these ancient Indian views of causality will be described in more detail. For now, suffice it to say that all parties to this debate assumed that causality was either linear or nonexistent—all, that is, except the Buddhists. With the teachings of Gotama the Buddha a radically new view of causality emerged.

The Mutual Causal Paradigm in the West

Assumptions of linear unidirectional causality in the West were not without exception. Alternative views arose, mainly among mathematicians and mystics, but they did not constitute a challenge to the dominant view sufficient to modify it. The visions of reality put forth by, for example, Meister Eckhart or Nicholas of Cusa implied a causal process that was not linear but circular or reciprocal. The ecstatic perspective dissolved categorical distinctions between cause and effect, and occasioned circular and seemingly paradoxical statements: "The eye by which I see God is the eye by which God sees me." Such departures, however, were neither presented nor perceived at the time as a philosophic challenge to the mainstream causal view, nor was an alternative elaborated until the mid-twentieth century.

Earlier in our century the work of physicists revealed how the position of the observer (as Albert Einstein showed) and how the act of observation (as Werner Heisenberg demonstrated) alter the perception of cause and effect. The relativization of subject and object weakened the linear causal view, but it remained for general systems theory to challenge it outright and articulate a coherent alternative.

As a metadiscipline based on the observation of invariances in many fields, general systems theory developed with the recognition that one-way causal concepts, while adequate for two-variable problems, could not be usefully applied to multivariable complex systems. Whether in the orbital patterns of atoms with more than two electrons or the electrochemical patterns of a living organism maintaining its equilibrium, variables appeared as mutually conditioned and irreducible to a linear causal chain. In consequence the systems view focused not on substance but on process—process in which cause and effect could no longer be categorically isolated.

"This scheme of isolable units acting in one-way causality has proved to be insufficient," wrote Ludwig von Bertalanffy, the biologist and father of general systems theory. "In the last resort, we must think in terms of systems of elements in mutual interaction".[12] The development of cybernetics during World War II helped in this thinking.

The invention and design of self-guiding antiaircraft missiles offered a conceptual breakthrough—a way of imaging "systems of elements in mutual interaction." The process called "feedback," by which the missiles could monitor and correct their trajectory, was found to be analogous to the biological system's capacity to maintain and organize itself in nature. It showed how orderly and purposeful patterns, be they molecules or mammals, could subsist and evolve without recourse to Unmoved Movers or final causes. Negative feedback could explain the operation of systems in equilibrium, maintaining themselves in homeostasis against the forces of entropy, while positive feedback clarified how systems could change, grow, and complexify. Both demonstrated how, through the exchange and processing of energy and information, systems function as integrated networks.

As systems scientists seek to express the import of these concepts and of the data emerging from their studies, terms like *cyclical causality, reciprocal* and *mutual causality,* and *interdetermination* are employed. To those systems theorists in the natural sciences, this causal view offers a convincing alternative to previous models of nature, either as a predetermined clockwork universe or as the blind, random play of chance. To those in the social sciences it demonstrates as well the error of behaviorism with its linear model of stimulus-response. It also permits social scientists to perceive and articulate the inadequacy of diagnosing social problems and mounting social programs in terms of isolated "causes," without regard for the mutual causation between, for example, schools, jobs, housing, and health. They see this mutual causal view as heralding an intellectual revolution and as central to a new cultural paradigm emerging in our time, one which, by that token, they describe as symbiotic, synergistic, pluralistic, mutualistic.[13]

While systems pioneer Anatol Rapoport offers the opinion that the ancient world lacked "the analytical tools" for such a process-oriented concept of causality,[14] others such as Magoroh Maruyama recognize that mutual causality has been the world view of many "unscientific" cultures. Indeed, Maruyama suggests that such a view has characterized much of human thinking in other parts of the world and throughout history, and that it is time that the modern West, scuttling its outmoded linear views, caught up with the rest of the world.[15]

The Buddhist Vision of Mutual Causality

With the emergence of this causal view in the West, it is rewarding to examine how mutual causality is presented and understood in a major religious and philosophic tradition—that of Buddhism. Buddhist thought offers a uniquely relevant perspective.

Its vision of interdependence, presenting reality as a dynamic interaction of mutually conditioning events, posits no prime cause or
unconditioned absolute to which occurrences can be traced in a linear fashion.

This causal vision, known as *paṭicca samuppāda*, or dependent
co-arising, underlies the Buddhist perception of the human predicament and of the liberation that is possible. It constitutes the
intellectual content of the Buddha's enlightenment—that part of his
transforming, intuitive realization that can be expressed in conceptual terms. It represents that character of reality, that truth about
the universe, to which Gotama awoke. It is, therefore, accorded
paramount importance in scripture; its understanding considered
requisite to release from suffering and basic to the moral and meditative practices which the Buddhist Path upholds. Upon occasion it
was identified with the Dharma itself, the order of things, the saving truth. "Whoever sees *paṭicca samuppāda* sees the *dhamma*, whoever sees the *dhamma* sees *paṭicca samuppāda*".[16] It is hard to find
another faith or value system where a doctrine of causality holds so
explicit and so central a position.

In this doctrine, reality appears as a dynamically interdependent process. All factors, mental and physical, subsist in a web of
mutual causal interaction, with no element or essence held to be
immutable or autonomous. Understanding this is important because, it is held, our suffering is caused by the interplay of these
factors and particularly by the delusion, craving, and aversion that
arise from our misapprehension of them. We fabricate our bondage
by hypostatizing and clinging to what is by nature contingent and
transient. The reifications we construct falsify experience, imprision
us in egos of our own making, doom our lives to endless rounds
of acquisition and anxiety. Being so caused, our suffering is not
endemic; it is not inevitable. It can cease, the causal play reversed.
This cessation is not effected by unity with or obedience to an
immutable being aloof from space-time, nor by the power of any
metaphysical substance or entity. Our hope hinges on no external
agency, but derives rather from the causal order itself where self
and act, project and perception are mutually determining. Hence
liberation entails a vision of the dependently co-arising nature of all
phenomena. This vision, which amounts to a reorganization of personality, is made possible by the cleansing of perception (through
meditation) and by moral conduct.

The Buddha's teaching of causality presents a radical contrast
with other views that were debated in his time in India. It departed

from previous causal notion as much as the general systems view of causality does from traditional Western thought. The Buddha cut through the debates about causation by focusing not on power but on process. In *paṭicca samuppāda* he presented causality not as a function of power inherent in an agent, but as a function of relationship—of the interaction of multiple factors where cause and effect cannot be categorically isolated or traced unidirectionally. No effect arises without cause, yet no effect is predetermined, for its causes are multiple and mutually affecting. Hence there can be novelty as well as order. Thus, Buddhist teachings presented a middle way between the positions of determinism and indeterminacy that had polarized the discussion of causality.

The centrality of this vision of causality to Buddhist thought and practice is not always obvious, because *paṭicca samuppāda* is not presented as a view that can be taught and learned in the conventional sense. Integral to the concept of dependent co-arising is the belief that the preconceptions and predispositions of the mind itself shape the reality it sees. This runs counter to commonsensical notions of a world "out there" distinct from and independent of the perceiving self. A genuine understanding of mutual causality involves a transcendence of conventional dichotomies between self and world, a transformation of the way experience is processed, which amounts to an overhauling of one's most ingrained assumptions. *Paṭicca samuppāda* is not a theory to which one assents, so much as a truth one is invited to experience, an insight one is encouraged to win, by virtue of disciplined introspection and radical attentiveness to the arising and passing away of mental and physical phenomena. The character of the reality which can break through once false constructs, dichotomies, and attachments are dissolved, has been variously termed *nirvana, emptiness, dharmadhatu, Buddha nature.* It gives rise to bliss and compassion, for, revealing the illusory nature of ego, it brings release from ego's strategies, cravings and fears. Although its experience has been described with differing metaphors and emphases, it involves, as did the Buddha's own enlightenment, a profound intuitive perception of dependent co-arising.

The Reciprocal Hermeneutic of Buddhism and General Systems Theory

Much can be discovered about mutual causality and its implications when we use perspectives of both general systems theory and early Buddhist teachings. In no other bodies of thought is such a view of causal process set forth so coherently and precisely. We can employ these two perspectives to illuminate the notion of mutual causality, each from a different angle, using different data. It is not my aim to compare systems theory and the Buddha Dharma. While their views of the nature of reality may often appear to converge and complement each other, they remain two different kinds of human enterprise.

Arising from the sciences as a cross-disciplinary tool, general systems theory represents a set of conceptualizations employed to increase understanding of natural events for purposes of explanation, prediction, and control. While these conceptualizations are increasingly appropriate to considerations of value and the human quest for meaning, the aim is hardly soteriological. The aim of the Buddha Dharma is. Like other religious systems, it presents a path of liberation. The world view it offers and the ethic it teaches provide a structure of transformation, whereby it is held that suffering can be transcended and consciousness opened to that which is of irreducible reality and value.

These two enterprises differ in method as well as purpose. Both claim to be empirical, basing their constructs on experiential evidence and relying on neither revelation nor a priori reasoning, but the kinds of data used are not the same. While general systems theory employs observations afforded by tangible scientific practices, Buddhist teachings draw from subjective experience and the intuitive insights which meditative practice can yield. Although the Buddha urged his followers to win these insights for themselves, to test them in the laboratories of their own consciousnesses, they represent data or observations that are not publicly testable because they can be known only introspectively. Respect for the intrinsic contrasts between these two bodies of thought is essential if we are to bring them together and examine their respective views of mutual causality.

Notes

1. Barks, *Open Secrets, Versions of Rumi*, Quatrain 511.

2. Kuhn, *Structure of Scientific Revolutions*.

3. Reese, *Dictionary of Philosophy and Religion*, p. 413.

4. Copleston, *History of Philosophy*, pp. 55–61.

5. Plotinus, *Ennead* 5.2.1. and 5.1.6.

6. Plotinus, *Ennead* 5.1.6.

7. Reese, *Dictionary of Philosophy and Religion*, p. 125.

8. Newton, *Opticks*, cited in Griffin, *Woman and Nature*, p. 235.

9. Laszlo, *Introduction to Systems Philosophy*, p. 104.

10. Hartshorne, *Philosophers Speak to God*, p. 502.

11. Stewart, *Does God Play Dice?* p. 83.

12. von Bertalanffy, *General Systems Theory*, p. 44.

13. Dubin, "Causality and Social Systems Analysis," pp. 107–113; Fuller, *Synergetics*; Maruyama, "Mutual Causality."

14. Rapoport, "A Philosophic View."

15. Maruyama, "Paradigmatology and its Application"

16. *Majjhima Nikāya*, I.191.

Part Two

Perceptions of Mutual Causality

2

The Buddhist Teaching of
Dependent Co-Arising

"Wonderful, lord, marvelous, lord, is the depth of this causal law and
how deep it appears. And yet I reckon it as ever so plain." "Say not
so, Ananda, say not so! Deep indeed is this causal law, and deep indeed it appears. It is through not knowing, not understanding, not
penetrating, that doctrine, that this generation has become entangled
like a ball of string, and covered with blight, like unto munja grass
and rushes, unable to overpass the doom of the waste, the woeful
way, the downfall, the constant faring on."

Two and a half millenia ago Gotama the Buddha put forth the
doctrine of causality called *paticca samuppāda*, or dependent co-
arising. It is basic to the Buddhist view of life. Indeed in no other
religion we know is a teaching of causation accorded so explicit and
fundamental a role. In this vision of reality, the existence of both
self and world are seen in terms of mutually conditioning psycho-
physical events, which arise and pass away, interdependently. It is
so comparable to the causal paradigm emerging in our own era that
it can appear to us like an ancient, forgotten city, overgrown by jun-
gle and awaiting rediscovery and restoration. Indeed the Buddha, in
speaking of his initial vision of *paticca samuppāda*, likened it to such a
city:

There arose in me vision, knowledge arose, insight arose, wisdom arose, light arose. Just as if, brethren, a man faring
through the forest, through the great wood, should see an ancient path, an ancient road traversed by men of former days.
And he were to go along it, and going along it he should see
an ancient city, an ancient prince's domain, wherein dwelt

men of former days, having gardens, groves, pools, foundations of walls, a goodly spot. And that man, brethren,
should bring word to the prince or to the prince's minister:
"Pardon, Lord, know this . . . I have seen an ancient city,
an ancient prince's domain, wherein dwelt men of former
days, having gardens, groves, pools, foundations of walls, a
goodly spot. Lord, restore that city." And, brethren, the
prince or his minister should restore that city. That city
should hereafter become prosperous and flourishing, popu-
lous, teeming with folk, grown, and thriven.[2]

The Central Role of the Causal Doctrine in the Dharma

The Pali term *paticca samuppāda* (Sanskrit: *pratitya samutpada*)
denotes the doctrine of causal process which the Buddha taught. In
the Dharma[3] (the teachings of the Buddha and the law of reality
which they convey), its chief emphasis is soteriological: It shows
how suffering arises and how liberation from suffering can be won.
As such this doctrine serves not only as explanation but as means
for liberation: Its very realization, existentially and intuitively, is
presented as transforming consciousness. Revealing itself as the
fundamental character of reality, of the way things are, *paticca
samuppāda* colors the Buddhist apprehension of all phenomena. It
underlies the Buddhist vision of the interdependence of life, and is
basic to its understanding of the plight and the promise that are
intrinsic to the human condition. As Louis de la Vallée Poussin, the
French Buddhologist, put it,

> Aucune théorie ne parait plus essentielle au bouddhisme que
> celle de la 'production conditionée' . . . aucune n'est plus sou-
> vent mentionée ou supposée dans les écrits canoniques,
> aucune ne peut être plus justement définie comme le *crédo* du
> bouddhisme.
>
> (No theory appears more essential to Buddhisim than that of
> 'conditioned production' . . . none is more frequently men-
> tioned or assumed in the canonical texts, none can be more
> justifiably defined as the *credo* of Buddhism.)[4]

In scriptural accounts of the enlightenment, *paticca samuppāda*
is the intellectual and expressible content of the insight to which
Gotama awakened, the realization by which he became the Buddha.

After years of yogic training, Gotama found the religious teachings of his time inadequate to reveal and resolve the canker at the core of human experience. When he sat under the *bodhi* tree to plumb for himself the root causes of human suffering, it was this vision of dependent co-arising which swept upon him. As such, *paticca samuppāda* is that abiding truth about reality which Buddhas, as they appear in the world, rediscover and make manifest.[5] Other religious teachers can witness to righteousness and the virtues of loving kindness and self-restraint, but only Buddhas, according to scripture, have won that causal vision and give that causal teaching by which such virtues are seen as integral to the nature of reality.

"Deep, delicate and subtle," it is hard to understand, difficult to see, and "beyond logic"[6]; yet when glimpsed and intuitively grasped, it is an integral component to enlightenment—as the stories not only of Gotama, but also of his first convert Kondañña and his eminent disciple Śariputra indicate.[7] The doctrine of *paticca samuppāda* is so central as to be, in words attributed to the Buddha, equated with the Dharma itself and set forth as prerequisite to the attainment of *nirvāna* (Pali: *nibbāna*).[8]

Its understanding represents wisdom (*paññā*) and constitutes 'right views', the first component of the Buddha's Eightfold Path.[9] *Paticca samuppāda* also serves as ground for morality. It is on this basis, as well as that of empirical evidence, that the Buddha attacked other contrasting causal views, for he saw these as providing neither rationale nor motivation for moral action.[10]

This doctrine, then, arose out of religious and ethical concerns, as the fruit of a quest for emancipation. It came out of confrontation with the brute fact of human suffering and the raw issue of the validity of moral action. To the Buddha and his followers this insight was integral to a transformation whose occurrence and promise changed the face of life. The scriptures make clear that a true, efficacious perception of *paticca samuppāda* entails the overhauling of one's most ingrained assumptions and cannot be won without the risks of existential commitment and meditative introspection:

> By him who knows not, who sees not as it really is (the causal uprising and ceasing) . . . training must be done . . . practice must be done . . . exertion must be made . . . there must be no turning back . . . there must be energy . . . there must be mindfulness . . . there must be earnestness.[11]

Such words remind us of the limits of scholarship. No textual exegesis or conceptual elaboration can substitute for the training and psychological investment considered requisite for an understanding of *paṭicca samuppāda*. We need, therefore, to be mindful that all conceptual treatments of dependent co-arising are by their nature limited and inadequate.

In this study I will examine *paṭicca samuppāda* on the basis of its earliest presentations in the *vinaya* and *suttas* (also known as *nikāyas*) of the Pali Canon.[12] I will show that this vision of reality goes beyond a linear view of causality to embrace a reciprocal or mutual relation between cause and effect. Later, in examining the implications of mutual causality, I will show how *paṭicca samuppāda* is fundamental to the Buddha's teachings about the character of the self, its capacity to know and act, and its relation to body, nature, and society. In doing so I will bring this causal doctrine into dialogue with general systems theory, so that together these two perspectives can enrich our understanding of mutual causality.

Paṭicca samuppāda presents a contrast with pre- and non-Buddhist Indian views of causality as radical as general systems theory's departure from the unidirectional causal constructs that have predominated in Western thought. To appreciate the distinctiveness of dependent co-arising within its historical and cultural context, let us look at the causal notions that were current in India in the sixth century B.C.E., at the time the Buddha began to teach.

Linear Causality in Pre-Buddhist India

The Buddhist view of causality represented a sharp divergence from other causal views current in ancient India and was articulated and defended in opposition to them. These included both the Vedic view and its non-Vedic alternatives. Together these constitute the contrasting philosophic backdrop against which *paṭicca samuppāda* was presented.

In discussing these non-Buddhist views of causality, I am dealing with identifiable and articulated philosophical perspectives rather than with the causal implications of myth and ritual. Within the philosophic context the Buddha Dharma represents a clear and radical departure from early Indian teachings. If this frame of reference were broadened to include other forms of religious expression, the divergence represented by the Buddhist causal view would not appear quite so radical. The ideas, stories and imagery surrounding the central Vedic ritual of the sacrifice, and especially the sacred role of fire, can suggest a cosmic vision where order and power are sustained in their operation by the reciprocal response of the life forms they occasion. The fire sacrifice nourishes, feeds back to, the gods that which their existence makes possible, and which they in turn require for their own continuity and efficacy.

An examination of such mutual causal implications discernible in Indian myth and ritual would necessitate a separate work. Here the focus is on the philosophic domain, where views of causality were explicitly expressed. I would note, however, that reciprocal causality appears to be perceived more readily by the mythic than the philosophic mentality. For this causal notion yields apparent paradoxes—cause turns into effect; the doer, by the doing, is done unto; hunter becomes prey. Implicit in mythic causality is the creative interplay of opposites. The founder of general systems theory attested to this acknowledging the debt he owed Nicholas of Cusa.[13] Because the mythic apprehension of reality, by virtue of its roots and forms, is less subject to linear causal assumptions, it has been able to reconcile polarities with greater ease than has rational discourse.[14] From this standpoint the Buddha's teaching does indeed represent a radical departure from the thought of his era, for it articulates mutual causality as a conscious and explicit philosophic view.

The Vedic philosophic view of causality, as intimated in the Rig Veda and elaborated by Upaniṣadic and Sāṃkhyan thinkers, is unidirectional. In the notions of svadhā (own power) and satkāryavāda (self-causation) the effect pre-exists in the cause. The effect represents potency inherent in the cause and unfolds and evolves from it sequentially, as curds from milk, rain from clouds. As such, effects and transformations represent new guises of the old. The logic of this view stems from the Vedic equation of the real with the immutable, an absolute aloof from change—a presupposition which characterizes the mainstream of subsequent Hindu thought.

This presupposition poses the problem of how to relate the true and the changeless to the existential experience of change. It renders questionable the reality of transformation. The appearance of novelty was interpreted either as the ripening of a previously existing condition (pariṇāmavāda) or as an outright illusion (vivartavāda). In either case, change, the realm of māyā, is seen as that which obscures the real and deludes the mind. The postulation of an absolute essence as the ground of phenomenal reality leads also to a distinction between substance and attribute. Change comes to be seen as the domain of properties superimposed on the underlying essence. The properties (*guṇas*) thus distinguished were seen as real by the Sāṃkhyans, as illusory by the Upaniṣadic and Vedantic thinkers, and by *both* as binding and perilous to the spirit.

Where an absolute is posited as the abode of pure being, it is also the locus of power and agency. This is true of Brahman. Although no world-creator role is accorded it, it is the source and progenitor of *māyā*. This is also the case in Sāṃkhyan philosophy. There, although *puruṣa* (cosmic Person) and *prakṛti* (nature) are dualistically conceived and accorded equal reality, the process of phenomenal change and evolution requires the presence of the changeless, pure spirit. Change, emanating from or impelled by an unalterable agent, is unidirectional. And this became, in non-Buddhist India as it did in the West, the predominant model for causality.

Yoga may appear on the surface to challenge this linearity. It can appear to represent a reverse movement from effect to cause. The yogi works back upstream against the form-spawning current of phenomenality; the process is one of involution in contrast to evolution. Even so, causation as production of change can be seen as remaining unidirectional. For in this yogic movement back from product to producer, from phenomenality to essence, from the Many to the One, the cause is not in turn modified by the effect. Change is undone, or seen through, rather than continuing to be operative.

In the intellectual ferment that characterized sixth century B.C.E. India, other views of causality contended as well. In opposition to doctrines which posited the causal primacy of *ātman*, Brahman or *puruṣa*, these alternative views took two main directions: materialist determinism, and accidentalism, or acausalism.

Among the materialists, the Cārvākas and Lokāyatas, an initial spiritual, transcendent cause was denied and events made explicable solely in terms of the inherent properties of matter (*svabhāva*, or "own nature").[15] Some materialists, in their rejection of a psychic component to experience, even denied any validity to inference. The reality they presented, however, instead of appearing chaotic and random, adhered to a strict determinism, the remorseless juggernaut of material inevitability. Most deterministic of all were the Ājīvakas, whose concept of fate (*niyati*) and material view of *karma* (action and the results of actions) allowed scope for neither will nor chance (*yadṛccha*).[16] These views, while deterministic, were also called *ahetuvāda* (non-causal way), probably because no causal role was assigned to mind or spirit.

At the other extreme from such determinism stood the views accorded to the *yadṛcchavādins* (accidentalists).[17] Also known by the Buddhists as *adhicca-samuppanikā* (fortuitous-originists), these thinkers held that "the soul and the world arise without a cause."[18] A further category, probably overlapping both views, included those whom the Buddhists referred to as *ucchedavādins* (annihilationists). This view, according to the *Brahamjāla Sutta*, accepted the premise of a soul, but saw it as finite and assumed, in opposition to the eternalism of Vedic thought, a radical discontinuity in the nature of reality.[19]

The early Buddhists sometimes categorized these contrasting causal visions in a fourfold fashion: as *sayam-katam* (self-caused), as *param-katam* (externally, or other- caused), as both, and as neither.[20] To the category of self-causation they assigned the *satkāryavādins* of Upaniṣadic and Sāṃkhyan persuasion, with their belief in an external and immutable essence. This Vedic view they also characterized as eternalist. By external causation, they refer to determinacy external to human will and present choice. In this category figured a variety of theories, including the materialist determinists as well as those adhering to belief in a creator God.[21] The third category, causation as both internal and external, probably represented, as Kalupahana suggests, the position of the Jainas.[22] These, in an eclectic mix, sought to accommodate change and relativity while maintaining belief in an eternal soul (*jiva*) and a deterministic view of *karma*. The fourth category of neither internal nor external causation reflects the position of the accidentalists.

The early Buddhists also used other terms and categorical divisions to classify the causal views with which they took issue. Since the nature of causality directly affected the character of *karma*, a pervasive concept of the time, the degree to which present action was predetermined was an urgent and lively issue. Consequently, alternate theories were categorized not only in terms of agency, but also in terms of determinism and responsibility. Such a classification of the views which the Buddhists rejected is: the karmic determinist or *pubbekataheto* ("due to what one did in the past"), the theistic determinist or *issaranimmanāheto* ("due to creation by God"), and the indeterminist or *ahetu-appaccayā* ("without cause or reason").[23]

All these contending non-Buddhist ideas of causality, whatever the differing schemas according to which they were ordered and labeled, are essentially linear. In the Vedic view, change, whether real or illusory, is seen as issuing from or occasioned by an eternal changeless substance. In the non-Vedic arguments, such causation is either denied outright or transformed into a radical determinism. Whether affirmed or attacked, causality is perceived as unidirectional.

Comparison with Western Linear Views

The early Indian debate about causality, which formed the philosophic backdrop against which the Buddha propounded a radically different causal vision, bears a schematic similarity to that of the West. Tracing these parallels will help us to see more clearly the distinctiveness of the Buddha's teaching from the causal assumptions to which we are accustomed in our own society.

Like the dominant Vedic notions of *svadhā* and *satkāryavāda*, based on the assumption of an absolute essence and the equation of reality with changelessness, the Greek postulation of permanent substance (with Parmenides) and then an Unmoved Mover (with Aristotle) led to a comparable unidirectionality of causal view. A major difference in the dominant Western view stems from its restriction, since the Renaissance, to efficient causation. With the rise of modern science, the other forms of causation which Aristotle had posited fell away as irrelevant or obstructive to the spirit of inquiry. Final and formal causes were rejected as beyond empirical verification, while material cause was taken for granted as the ground of all research.[24] By contrast, *svadhā* and *satkāryavāda* go beyond efficient causation to partake of the nature of formal and material cause. While efficient causation is essentially external, the Vedic notion refers primarily to the self-evolution of the primal cause. Yet the predominant Eastern and Western mainstream views are comparable to the extent that they originated in presuppositions of a prime cause, an unalterable absolute. From this derive their linearity and their distinction between substance and attribute.

In the West as in ancient India, reactions against the dominant causal view moved in two opposing directions. There were those who denied any objective causality at all; perceiving that the mainstream view ultimately rested on the assumption of a prime mover, they rejected that assumption as an unsubstantiated inference, and so rejected both causality and inference as well. And, on the other hand, there were those who, accepting causality, restricted its operation to the purely physical plane.

Among the former we find such thinkers as Locke and Hume, whose radical empiricism reduced causality to a subjective category, the perception of constant conjunction. Observed reality became in their eyes a temporal succession of events to which objective production could not be legitimately attributed. This view of causality as mere sequence led to a modern acausalism which substitutes description for explanation and which is comparable to the accidentalists of the Buddha's time.[25] Twentieth century scientific observations seemed to confirm the accidentalist or indeterminate view. Because subatomic particles do not follow trajectories comprehensible in terms of linear, efficient causation, reality itself appeared random.

The other and opposite reaction to the dominant linear model of causation involved a shift to material determinism. To many in both ancient India and the modern West, the rejection of a first cause, unconditioned and supraphysical, entailed wholesale rejection of the causal efficacy of mind. Like the Ajivikas of the Buddha's era, many modern determinists have come to see causality as material process alone. The most clearly articulated view of this kind is the Marxist, which explicitly perceives change as rooted in physical conditions. But belief in the determining role of the material and measurable, the assumption that it is more real than the mental, dominates a large portion of the non-Marxist world as well.

Since the rise of modern science, determinacy had become identified with efficient causation, one thing shaping or pushing another thing. This made mainstream Western causality susceptible to materialism and useful as a defender of it. In contrast, the Vedic view had maintained its view of the causal supremacy of spirit, and the materialists of the Buddha's time stood outside of and in contrast to it.

In both the West and ancient India, presuppositions characteristic of the predominant view—that is, unidirectionality and the dichotomy between substance and attribute—tended to be assumed by those who reacted against it. In each culture, perception and critique of these presuppositions was necessary for a breakthrough to a radically new causal vision.

In the modern West such a critique has accelerated in the last generation. Not only do scientists find linear, one-way causality inadequate as a conceptual tool for understanding complex systems, they also challenge its philosophic and ontological implications. A primary problem is that of novelty, for they see in the traditional view an implicit denial of the qualitatively new. Mario Bunge criticizes linear causality for presenting a perspective on reality in which "only old things can come out of change." According to the linear view, he says, effects essentially pre-exist in their causes; they are passive and incapable of adding "something of their own" to the causal bond. "[Such] processes can give rise to objects new in number or new in some quantitative respects, not however new in kind."[26]

In ancient India the Buddhists provided such a critique of traditional causal presuppositions, and on similar grounds. The Buddha also perceived that the causal views of his time disallowed novelty and meaningful change, but he expressed his judgment in more existential and ethical terms. He opposed these causal views, he said, because they provided "neither desire to do, nor effort to do, nor necessity to do this deed or abstain from that deed. So then, the necessity for action or inaction [is] not found to exist in truth or verity."[27]

Scriptural Presentations of *Paṭicca Samuppāda*

A concise and literal English rendering of this Pali term is difficult. *Uppāda*, the substantive form of the verb *uppajjati*, means "arising"; *sam-uppāda*, "arising together." *Paṭicca*, as the gerund of *pacceti (pati + i*, to "come back to" or "fall back on"), is used to denote "grounded on" or "on account of." Literally, then, the compound would mean "on account of arising together," or, since it is used as a substantive, "the being-on-account-of-arising-together." Buddhaghosa defines *paṭicca samuppāda* as "that according to which co-ordinate phenomena are produced mutually."[28] English translations of the scriptures most frequently render it as "dependent co-arising," "dependent co-origination," "conditioned genesis," or "conditioned co-production." Another Pali compound used in the canonical texts to refer to the Buddha's view of causality is *idapaccayatā*, literally "this-conditionality." Sometimes translated as "the relatedness of this to that" and as "relativity," it is used synonymously with *paṭicca-samuppāda*.

The meaning of *paṭicca samuppāda* cannot be apprehended aside from the doctrine of *anicca*, impermanence. The first of the three characteristics (*ti-lakkhaṇa*) of existence, it is usually treated as the basis for the other two, *dukkha* (suffering) and *anattā* (no self). Although masked by the appearance of continuity, impermanence is real and pervasive, as is learned in the meditation which the Buddha taught.[29] There in *Satipaṭṭhāna* or mindfulness practice, we perceive that change, the ceaseless arising and passing of events, constitutes our existence, and that there is nothing in our experience or self that is aloof from change. All that we perceive and feel and think is *anicca*. No factor external to change, no absolute that is not definitive of process itself, secures our existence. Taking a small piece of cow dung in his hand, the Buddha said, "Bhikkhus, if even that much of permanent, everlasting, eternal individual selfhood (*attabhava*), not inseparable from the idea of change, could be found, then this living of the holy life could not be taught by me".[30]

Within this realm of flux the causal orderliness which the Buddha taught inheres. No immutable essence is posited from which *paṭicca samuppāda*, as a regulative principle, emanates. Rather it is the pattern of change itself. As such, it represents a dual assertion—of change *and* order, or order within change. In the linear view of causality, order requires permanence, a static basis impermeable to change. But here order and impermanence go hand in hand.

The dual perception of impermanence and order suffices to demonstrate the distance between the Buddha's causal teachings and other causal concepts of his time. This can be seen succinctly and schematically in a dialogue with the disciple Kassapa.[31] He questions the Buddha on the origin of suffering, using the fourfold form, or tetralemma, that will become characteristic of Buddhist dialectics (*A;* not *A;* both *A* and not-*A;* neither *A* nor not-*A*). This dialogue is essentially repeated as having occurred with others, attesting to its significance. With the wanderer Timbaruka, for example, the question is not the cause of suffering but the cause of pleasure and pain.

Here, to Kassapa's question, "Is suffering wrought by oneself?" the Buddha answers no, for that would imply, he explains, the eternalist theory: a changeless self. "What then, Master Gotama, is one's suffering wrought by another?" The Buddha again says no;[32] that question assumes one is impotent in a predetermined universe. Similarly he denied, in the third query, that suffering is caused (made) both externally and internally. All three of these questions presuppose (the verb used is "wrought" or "made," not "conditioned") that causality requires an enduring substance which as agent produces another—a view undercut by the perception of *anicca* and *anattā*.

The fourth and last question offers the only alternative that Kassapa sees: acausality. "Has suffering, wrought neither by myself nor another, befallen me by chance?" Again the Buddha's negative reply. In his view the denial of permanence and substance, represented by *anicca* and *anattā*, does not mean the rule of chance. Kassapa, confused, wonders whether the Buddha accords reality to the concept they are discussing. "The Master Gotama neither knows nor sees suffering." "Nay, Kassapa, I am not one who knows not suffering nor sees it. I am one that knows suffering, Kassapa, I am one that sees it." And he then teaches the interdependence of conditions, which he perceived in his enlightenment.

In this teaching he shows how factors of existence, such as ignorance, sense perception, feelings, craving, condition each other to produce suffering and how, by virtue of that conditionality, suffering in turn can be undone. This conditionality represents the order within the flow of existence. According to the chronology the scriptures present, this interrelated series of psycho-physical factors is set forth as the first perception and enunciation of *paticca samuppāda*. It features in accounts of the Buddha's enlightenment and represents the cognitive content of his insight. It is likely that this formulation by a series of conditioned factors is a later, formalized illustration of *paticca samuppāda*, which became identified with the insight itself as the teachings were passed down.[33]

That event, as described, begins in confrontation with suffering, as does the later formulation of the Four Noble Truths. Facing the dimensions of pain, respecting its reality, the Buddha seeks to trace its arising: "What now being present, is decaying and death also present; what conditions decaying and dying?"[34] Birth is the condition of decay and dying. The question is repeated for birth, and with each successive answer it is asked again. "What now being present, is craving also present? What conditions craving?" and "feeling"? and "contact"? on back to *nāmarūpa* (name and form) and *viññāna* (consciousness or cognition) itself. In what is considered the oldest account, these factors amount to ten; most other passages add the conditioning factors of *sankhāra* (volitional formations) and *avijjā* (ignorance) to make a total of twelve.

The conditional factors enumerated in this series came to be known as *nidānas*. Sometimes translated as "cause," the term *nidāna* (stemming from *ni + dā*, to bind or fetter) denotes basis, constraint, or occasion. It came to be used synonymously with *paccaya*, the relational term whose adverbial form is used in the series and translated as "conditioned by." In some passages, such as the *Dvayātānupassana sutta*, the equivalent term for these factors is *upadhi*. Appearing elsewhere in scriptures to denote passion and limitation, *upadhi*, like *paccayā*, literally means "support" or that "which is placed under."

The serial enumeration of these *nidānas*, *upadhis*, or *paccayas* appears in a variety of forms. Some exclude *sankhāra* and *avijjā*; some change the order; and some include factors of pleasure and bliss. The predominant form which became standard, is twelvefold as follows.[35] Connecting each is the term *paccayā* in the ablative, as in *avijjā-paccayā saṅkhārā*, "conditioned by ignorance, the formations."

avijjā (ignorance)
sankhārā (volitional, or karmic formations)
viññāna (consciousness or cognition)
nāmarūpa (name and form, or the psycho-physical entity)
saḷāyatana (the sixfold senses)
phassa (contact)
vedanā (feeling)
tanhā or *trṣna* (craving)
upādāna (grasping)
bhava (becoming)
jāti (birth)
jarāmaraṇa (decay and death)

While each link arises *paccayā*, by means of or conditioned by the preceding one, a variation occurs in the third and fourth *nidānas*. There a number of texts circle back, and after stating that *nāmarūpa* is conditioned by *viññāna*, reinsert the latter as conditioned in turn by *nāmarūpa*.

So presented, with *paccayā*, the series represents *dukkha-khandassa samudaya*, the "arising of this heap of suffering." Since suffering is seen as conditioned, it can be undone as is affirmed by the third Noble Truth. If conditioned by *A*, B arises, then with the cessation of A, B ceases. The series then is recited in the form of *avijjā-nirodhā saṅkhārā nirodho*. Here the term *nirodhā*, *"with the ceasing of"*, replaces *paccayā* is repeated in the nominative form to show that this entails the cessation of the next factor. In this form the series represents *dukkha-khandassa nirodha* or the "ceasing of this heap of suffering." Redactors often substituted these two forms of the *nidāna* series for the second and third Noble Truths.

The series, whether *samudaya* or *nirodhā*, is also presented both in forward order (from that which conditions to that which is conditioned) and reverse order. These directions are termed *anuloma* and *paṭiloma*, with and against the grain.

The variations in the number and kind of causal factors indicate that the conditional relationship of these causal factors is significant, not the separate factors themselves. Emphasis is on the transiency and relationality which characterize them and which provide scope for meaningful change. The factors which we experience as basic to life and which give rise to our pain condition each other. All are linked, none are permanent, hence the possibility of release.

This emphasis can be discerned from the outset in the account of the Buddha's enlightenment right after he had traced the factors conditional to suffering.

> Coming to be, coming to be! . . . Ceasing to be, ceasing to be! At that thought, brethren, there arose . . . a vision of things not before called to mind, and knowledge arose, light arose. . . . Such is form, such is the coming to be of form, such is its passing away. . . . Such is cognition, such is its coming to be, such is its passing away. And [he abided] in the discernment of the arising and passing away.[36]

The nonsubstantial character of reality which it affirms makes this teaching hard to convey. It goes against the grain of both our sensory experience and our desire for security. Recognizing this, the Buddha was tempted not to teach.

> I have penetrated this truth, deep, hard to perceive, hard to understand, calm, sublime, beyond logic, subtle, intelligible only to the wise. But this is a race devoting itself to the things to which it clings. . . . And for such a race this were a matter hard to perceive, to wit, that this is conditioned by that (*ida paccayatā paṭicca samuppādo*). . . . And if I were to teach the truth, and other men did not acknowledge it to me, that would be wearisome to me, that would be hurtful to me. . . . This that through many toils I've won—enough! Why should I make it known?[37]

But although he pondered thus, his "heart inclining to be averse from exertion," he remembered the suffering and the need of beings. According to the legend it was the god Brahma who reminded him: "[T]here are those perishing from not hearing the truth; they will come to be knowers of the truth . . . there are those who will understand".[38] Thereupon, in compassion, the Buddha set forth to teach.

When he found his former companions and delivered his first teachings, the order and emphasis accorded them in the texts is significant. Note that of the elements of his sermon it is *paṭicca samuppāda* that is identified as unique to the Buddha. First he "discoursed in due order,"

> that is to say, he gave them illustrative talk on generosity, on right conduct, on heaven, on the danger, the vanity and the defilement of lusts, on the advantages of renunciation. When the Exalted One saw that they had become prepared, softened,

unprejudiced, upraised and believing in heart, then he proclaimed that Truth which the Buddhas alone have won; that is
to say, the doctrine of Sorrow, of its origin, of its cessation,
and the Path.[38]

Here a key phrase is employed, "whatsoever is subject to the condition of origination is subject also to the condition of cessation." At
this point his first convert Kondañña is enlightened. "Truly Kondañña has perceived it!" said the Buddha.[40]

   The teachings of *paṭicca samuppāda* in the form of the *nidāna*
series occurs chiefly in the accounts of the Buddha's enlightenment
and in passages where he distinguishes the Dharma from other
views of karma and determinacy. In these early texts the series is
not presented as a portrayal of rebirth or a sequence of lives. That
interpretation, as I detail in the next chapter, arose later with the
Abhidharma, or Buddhist scholastic thought. Nor is the series in
the *suttas* and *vinaya* imaged in circular form. Only in later descriptions and iconography is it applied to the symbol of the wheel. In
the *cakra* (wheel), which has featured in Indian culture since the
time of the chariot-driving Aryans, *avijjā* and *jarāmaraṇa* meet in
contiguity, the circle thus formed conveying the endlessness and
beginninglessness of causal interaction. Then, as portrayed in Ma-
hayanist art, this causal series becomes the wheel of life itself held
in the claws of Yama, god of death.[41]

   In addition to the interdependent chain of *nidānas* and to the
second and third Noble Truths, which it represents and sometimes
replaces, *paṭicca samuppāda* receives in the early texts another fre-
quent and much briefer formulation. It consists of a four-part formula that sometimes stands alone and sometimes accompanies the
nidāna series, either preceding or following it.

> imasmiṃ sati idaṃ hoti
>   imassupādā idaṃ uppajjati
> imasmiṃ asati idaṃ na hoti
>   imassa nirodhā idaṃ nirujjati.

(This being, that becomes; from the arising of this, that arises; this
not being, that becomes not; from the ceasing of this, that ceases.)[42]

Frequently this short formula appears in the texts in conjunction with the denial that anything ever exists eternally or perishes
absolutely. "This" (*idam*) arises and passes away in interdependence

with other similarly transient phenomena; its manifestation is not related to any immutable essence or entity, nor is it conditional on anything external to change. The conditionality, *ida-paccayatā*, to which this and other expressions of *paṭicca samuppāda* witness, is that of a universe in process where all is interrelated and mutually affecting.

No mention is made of *dukkha* here, nor is this formulation tied in the texts to explanations of suffering. Rather it presents, simply and baldly, the interdependence of phenomena which the Buddha perceived. *Paṭicca samuppāda* is frequently assumed to consist in an explanation of suffering alone. But that does not define or delineate the content of the insight that occurred in the enlightenment. It was not *dukkha* that the Buddha beheld beneath the *bodhi* tree—that fact he already knew, and it impelled his search. It was *samudaya* and *nirodhā*, the conditioned arising and ceasing, that broke upon him there. Nor did this relation of arising and passing away come to be presented exclusively in terms of suffering. T. W. Rhys Davids concluded that of all the ninety-three suttas dealing with *paṭicca samuppāda* in the *Saṃyutta Nikāya*, only one-sixth have *dukkha* as their subject. A number of others employ it to exhort against craving; but by far the largest proportion, fifty-six, present *paṭicca samuppāda* as the causal relation between all phenomena and the principle which all followers must master.[43]

This chapter has focused on those portions of the Dharma that are seen as explicit formulations of *paṭicca samuppāda*. Such a focus is inadequate to convey the pervasive presence of this concept of causality in the teachings of the Buddha. It imbued all his utterances, shaped the metaphors and parables he employed, and underlay, as we shall show, the views of personhood, of karma and social responsibility which he taught. Dependent co-arising is implicit throughout. In Part Three of this book many of these less explicit allusions to *paṭicca samuppāda* will be brought out.

Notes

1. *Saṃyutta Nikāya*, II.91.

2. *Ibid.*, II.105.

3. Because popular English usage today has adopted the word *dharma* in this Sanskrit form, I will use that instead of the Pali form (*dhamma*). For the same reason, I will use *karma* instead of the Pali *kamma*.

4. Poussin, *Théorie des Douze Causes*, p. v. My translation.

5. *Saṃyutta Nikāya*, II.25.

6. *Dīgha Nikāya*, II.36.

7. *Vinaya*, Mahavagga I.1,39.

8. *Majjhima Nikāya*, II.32; *Saṃyutta Nikāya*, II.124.

9. *Saṃyutta Nikāya*, II.15.

10. *Aṅguttara Nikāya*, I.174.

11. *Saṃyutta Nikāya*, II.131,2.

12. The *suttas* (Sanskrit: *sutras*) or the recorded discourses attributed to the Buddha, and the *vinaya* or books of monastic discipline, are the first two and the oldest of the three "baskets" of the Pali canonical scriptures.

13. von Bertalanffy, *Perspectives on General Systems Theory*, p. 53ff. By the same token, Stewart Brand sees systems-cybernetics as presenting "wholesome paradoxes that (thank God) undermine human conscious purpose" (*II Cybernetic Frontiers*, inside front cover).

14. Dudley, "Mircea Eliade as Anti-Historian," p. 356.

15. Kalupahana, *Causality*, 29–31.

16. *Ibid.*, p. 37.

17. Jayatilleke, *Early Buddhist Theory of Knowledge*. pp. 444–45.

18. *Dīgha Nikāya*, I.28.

19. *Ibid.*, I.34.

20. *Saṃyutta Nikāya*, II.18.

21. Kalupahana, *Causality*, p. 5.

22. *Ibid.*, Chapter II.

23. *Aṅguttara Nikāya*, I.173.

24. Bunge, *Causality*, 32–33.

25. *Ibid.*, pp. 29, 333.

26. *Ibid.*, pp. 203, 4.

27. *Aṅguttara Nikāya*, I.174.

28. Kalupahana, *Causality*, 54, 202.

29. *Dīgha Nikāya,* II.290.

30. *Saṃyutta Nikāya,* III.144.

31. *Ibid.,* II.18.

32. The Buddha's negative replies in these passages is literally *ma he-vam,* which is usually translated "not so" or "not so, verily." Actually, the form suggests prohibition rather than denial, as in "do not say so." Thus emphasis is on the wrongness of question and the kind of answer it invites—"don't put it that way"—rather than on its negation. (Kalupahana, *Causality,* p. 143.)

33. Mizuno, *Primitive Buddhism,* 132f.

34. *Saṃyutta Nikāya,* II.10.

35. *Ibid.,* III.26, II.30, II.25.

36. *Dīgha Nikāya,* II.33.

37. *Ibid.,* II.36.

38. *Ibid.,* II.37–39.

39. *Ibid.,* II.41.

40. *Vinaya,* Mahavagga I.1.

41. From the Rig Veda's description of the wheel of Surya, the sun, to Gandhi's spinning wheel, which became the symbol of national independence, the *cakra* (Pali: *cakka*) has been a dominant motif in Indian culture. As such it signifies both power and unity. It was adopted early on by the Buddhists to represent, most preeminently, the Wheel of the Law or the Dharma (Pali: *Dhamma Cakka*). The Buddha's teaching constitutes its "Turning" and makes him the *Dhamma Cakkavatti* or the sovereign of the Wheel of the Dharma. Incorporating the twelve *nidānas* in a circular form, the wheel also became the *Bhava Cakka* or Wheel of Life, conveying both the rebirth and the interplay of causal factors. Used first metaphorically by Buddhaghosa to indicate the beginninglessness and interdependence of *paṭicca samuppāda* (*Visuddhimagga,* I.198: II.576–8), this application of the wheel symbol was amplified by the Sarvāstivādins in the *Divyavadāna* (Karunaratne, p. 25) and in a manner which was later adopted by the Tibetans. There, in Tibetan art, it features three concentric circles: at the center and representing lust, hatred and delusion, a cock, snake and pig pursue each other, while the next circle pictures the six realms of existence, from animals to humans to gods and hungry ghosts; enclosing these and arrayed around the rim of the wheel are portrayals of the twelve factors of dependent co-arising.

42. *Samyutta Nikāya*, II.28,65; *Majjhima Nikāya*, I.262, II.32 *inter alia*. In the Pali the same demonstrative pronoun "this" is employed throughout, but in translation "that" is alternatively inserted for clarity.

43. Dīgha Nikāya, pp. 42–43.

3

Dependent Co-Arising as
Mutual Causality

This were a matter hard to perceive, namely this conditionality, this
paṭicca samuppāda ... against the stream of common thought,
deep, subtle, difficult, delicate. . . . [1]

The Buddha asserted that his teaching of causality was hard to
understand. Scholars of the Dharma have found this to be true.
Their efforts to grasp and convey the significance of *paṭicca
samuppāda* have led to differences and, in the opinion of Ven.
Nyanatiloka, many distortions.

> None of all the teachings of Buddhism has given rise to greater
> misunderstandings, to more contradictory and more absurd
> speculations and interpretations than the Paṭicca Samuppāda,
> the teaching of the Dependent Origination of all phenomena
> of existence.[2]

Theodor Stcherbatsky, the Russian scholar who devoted years to the
study of Buddhist logic, expresses his view of interpretations of
paṭicca samuppāda with similar vehemence. "There is perhaps no
other Buddhist doctrine which has been so utterly misunderstood
and upon which such a wealth of unfounded guesses and fanciful
philosophizing has been spent."[3]

While interpretations of the doctrine of dependent co-arising
have varied, most scholars have recognized it as central to the Buddhist view of reality. By virtue of the universality and impersonality
of the causal process it perceives, it has also been acclaimed as a
milestone in the history of human thought. Relatively few scholars,
however, have identified or emphasized the reciprocal nature of the

causality it presents. Generally, it has not been seen as an issue, and therefore has not been presented as either distinctive or significant.[4]

The reciprocity of causal process is integral to the Buddha's teaching of *paṭicca samuppāda*. It is inherent in the doctrine of *anicca* and the denial of a first cause, evident in the interdependence of causal factors, and reflected in the linguistic structures employed.

From Substance to Relation

Maruyama has pointed out that "the unidirectional causal paradigm originated [in a logic] based on the concepts of 'substance' and 'identity'."[5] The early Greek notion of the universe as composed of basic substances (Anaximander's conception of one proto-substance and Anaxagoras's idea of a power-substance identified with soul, order, and rationality) led, Maruyama argues, to the classifications and deductive thinking of Aristotle. There the stuff of the universe is ordered and ranked in terms of nonoverlapping abstract categories, and circular reasoning is forbidden. In the East, Vedic thought is essentialist and substantialist in that the Ātman, the locus of reality and power, is perceived as a subtle substance underlying and permeating the phenomenal world. Whether substance is perceived monistically as in the Upaniṣads or pluralistically as in Mīmāṃsā, (a classic Brahmanic school of thought), it is the ultimate material of the world and the locus of agency.

Where reality is seen as substance, subtle or gross, causal efficacy is attributed to potency inherent in the objects manifesting or comprising the basic stuff of the world. In other words, reality is seen, not as constituted primarily of relationships, but constituted primarily of entities—substances that can impinge on others and transmit properties to them.

To be an entity caused or modified by another particular entity or state means to undergo its power, to receive qualities from it. Such a view involves a dichotomy between substance and attribute. Change, as causation between substances, consists in the unfolding or transmission of properties, whether envisaged as attributes in the Aristotelian sense or as *guṇas* in the Vedantic or Sāṃkhyan sense. In either case, substance is seen as a carrier of attributes, even though this has no basis in experience. For, as Bunge points out in his critique of linear causality, "save by abstraction we never meet anything devoid of qualities and standing apart from change; nor do we find, except by abstraction, qualities outside objects endowed with them."[6] Yet substance—whether its properties are transmitted and altered by pushing from without as in efficient causation, or by ripening from within as in *pariṇamavāda*—is basic to agency in the linear view.

The Buddhist perception of process cuts the ground from under such a view. The doctrines of *anattā* and *aniccatā* dissolve all notions of enduring, isolable entities and leave no basis for a dichotomy between substance and attribute. Causal formulations and questions which presuppose such substantiality are, from the Buddha's perspective, "not fit." When the follower Phagguna kept asking him to identify the causal agent that produces consciousness, contact, feeling, and other elements of the *nidāna* series, the Buddha criticized the question. Only when the question is rephrased will he provide an answer—and when he does, he substitutes verb for noun, action for substance.

> "Who now, Lord, is it who craves?" "Not a fit question, said the Exalted One. I am not saying [someone] craves. If I were saying so, the question would be a fit one. But I am not saying so. And I not saying so, if you were to ask thus: 'Conditioned now by what, lord, is craving?' this were a fit question. And the fit answer there would be: 'Conditioned by feeling is craving'."[7]

In the early Buddhist view, the tendency to substantialize and hypostatize the co-arising factors of existence creates the human predicament. Reifying them, we lay ourselves open to attachments and aversions—hence our need to experience their transience. As it says in the *Dvayatānupassanā sutta*, he proceeds correctly "who sees no essence in the *upadhis*" (or factors of experience).[8]

To interpret the Buddhist position as one which replaces being with nonbeing as the causal substratum is a mistake. This move was made by the 19th-century French scholar Burnouf and his colleague Goldstuecker, who saw in Buddhist causality the factors of existence as emerging in degree from "le non-être" (non-being) and "le néant" (nothingness), as from a primary, undifferentiated stuff.[9] Hermann Oldenberg, writing a generation later, pointed out the error. Emphasizing the centrality of *anicca*, he affirmed that *paṭicca samuppāda* is a function of relationship and that the "becoming" of things arises from "their standing in that mutual relation".

> We prefer to avoid every expression which would make Buddhism regard non-being as the true substance of things, and to

express ourselves thus. The speculation of the Brahmans apprehended being in all becoming, that of the Buddhists becoming in all apparent being. In the former case substance
without causality, in the latter causality without substance.[10]

The doctrines of *anicca* and *anattā* desubstantiate reality. The Buddhist vision of process, to which they attest, is fundamental to dependent co-arising and makes it radically different from concepts
which presuppose that causality is something occurring between
substances. To understand it we must move, as Frederick Streng
points out, beyond "conventional views of causality".

> All [Indian Buddhists] recognized that life could not be prop-
> erly understood . . . without seeing beyond conventional
> views of causality. The usual common knowledge procedure
> for understanding causality is to conceive of causal relations as
> an intermediate force between two separate entities, e.g. an
> agent and a result of an agent's action. This set of notions,
> however, from the Buddhist perspective is a mental projection
> imbued with illusory tendencies. . . . As long as one thinks in
> terms of self-existent entities . . . there is an effective "being
> stationed" (*pratiṣṭhitam*) by a subject-object dichotomy.[11]

No First Cause

Linear causality offers us causal chains by which we can endeavor to understand how things have arisen. D is caused by C and
C is produced by B, which in turn is the result of A and so on. Thus
causal action can be traced backwards, whether from the ghee to
the uncurdled milk or from the final pattern on the billiard table to
impact on the first ball. But what produced the milk? Who held the
billiard cue? And the same question can be asked about the cow
and the pool player. Linear causal chains require either a first cause
or infinite regress. Either we end up with an Unmoved Mover,
which is a metaphysical assertion, or with a dizzying *regressus ad
infinitum*. Instead of explaining the unknown in terms of the
known, both, as Bunge points out, do the opposite.[12]

In spite of its difficulties, the notion of a first cause is inherent
in the unidirectional view, both as a logical necessity and as a religious predisposition. Many scholars of Western and Hindu background, betraying the linear assumptions of their own traditions,
have ascribed it to the Buddhist doctrine. Because *avijjā* (ignorance)

frequently stands at the start of the series of *nidānas*, the conditioned factors of existence, they have taken it as a prime cause.

Such a move has been made by a number of noted figures in the field—from Brian Hodgson, the founder of Western Buddhist studies, who presents *avijjā* as "the first act" of the not-yet-individualized soul,[13] to T. W. Rhys Davids and William Stede who, in their Pali-English dictionary, qualify *avijjā* as "the primary cause of all existence." Even Stcherbatsky, who at some points acknowledges the principle of interdependence in Buddhist causality, falls into the habit of seeing *avijjā* as "the primary cause (being) the first and fundamental member of the Wheel of Life."[14]

Nyanatiloka bemoans the "absurd speculations" about *paṭicca samuppāda*. This is especially true, he goes on to say, "with regard to Western scholars and writers on Buddhism," who interpret

> *avijjā* as a causeless first principle out of which conscious and physical life has evolved. That all in spite of the Buddha's repeated express declaration that an absolute first beginning of existence is something unthinkable (Anamatagga-Samyutta), and that all such like speculations may lead to imbecility [*Aṅguttara Nikāyua*, IV. 27] and that one never could imagine a time when there was no Ignorance and no Craving for existence [*Aṅguttara Nikāyua*, X. 61].[15]

Such an error is not restricted to Westerners nor to our era. It was current in the early centuries of Buddhism, to judge by the arguments against it in the scriptures (such as *Aṅguttara Nikāya* IV, 27; V, 113, 116; X, 61). Buddhaghosa is more explicit in countering the tendency to attribute causal primacy to ignorance. He stresses that the starting point which *avijjā* occupies in the causal series is figurative only, and a pedagogical device.

> But why is ignorance stated as the beginning here? How then, is ignorance the causeless root-cause of the world . . . ? It is not causeless. For a cause of ignorance is stated thus 'With the arising of cankers there is the arising of ignorance' [Majjhima Nikāya, I. 54]. But there is a figurative way in which it can be treated as the root cause. What way is that? When it is made to serve as a starting point in an exposition of the round [of becoming].[16]

> There is no single or multiple fruit of any kind from a single cause . . . [but] the Blessed One employs one representative

cause and fruit when it is suitable for the sake of elegance in instruction and to suit the idiosyncrasies of those susceptible of being taught.[17]

When treated by scholars as a first cause, *avijjā* becomes a generalized principle or a primordial state. In contrast, Oldenberg argues that the early texts present ignorance as the nonpossession of a specific knowledge. There *avijjā* consists in not-knowing the Four Noble Truths, ignoring the causes for the arising and cessation of suffering.[18]

Far from being a causeless first principle, "ignorance," as the Buddha taught, "is causally conditioned."[19] Indeed there is, in the *suttas* and *vinaya*, no entity, essence, or condition which is presented as a primordial and uncaused starting point. The Buddha not only declined to teach the existence of a first cause, but, indeed, discouraged any such inquiry.

> Would you, O monks, knowing and seeing thus probe [lit. "run behind"] the prior end of things . . . or pursue [lit. "run after"] the final end of things?[20]

> Incalculable is the beginning, brethren, of this faring on. The earliest point is not revealed of the running on, the faring on, of beings cloaked in ignorance, tied to craving.[21]

The term translated here as "incalculable" is *anamata*, which means "cannot be thought." Beginnings are unthinkable not only because they are distant in time, but also because the thinking mind is part of the causal arising, emerges from it and contributes to it, and cannot stand outside the "faring on" to trace its origin.

Passages such as these suggest that the Buddha's noted silence on matters that are "indeterminate" relates to *paṭicca samuppāda*. Speculation on abstract matters, as he made clear, can be fruitless, a distraction on the path, and can lead to dissension. Perhaps the Buddha saw another danger there as well—that of assuming or seeking a first cause. When asked how diverse opinions arose on matters eternal, and disputation on such topics as the origin and duration of the world, the Buddha answered that they arose through ignorance of the arising and ceasing of causal factors.[22] This suggests that such metaphysical argumentation is, in his view, conditioned by the assumption that a first cause can exist and be identified—an assumption undercut by *paṭicca samuppāda* and its stress on complete conditionality.

The interrelatedness of all causes, wherein no one factor emerges as solely determinative, is expressed in many a metaphor and analogy in the early scriptures. Take a plant: No neat linear chain can present the conditions which permit it to grow. The seed is not enough; soil is required and moisture.[23] Similarly, from the conjunction of events, that is, from relationship, fire ignites. "From the adjusted friction of two sticks, heat is born, a spark is brought forth, but from the separating and withdrawing of just those two sticks, the heat which was consequent, that ceases, that is quenched."[24] So also is a house constructed. There the rafters, "all converging to the roof-peak, resorting equally to the roof-peak," support each other in mutual dependence, none able to stand alone.[25] Buddhaghosa, arguing against the primacy of any one causal factor, used the simile of the creeper. The creeping vine runs along the ground and, like the teaching of *paṭicca samuppāda* itself, can be seized at any point.

> Namely, from the beginning, from the middle up to the end, from the end, from the middle down to the beginning. . . . Why does the Blessed One teach [dependent origination] thus? Because the dependent origination is entirely beneficial: starting from any one of the four starting points, it leads only to the penetration of the proper way.[26]

Syntax of Interdependence

The very language and grammatical forms used in the teachings of *paṭicca samuppāda* imply that it entails a nonlinear kind of causality. The departure from linear assumptions, and the emphasis on relationship rather than substance, is discernible both in the choice of terms and their inflection.

Take the series of *nidānas*. On the night of his enlightenment the Buddha contemplated these factors of existence to understand how suffering arises. The semantics of the questions he asked himself is noteworthy: "What now being present, is craving also present? What conditions craving?"[27] He does not seek to determine what makes, generates, or produces a given factor; the issue is rather what is present when *A* is present and what conditions *A*. The assertions, then, which follow these questions, and feature in his subsequent teaching of the causal doctrine, take the form of an enumeration of conditions: "conditioned by *A*, *B* arises." More literally it is "conditioned by" or "depending on *A*, *B*" (*viññāna-*

paccayā-nāmarūpa, conditioned by consciousness, name-and-form), since in translation the word "arises" is inserted.

The causal term employed is *paccaya*, which literally means "support." Like *paṭicca*, it stems from the verb *pacceti*, to come back to or fall back on. In the Abhidharma *paccaya* came to be used as a generic category embracing all forms of relation, the events to which they give rise being termed *paccayuppanna*. The ablative *paccayā*, used in this series, is an adverbial form denoting "by means of," or "depending on," to which the usual translation "conditioned by" is not inappropriate. In contrast to the Vedic theories of *svadhā* and *satkāryavāda*, this language does not present a causation wherein *B* issues from a potency of *A* or represents a self-evolution of *A*. It points to the function, not of that which genetically produces out of inherent power, but of that which in relationship, by its presence, occasions and supports. If causation as production had been meant, the teaching could have used a verb like *kar* (make) as in *satkāryavāda*. With the use of *paccaya*, however, it presents causation not in terms of unilateral power but in terms of relationship—that which "being present," facilitates, catalyzes, or occasions.

The process nature of the reality to which this usage of *paccaya* points, and the departure from efficient causation it entails, are stressed by Caroline Rhys Davids and S. Z. Aung.

> *Paccaya* . . . implies that, for Buddhist philosophy, all modes of relation have causal significance, though the causal efficacy . . . may be absent. To understand this we must consider everything, not as statically existing, but as "happening" or "event." We may then go on to define *paccaya* as an event which helps to account for the happening of the *paccayuppanna*, i.e. the effect, or "what-has-happened-through-the-*paccaya*." . . . Dropping our notion of efficient cause (A as having power to produce B), and holding to the "helping to happen" notion, we see . . . *paccaya* as . . . helping (*upakaraka*).[28]

I noted in the last chapter that *ida-paccayatā* is used as a synonym for *paṭicca samuppāda* and referred to its translation as "this conditionality." Aung and C. Rhys Davids are perhaps more accurate in expressing it as "the conditionedness of this." Using *A* to represent "cause" and *B* "effect," they say, in the same passage quoted above, that

"This (*ida*) refers to B, but the compound refers to A: A is the "*paccaya*-of-*this*." The abstract form is the only philosophic way of expressing *paccaya*.[29]

Now let us turn to the short four-part formula which, as specified in Chapter 2, represents a capsule version of *paticca samuppāda*: This being, that becomes; from the arising of this, that arises; this not being, that becomes not; from the ceasing of this, that ceases.

Here again the language does not state that A makes or produces B or that B emerges from A; the locative of the participle is used, suggesting that in the happening (or not happening) of A, B happens (or does not happen). This relation is closer to a "when" or an "if" connection, than to a "because," (and indeed both "if" and "when" are sometimes used in translations, "if this is, that comes to be"). The "because" relation tends to be more indicative of linear production—as in the phrase, "the iron is red because it is in the fire" (i.e. the fire *makes* the iron red), contrasted with "it being Sunday, the library is closed" (i.e. Sunday does not close the library).

In Pali, the notion of making something be or happen is conveyed by the causative form of the verb. As G. C. Pande has pointed out, this formula does not read *idaṃ uppannaṃ idaṃ uppādeti* (the causative form of *uppajjati*), which would translate "this, arising, makes that to arise".[30]

These events are not merely contiguous or coincidental. The Pali does not read *idaṃ uppannaṃ idaṃ uppajjati*, with the first clause in the nominative; that would suggest coincidence, or mere sequence. But the first clause appears in the locative absolute, indicating that B happens *in relation to* the happening of A. The happening of A provides a locus or context in which B can happen. So more is involved than a contiguity of events, as in Hume's view. In Hume's interpretation of causality, which is sometimes mistakenly equated with the Buddhist, events flow past and are essentially, objectively unrelated. Our mental operations infer causal connection. In contrast, the Buddha's view perceived ontological as well as epistemological connection, as witnessed by the locative form.

In arguing that Buddhist causality is presented in these texts as an objective phenomenon rather than a subjective projection, Kalupahana calls attention to the second and fourth phrases of the formula.[31] The teaching does not simply state that "when this is, that is and when this is not, that is not," it also includes verbs of transformation, of arising and ceasing. These are not, as Kalupahana points out, merely repetitions of the preceding phrase. With the change of verb (from being to arising, from not-being to ceasing) they stress the possibility of novelty, of new generation and new cessation.

A perhaps more telling argument for the objective status of *paticca samuppāda* resides in the texts' assertion that this causal law exists independently of the Buddhas; it has a reality external to their perception of it. "Whether, brethren, there be an arising of Tathāgatas, or whether there be no such arising, this nature of things just stands, this causal status, this causal orderliness."[32] The enlightened ones do not invent it or infer it, but rediscover it. More than a private interpretation of reality, it led the Buddha to speak of it in terms of "the nature of things" (*dhammatā*).[33]

Two more etymological points remain to be made. *Paticca* and *paccaya*, terms basic to Pali expositions of dependent co-arising, both stem, as I noted, from the verb *pacceti*. Composed of *pati + i*, it means to come or go back to. Present, then, is the notion of return or reverse movement which the preposition *pati*, "back to," denotes. As I turn in the next chapter to systems theory, I will show how central to its notion of mutual causality is the concept of feedback. The effects of any action are fed back into the organism, and by virtue of this feedback systems are interdeterminative. The perception of return in causal flow is present linguistically in these central terms of *paticca* and *paccaya*. It also is discernible in our own language in the very word "relation"—*re-latus*, meaning originally, "that which is carried back." *A*, in relating to *B*, brings it back to itself; self-reference, which the cybernetic view of things makes explicit, is implicit in these Pali terms, as well as in the roots of our own speech.

Nidāna and *upadhi* are terms applied to the factors which condition existence, be they mental or physical. Present in the etymology of both is the notion of constraint. *Upadhi*, the earlier term, connotes not only basis or foundation, but also impediment, bond, restriction. As for *nidāna*, it stems directly from the verb to bind or fetter (*dā, dyati*).

The notion of constraint imbedded in these terms underscores the character of causality. When causal efficacy is attributed to relation rather than to substance, then, as systems theorists have pointed out, it operates in terms of the constraints these relations impose on phenomenality (see p.78). Systems self-organize and evolve by virtue of invariant relations whose constraints, channeling flows of energy and information, are of a morphic nature.[34]

Reciprocity of Causal Factors

The conditioned factors of existence are presented in serial form; indeed language itself constrains us to express things sequentially. Although some scholars have interpreted these factors as a linear causal chain, textual evidence abounds that their relationship is one of mutual dependence. This interdependence is implicit in a relational view of reality and in the absence of a first cause; here in the interaction of the *nidānas*, or *upadhis* their reciprocity is more explicit.

An early text on dependent co-arising, the *Dvayatānupassanā sutta*, presents each *upadhi* as the cause of the others:

> Whatever pain arises is all in consequence of *avijjā* . . . from the complete destruction of *avijjā* there is no origin of pain. . . .

> Whatever pain arises is all in consequence of the *saṅkhārās* . . . from the complete destruction of the *saṅkhārās* there is no origin of pain. . . .

> Whatever pain arises is all in consequence of *viññāna* [and so on].[35]

These phrases are repeated for all the rest. Here the series clearly represents no linear chain: Each *upadhi*, in giving rise to all pain, gives rise to the others. Occasioning and occasioned by each other, their causality is mutual. Like a house of cards, the constellation of factors that condition our existence can be disrupted and collapsed at any point.

Sheaves or bundles of reeds propped together, leaning on one another, is a simile used in the scriptures. Such is the relation ascribed to *viññāna* (consciousness) and *nāmarūpa* (name-and-form). It is with these two factors that the causal series frequently interrupts its enumeration and, after stating that *nāmarūpa* arises conditioned by *viññāna*, circles back and states that *viññāna* in turn arises conditioned by *nāmarūpa*. Here causal reciprocity is so explicit that a number of scholars have been struck by it and some, like Keith and Thomas, have seen in it a logical objection to dependent co-arising.[36] Koṭṭhita, discussing the matter with Śariputra, the most scholarly of the Buddha's disciples, says,

> Lo! now we understand the venerable Śariputra's words thus . . . Name-and-form is conditioned by consciousness,

consciousness is conditioned by name-and-form. How, friend
Śariputra, is the meaning of what you have said to be regarded?

Well, friend, I will make you a simile, for through a simile
some intelligent men admit the meaning of what has been
said. It is just as if, friend, there stood two sheaves of reeds
leaning one against the other. Even so, friend, name-and-form
comes to pass conditioned by consciousness, consciousness
conditioned by name-and-form, sense conditioned by name-
and-form, and so on. . . .

If, friend, I were to pull towards me one of those sheaves of
reeds, the other would fall; if I were to pull towards me the
other, the former would fall.[37]

A similar image, a tripod of three sticks, is used to illustrate the
relationship between the *khaṇḍas*, the aggregates of which the sense
of self is composed.[38]

In the causal series the reciprocity between *nāmarūpa* and
viññāna is emphasized most, probably to contrast it with the Brahmanical view, which gave consciousness ontological and axiological
primacy over material manifestations. But its causal relations with
other factors are seen as mutual also, as is implied in Śariputra's
inclusion of "sense and so on" in his simile of the reeds.

Take the relation of consciousness to the preceding *nidāna*, by
which it is conditioned: *saṅkhārā*, volitional formulations. While
these formations are presented in this series as formative of consciousness, they are in turn conditioned by it. This notion is present
in its meaning, which derives from *saṅkhata*, "compounded" or
"put together." It is our conscious acts and intentions which modify
the volitions which in turn shape our consciousness.

That which we will, brethren, and that which we intend to do
and that wherewithal we are occupied: this becomes an object
for the persistence of consciousness.[39]

The same causal mutuality can be seen in the relation of
saṅkhārā to the factor which precedes it in the series, *avijjā*. While
our ignorance shapes our volitions, these do not evolve unidirectionally from a preexistent state of ignorance, as Burnouf, Coomaraswamy, and others interpreted, but they in turn feed and
perpetuate our ignorance. This point is stressed in the *Kathāvatthu*

of the Abhidharma.[40] In opposition to the view attributed to the Mahāsaṅghikas, that "whereas actions are conditioned by ignorance, we may not say that ignorance is conditioned by actions," the Theravadins responded that *avijjā* was co-existent with *saṅkhārā*, and that just as *viññāna* and *nāmarūpa* are reciprocally caused, so can be ignorance and volition or grasping and craving. "Then the conditioning relation can be reciprocal," states the text.[40]

The Pali term is *aññamañña*. Literally "one another," it appears on translations as "reciprocal" and "mutual." While it came to be used technically by the Abhidharmists as a specific type of causal relation, Buddhaghosa used the term to qualify the import of the causal doctrine as a whole.[41] He defines *paṭicca samuppāda* as the mode of causality according to which "phenomena arise together in reciprocal dependence (*aññamañña paṭicca*)"

In the early texts this reciprocity, which characterizes the interaction of *viññāna* and *nāmarūpa*, and *viññāna*, *saṅkhārā*, and *avijjā*, functions also in the arising of *tanhā* or craving. While eighth in the *nidāna* series, as arising conditioned by feeling, it is a key factor in our suffering, as the second and third noble Truths declare. This has led students of Buddhism to wonder which is considered more causative of humanity's fallen state, ignorance or desire. Is it ignorance, as in the Platonic view, or is the vision more like the Pauline in seeing the egocentricity of craving as fundamental? From the viewpoint of the Nikāyas, the answer is both. *Avijjā* is emphasized by being most frequently placed first in the *nidāna* series; *tanhā* is emphasized in the Noble Truths and, on occasion, as the first element in *dukkhasamudaya*.[42] Buddhaghosa points out that both can be "starting points" of the teaching.[43] That neither can be reduced to the other is suggested by the phrase quoted above, descriptive of *saṃsāra*: It is the faring on of beings "cloaked in ignorance, tied to craving".[44] Neither factor is reducible to the other because they are mutually generative: As ignorance propels our craving, so does craving mire us in ignorance.

In similar fashion do *tanhā* and the notion of self (*attā*) reflect a process of mutual causation. All the components of the sense of separate selfhood, categorized in the *Mahātānhasankhaya sutta* as material food, sense perception, volitions, and thoughts, have "craving as the provenance, craving as source, craving as birth, craving as origin."[45] The mythical account of genesis in the *Aggaññasutta* illustrates how craving leads to the illusion of ego. Feeding greedily on the fruits of earth, beings grew more conscious and prideful of their individual attributes.[46] The notion of having an enduring self is one

of the four forms of grasping (*upādāna*), which in the series arises
conditioned by craving.[47] Yet just as craving feeds it, so does the
illusion of self in turn feed craving.

> Now Rahula, when a monk by perfect wisdom realizes with
> regard to the elements [which comprise the human being] 'this
> is not mine, this is not I, this is not my *attā*,' then does he cut
> himself off from craving, loosen bonds and by overcoming the
> vain conceit [of attā] make an end of suffering.[48]

Thus do *tanhā* and *attā* appear as interdependent, their causal relationship reciprocal. As with the bundles of reeds, the removal of
one collapses the other.

In the "Great Discourse on the Destruction of Craving,"
quoted above, sensory perception is seen as formative of the sense
of self, along with physical sustenance, volitions, and mental constructs. This teaching is made vivid by the metaphor of food (*āhāra*).
"These four foods sustain creatures that have come to be."[49] The
food image suggests that the reality with which we deal is something we process—we ingest it and pass it through our system. We
cannot confront it as something "out there," cleanly and neatly separable from our observing consciousness. Rather it is in us, of us,
shaping our very perceptions.

The *nidāna* series, therefore, appears not as a linear causal sequence so much as a network of interacting and mutually affecting
conditions. Anagarika Govinda, the German-born monk and lama,
writes of the "dynamic character" of *paţicca samuppāda*:

> Every link can be combined with another . . . and, indeed, in
> whichever succession one chooses. . . . In this way we have
> neither a purely temporal, nor yet a purely logical causality,
> but a living, organic relationship, a simultaneous correlation,
> juxtaposition and succession of all the links, in which each, so
> to say, represents the transverse summation of all the others,
> and bears in itself its whole past as well as all the possibilities
> of its future. And precisely on this account the entire chain at
> every moment and from every phase of it, is removable.[50]

Abhidharmist Interpretations

My study of Buddhist causality is based on the *suttas* and *vinaya piţaka* of the Pali Canon, those first two "baskets" of scripture

which represent the earliest written records we have of Buddhist teachings. They represent what Buddhist scholar Mizuno terms "primitive Buddhism" and Edward Conze, "archaic Buddhism." The texts of the third basket, the *Abhidharma Piṭaka,* a scholastic elaboration of the philosophic aspects of the teachings, represent a later development in Buddhist thought, as evidenced by their terminology and content.[51]

In the Abhidharma, both of the Theravadin and Sarvastivadin schools, analytical theorizing about the nature of causal relationships is conducted and brought to a high degree of sophistication and complexity. That development, with the density and intricacy of its language and logic, influenced many later scholarly views of Buddhist causality as a whole. Yet in that development certain shifts occurred, subtle but significant differences in the way *paticca samuppāda* is presented.

These differences are often overlooked. Many teachers of Buddhism today and even scholars of the stature of Stcherbatsky and Conze have imputed to the earlier teachings speculative elements that did not appear until the Abhidharma. Because these differences have colored interpretations of the Buddha's teachings and because they represent a partial shift to a more linear view of causality, it is important to specify and summarize them here. They are fourfold: (1) the notion of momentariness; (2) the postulation of unconditioned dharmas; (3) the distinction between substance and attribute; and (4) the presentation of the *nidāna* series as a sequence of three lives.

The Notion of Momentariness

The early texts stressed the impermanence and interaction of phenomena, but did not try to analyze their ontological nature. The Abhidharmists sought to determine the intrinsic character of the elements in interaction, that is, the dharmas. These represent the psycho-physical units of experience, the fundamental building blocks into which conventional reality can be dissected. As such they were differentiated, enumerated, and classified and elaborate theories mounted as to their nature, number, and duration. These theories tended to hypostatize the dharmas as discrete entities, as "facts which are ultimately real."[52] As Streng has noted, this represents "an unfortunate drift back into essentialist thinking."[53]

In the Abhidharmist effort to accommodate this substantialism to a dynamic vision of reality, these dharmas came to be seen as instants, replacing each other with lightning rapidity, too brief to interact or do more than succeed each other in time. As a consequence, impermanence (*aniccatā*) became momentariness (*khanikā*), and causation became mere sequence. The dharmas are seen as too instantaneous to have any connection beyond that of succession.[54] This notion is close to Hume's view of causality, one which is often compared to the Buddhist, but the similarity with Hume extends only to the Abhidharma and not to earlier Buddhism.[55]

In the early texts, as Kalupahana argues, phenomena are presented as impermanent but not as momentary. There "empirical things . . . are observable facts existing for some time, and they can act successively or simultaneously because they are not momentary."[56] In addition to the time factor, there are critical questions of ontology and epistemology. The point is not so much how long a thing endures, but whether causality is posited in terms of things or relations. A reason why momentariness or *khanikā* does not appear and is not likely to appear in the early texts is because the earlier Buddhists did not attempt a metaphysical analysis of reality in terms of discrete entities. While the self, for example, was broken down into the five aggregates, the emphasis was less on the distinct nature of these components than on their impermanence.

The Postulation of Unconditioned Dharmas

Another Abhidharmist modification is the postulation that there are aspects of reality, or dharmas, which are unconditioned, namely *nibbāna* and *akaśa* (space). This represents a shift in the usage of the term *asaṅkhata* (Sanskrit: *asaṃskṛta*). In the earlier scriptures *saṅkhata* means "put together," "compounded," "organized"— and therefore subject to dissolution. The word did not mean conditioned, nor did its opposite, *asaṅkhata* (applied to *nibbāna*) mean unconditioned. Indeed nothing is seen in the early texts as unconditioned, removed from the realm of causality. As Kalupahana asserts, the pre-Abhidharmist texts qualify no entity, essence, or state as *apaṭicca samuppāna*.[57] Nor is emancipation in the early texts presented as an escape from causality. It is reached rather by employing causation, by using the leverage of conditionality. *Nibbāna* is presented as attainable, not by exiting from the series of conditioned *nidānas*, but by substituting through practice *nirodha* for *samudaya*. "I say that liberation is causally associated, not uncausally associated," said the Buddha.[58]

With the Abhidharma *asaṅkhata* begins to be used to denote "unconditioned," as is evident, for example, in the classification of dharmas in the *Dhammasaṅgaṇi*.[59] There, only *nibbāna* is in that category, while the lists of other schools include *akaśa* as well.[60] As such, the meaning of *asaṅkhata* comes to be used synonymously with *ahetujam*, "not the product of a cause."[61]

This move is understandable in terms of the shift toward a more substantialist and linear view, where effects preexist in their causes, and are produced by them. Since *nibbāna* cannot be produced in this way, it is imagined that it must then be removed completely from the causal realm—and posited as unconditioned. Such a move encourages interpretations which tend to equate *nibbāna* with a metaphysical absolute. It also has the effect of taking release and assigning it to another dimension than the world of contingency and need in which we live. That this shift has influenced scholars' views of Buddhist teachings as a whole is evident in Conze, who states that it is "the basic teaching of the Buddha" that "salvation can only be found through escape to the Unconditioned."[62]

The Distinction Between Substance and Attribute

For its purposes of analysis the Abhidharma posited categorical distinctions between dharmas (things or psychophysical events), which did not figure in the Buddha's recorded teachings. The distinction was made between conventional or relative reality and Ultimate Reality (*paramattha desanā*), suggesting the existence of an absolute truth or realm apart from the world of appearances.[63] A similar categorical distinction arose between the mental and physical realms, the Abhidharma itself being presented as *nāma-rūpapariccheda*, the analysis into mind and matter.[64] Mind (*citta*) and its mental properties (*cetasika*) were defined as nonmaterial (*arūpa*) (with *nibbāna* in some texts assigned to the mental realm) in contrast to the nonmental (*acetasika*) character of matter.

This dualistic drift fostered attitudes toward the body and the phenomenal world, that have characterized the Theravada and influenced other forms of Buddhism as well. It also caused philosophic problems for the scholastics, which Kalupahana examines at length and which relates to a third distinction the scholastics made: a thing (*dharma*) and its characteristic (*lakkhaṇa*).[65] This opens the way to the notion of an underlying substance, which serves to provide the continuity that was lost in the arising of the idea of momentariness. As we are reminded by critiques of linear causality in our own century, the distinction between substance and attribute leads to a unidirectional view of causal action (see Chapter 5).

The Presentation of the Nidāna Series as a Sequence of Three Lives

The fourth departure from earlier causal views, which we should note in the Abhidharma, is the presentation of the *nidāna* series in terms of three successive lives. As such it comes to represent the cycle of rebirth and is termed the "Twofold Causation extending to the Three Times," (twofold meaning *samudaya* and *nirodha*). In this interpretation, which is often equated with the Buddha's teaching of dependent co-arising itself, the first two factors, *avijjā* and *saṅkhārā*, are taken to represent causes incurred in a former life. The next seven represent present existence, *viññāna* through *vedanā* being the present fruits of past causes, while *taṇhā* and *upādāna* are the present causes of the future. The last three, *bhava, jāti,* and *jarāmaraṇa,* figure as the future fruits of present action, or a third life.

This view was not taught in the *suttas* and *vinaya*.[66] There the *nidānas*, functioned more as examples of how life is conditioned than as precise and specific determinants. According to Mizuno, the reference to *viññāna* as rebirth-consciousness was meant as a popular illustration only, and the series of factors themselves, which reveal no single authoritative version, exhibit too much variety to denote a rigid schema of three lives. Their number, their order, and their character vary in the early texts, as we have noted—some series amounting to ten, some to twelve or more, some preceding consciousness with contact and feeling, some including factors of joy and faith.[67] The order and precise composition of the sequence clearly do not constitute the main tenet of the teaching.[68] In the Abhidharma, however, these terms are accorded particular importance and specificity, as one form of the series, the one that occurs most frequently in the Nikayas, is taken to represent the sequential unfolding of cause and effect through a person's successive lives. What had been, as Mizuno suggests, a popular metaphoric and mnemonic device is here literalized. Like the view of *nibbāna* as unconditioned, it is likely that this development arose partially as a result of the tendency to substantialize the dharmas. In any case the Abhidharmists accorded to each *nidāna* an ontological significance not evident in the *suttas* and *vinaya*, and their three-lives interpretation tends to present the series as a linear causal chain. As such it obscures the reciprocal dynamic we examined above, the ways in which, within a given life, indeed a given moment, one's volitions and thoughts, craving and ignorance, interdetermine each other.

Paṭicca Samuppāda as Interdependence

Despite later divergences of some Abhidharmist and scholarly interpretations, it is clear that *paṭicca samuppāda* in the early texts teaches "the interdependent structure" of reality. In the words of Mizuno,

> The Buddha awoke to the interdependent structure of the world and attained enlightenment under the bodhi tree. From this standpoint, we may say that Buddhism stands basically on the thought of interdependence.[69]

The Buddha said that it was difficult to understand. Hardly self-evident from the conventional viewing of things, *paṭicca samuppāda* is, as the texts reiterate, deep and subtle, hard to perceive, and requiring insight. In the accounts of the enlightenment and subsequent causal teachings, a phrase recurs which refers to the kind of thinking involved in the perception of mutual causality. This is *yoniso manasikāra. Manasikāra* is from a verb meaning to "ponder," to "take to heart," and denotes deep attention or attentive pondering. Here this pondering is qualified by *yoniso*, the ablative of *yoni. Yoni*, literally, is "womb." By extension it came to mean "origin," "way of being born," and "matrix."

Yoniso manasikāra offers multiple and fruitful connotations for the way we can think about dependent co-arising. Referring to womb it connotes generation, the arising of phenomena. As "matrix," it suggests the web of interdependence in which these phenomena participate. It is not a dissecting or categorizing exercise of the intellect. Synthetic rather than analytic, it involves an awareness of wholeness—a wide and intent openness or attentiveness wherein all factors can be included, their interrelationships beheld.

Herbert Guenther, suggesting that such a style of thought is not characteristic of the West, stresses the doctrine's divergence from the linear perspective.[70]

> In talking about causality in Buddhism, it is of the utmost importance to be aware of the points of divergence from our ways of thinking. The conceptual framework of Buddhist associative and co-ordinative thinking was something different from the traditional European causal and nomothetic thinking. [It posits] a network of interdependent, co-existing and freely

cooperating forces and in this network at any time any one factor may take the highest place in a hierarchy of causes and effects.

Commenting on the role that this accords to conscious beings, Guenther goes on to say,

> It is he who as 'causal agent' creates his world which, in turn, is a 'causal agent' creating him. This is so, because 'causality' in Buddhism is, as has been noted, an interlocking system and not a linear sequence of cause and effect.

This causality is, then, both relative and objective: Objectively inhering in the nature of things, it is relative, not as a subjective opinion but by virtue of the interdependence of phenomena. This notion of interdependence so pervades the Buddha's teachings that even his giving of the Law itself is presented as conditioned. No unilateral revelation from on high, its appearance arises from the very conditions to which we all are subject. It is not the product of another purer realm, a dimension divorced from despair, but occurs in dependence on the very turmoil of birth, decay, dying, that is the definition of *saṃsāra*. In an utterance predictive of Nagarjuna's later affirmation of the dialectical interplay between *saṃsāra* and *nirvāna*, the Buddha says:

> If these three things were not in the world, my disciples, the Perfect One, the holy supreme Buddha, would not appear in the world, the law and the doctrine, which the Perfect One propounds, would not shine in the world. What three things are they? Birth and old age and death.[71]

This view of causality has far-reaching implications for an understanding of the self and its world, for the perception of the plight and promise intrinsic to human existence. These implications, evident in the Buddha's other teachings, will be drawn out in the final section of this work, along with those discernible in a similar view of causal process—that of general systems theory.

Notes

1. *Dīgha Nikāya*, II.36

2. Nyanatiloka, *Guide Through the Abhidharma Pitaka*, p. 139.

3. Stcherbatsky, *Buddhist Logic,* I.141.

4. While Kalupahana's study of Buddhist causality in the early scriptures is very helpful in clarifying many of its features, its reciprocal nature is mentioned only in passing (*Causality,* p. 59) and its contrast with linear causality left implicit. This is true also of Rahula (*What Buddha Taught,* p. 53). Govinda, Streng, and Guenther, as well as Oldenberg and C. Rhys Davids, do call attention to the distinctiveness of the mutuality of causes in *paṭicca samuppāda,* but their work does not examine in depth of the textual bases for this non-linearity, or of its significance in relation to the other teachings of the Buddha.

5. Maruyama, "Symbiotization of Cultural Heterogeneity," pg. 239.

6. Bunge, *Causality,* pg. 199.

7. *Saṃyutta Nikāya,* II. 13.

8. *Sutta Nipāta,* p. 363.

9. Burnouf, *Introduction à l'histoire du bouddhisme indien,* pp. 485, 507.

10. Oldenberg, *Buddha: Life, Doctrine, Order,* pg. 259, 251.

11. Streng, "Reflections" pg. 79.

12. Bunge, *Causality,* pp. 134–36.

13. Cited in Burnouf, *Introduction à l'histoire du bouddhisme indien,* pg. 506.

14. Stcherbatsky, *Buddhist-Logic,* I, p. 142; *Central Conception of Buddhism,* p. 30. Burnouf also saw ignorance as "le point de départ de toutes les existences" (485) *Introduction.* Other scholars who interpret *avijjā* in terms of a first cause, from which all else ensues in a linear sequence, include H. C. Kern (cited in Nyanatiloka, *Guide through the Abhidarma Pitaka,* p. 140) and A. K. Coomaraswamy.

15. Nyanatiloka, *Guide through the Abhidharma Pitaka,* p. 139.

16. *Ibid.,* p. 602.

17. *Ibid.,* p. 623.

18. Oldenberg, *Buddha: Life, Doctrine, Order,* pg. 241. On this subject Caroline Rhys Davids expresses similar views and is more specific in countering the notion that ignorance can be construed as a first cause. Her position is in harmony with her repeated use of the term "mutually dependent" in her discussion of *paṭicca samuppāda* ("Paṭicca Samuppāda").

19. *Aṅguttara Nikāya*, V.113.

20. *Majjhima Nikāya*, I.265.

21. *Saṃyutta Nikāya*, II.176.

22. *Ibid.*, III.33.

23. *Ibid.*, I.134; III.54.

24. *Ibid.*, II.96.

25. *Ibid.*, II.262.

26. Buddhaghosa, *Visuddhimagga*, pp. 600–1.

27. *Saṃyutta Nikāya*, II.11.

28. Rhys Davids, C., and Aung, *Points of Controversy*, pp. 390–91. The term *upakaraka* is used by Buddhaghosa to emphasize that the causal function of the factors of existence is that of "assisting" (*Visuddhimagga*, p.533, 612).

29. Rhys Davids, C., and Aung, *Points of Controversy*, p. 391.

30. Pande, *Studies in Origins of Buddhism*, p. 426, n. 135.

31. Kalupahana, *Causality*, p. 95.

32. *Saṃyutta Nikāya*, II.25.

33. *Saṃyutta Nikāya*, II.25; *Anguttara Nikāya*, V.2, 3; *Majjhima Nikāya*, I.324.

34. Whyte, "Structural Hierarchy" p. 275; Ashby, "Principles of Self-Organizing System," p. 131.

35. *Sutta Nipāta*, pp. 729–34.

36. Keith, *Buddhist Philosophy*, pg. 101; Thomas, *History of Buddhist Thought*, pp. 67–68.

37. *Saṃyutta Nikāya*, II. 113.

38. Nyanatiloka, *Guide Through the Abhidharma Pitaka*, p. 101.

39. *Saṃyutta Nikāya*, II.64.

40. *Katthāvatthu*, XV.2.

41. *Samangavilasini* II.6, quoted in Kalupahana, *Causality*, pp. 54, 202.

42. *Saṃyutta Nikāya*, II.84

43. Buddhaghosa, *Visuddhimagga,* I.603.

44. *Saṃyutta Nikāya,* II.178.

45. *Majjhima Nikāya,* I.261.

46. *Dīgha Nikāya,* III,88f.

47. *Ibid.,* II.58.

48. *Saṃyutta Nikāya,* II.253.

49. *Majjhima Nikāya,* I.261.

50. Govinda, *Psychological Attitude Early Buddhist Philosophy,* p. 56.

51. Reasons for adducing that the Abhidharma represents thinking that is subsequent in time to the *suttas* and *vinaya* are offered in Pande, *Studies in Origins of Buddhism,* Part I; Mizuno, *Primitive Buddhism,* Chapter I; Rhys Davids, T., *Buddhist India,* 72f; and Lamotte, *Histoire du bouddhisme indien, 168f.*

52. Conze, *Buddhist Thought,* p. 197.

53. Streng, *Reflections,* p. 74.

54. In struggling to explain how distinct entities which are instantaneous can enjoy causal relationship, or anything beyond sequential occurrence, the Sarvāstivādin Abhidharmists posited an enduring substratum, a *svabhava.* This led them back into an essentialist dichotomy between substance and quality and opened them to charges of vitiating the Buddha's doctrines of *anicca* and *anattā* (Stcherbatsky, *Central Conception of Buddhism,* pp. 30–31). The Sautrantīkas reacted against the substantialism of the Sarvāstivādin view by accentuating the instantaneity of dharmas, seeing them as point-instants so momentary that they self-destruct upon occurrence. Having done that, the Sautrantīkas made no serious effort to construe a causal connection.

55. Stcherbatsky refers to the theory of momentariness as "the foundation upon which the whole of the Buddhist system is built (*Buddhist Logic,* p. 119). The Buddhist theory of causation is a direct consequence of the theory of Universal Momentariness" (*Conception of Buddhist Nirvana,* p. 2). Similarly Conze presents "the Buddhist definition of causality" as "the inevitable corollary of the doctrine of momentariness" (*Buddhist Thought,* p. 149). Consequently both scholars see *paticca samuppāda* as similar to the causal view of Hume (Stcherbatsky, *Conception of Buddhist Nirvana,* p. 23; Conze, *Thirty Years of Buddhist Studies,* p. 239). N. Dutt also mistakenly ascribes the notion of momentariness to the early teaching (*Early Monastic Buddhism,* pp. 215, 219).

56. Kalupahana, *Causality*, p. 153.

57. *Ibid.*, pp. 85, 140–41.

58. *Saṃyutta Nikāya*, II.30

59. Nyanatiloka, *Guide through Abhidarma Pitaka*, p. 84.

60. Warder, *Indian Buddhism*, p. 308.

61. *Milindapanha*, pp. 268–71; Conze, *Buddhist Thought*, p. 159.

62. Conze, *Thirty Years of Buddhist Stuidies*, pp. 210–11; Similarly, Keith accepts as characteristic of all Buddhist teachings the scholastic categorization of *nibbāna* as unconditioned. Setting this beside scriptural emphasis on the universality of dependent co-arising, he finds contradiction. Unfortunately, this does not prompt him to question his interpretation, but confirms for him the "vagueness of the canonical view." "In the face of this to assign to Buddhism faith in the uniformity of causal process or of nature is absurd" (Keith, *Buddhist Philosophy*, p. 113).

63. *Dhammasangani*, A 21.

64. Kalupahana, *Buddhist Philosophy*, p. 98.

65. Kalupahana, *Causality*, Chapter 8.

66. Mizuno, *Primitive Buddhism*, p. 132; Pande, *Studies in Origins of Buddhism*, p. 416; Conze, *Buddhist Thought*, p. 157.

67. Such variations in the *nidāna* series are to be found, *inter alia*, in *Saṃyutta Nikāya*, II.66, 100; III.26; *Digha Nikāya* II.59; *Majjhima Nikāya* I.91, *Sutta Nipāta* 723f.

68. Rhys Davids, T., *Dialogues of Buddha*, p. 45.

69. Mizuno, *Primitive Buddhism*, p. 116.

70. Guenther, *Buddhist Philosophy*, pp. 75–76.

71. *Aṅguttara Nikāya*, III, quoted in Oldenberg, *Buddha: Life, Doctrine, Order*, p. 217.

4

General Systems Theory

The ideas were generated in many places: in Vienna by Bertalanffy, in Harvard by Wiener, in Princeton by von Neumann, in Bell Telephone labs by Shannon, in Cambridge by Craik, and so on. All these separate developments dealt with . . . the problem of what sort of thing is an organized system. . . . I think that cybernetics is the biggest bite out of the fruit of the Tree of Knowledge that mankind has taken in the last 2000 years.

—Gregory Bateson[1]

A leap from reflections on early Buddhist scripture to a presentation of general systems theory[2] is not quite the category-defying acrobatics that it might appear at first glance. Although these two bodies of thought represent very different human enterprises, with differing goals and methods, I dare say the Buddha himself would not regard it as unseemly to consider his teaching side by side with concepts spawned by modern science. He regarded no data, however mundane, as irrelevant to the idea of dependent co-arising, drew copiously on what his era knew of natural phenomena, and considered himself, in contrast to other teachers, as an empiricist relying on that which is known and testable by experience. The interdependence he perceived between the mental and the physical and between thought and perception broadens those areas of inquiry to which his teachings can be seen as relevant. It is not inappropriate, therefore, to consider his teachings in tandem with notions derived from the natural sciences.

In contrast to the linear paradigm that has predominated in Western culture, general systems theory presents a mutual or reciprocal view of causality. Together, these two perspectives, systems and Buddhist, can inform and enrich our understanding of this very different kind of causal process. Before examining how systems theorists see this causal process function, let us review general systems theory: its history, its main concepts, and its terminology.

Science's Problems with the One-Way Causal Paradigm

General systems theory originated in the effort to perceive and understand scientifically phenomena which eluded the mechanistic model of reality. That model represents, as the Austrian biologist Ludwig von Bertalanffy characterizes it, "the analytic, mechanistic, one-way causal paradigm of classical science."[3] It assumed that reality could be analyzed. It supposed that a whole could be understood in terms of its parts, that the nature and function of a substance or an organism could be comprehended by reducing it to its material, externally observable components.

Such analysis provided impressive scientific gains. The dissection of life afforded glimpses of its construction at a given moment in time, and a limited but telling capacity to predict and control. This capacity was achieved at some cost, however. Overarching patterns of relationship were disregarded as immeasurable, if not irrelevant. Considerations of purpose and plan were, along with final causes, banished as nonempirical. It was assumed that all causes and potentialities could be traced back, linearly, to initial conditions, that they are reducible to forces long set in motion. When it appeared, under closer observation, that phenomena did not behave that way, a corollary view arose which discarded causality altogether and saw the world as random.

The unidirectional paradigm eventuated in two alternatives: Either we live in a clockwork universe, predetermined by initial conditions, with no scope for genuine novelty, or it is a blind and purposeless play of atoms, "a tale told by an idiot" and determinable only statistically, by the laws of chance. These alternatives were bleak to the spirit, a factor in the psychic dislocation experienced in the modern world. The linear causality on which they were based also proved increasingly inadequate to scientific problems and evidence. We can note three areas where this inadequacy was manifest and where it gave impetus to systems thought.

The assumptions of classical science appeared sufficient to understand carefully isolated phenomena and causal relationships between one thing and another. Scientists had difficulty applying unidirectional causal notions to situations displaying more than two variables; that is, to any process that is more complex, for example, than a hydrogen atom, which has one electron orbiting its nucleus.

To map multivariable complexes in terms of linear relations involved piecemeal analysis, where the forces at play are reduced to sequences of interacting pairs.[4] While this can afford some useful information, it cannot map the flow of the whole interactive complex. As scientific tools opened vistas and yielded for any given event increasingly complex data, they impelled the search for new ways to conceptualize causal interaction.

A second area to which traditional causal concepts came to be seen as inadequate relates to entropy, or rather to the evidence for anti-entropic processes. The Second Law of Thermodynamics states that in every transformation of energy part of that energy is lost; therefore differences in heat become gradually equalized and the universe is seen as tending ultimately toward sameness, randomness, and disorganization. Regarded as "one of the most fundamental of all laws of nature," it has never been contradicted or disproved.[5] It is, however, inadequate to explain the evidence that in parts of the universe, such as all living organisms, forms differentiate and evolve in complexity. Instead of running down, they build up. Self-organization was first studied in biological phenomena, from the 1920s on, but by the 1970s physicists, inspired by conceptualizations afforded by systems-oriented life scientists, noted comparable processes at work in suborganic phenomena as well, particularly high-energy plasma.[6] The anti-entropic evolution of order cannot be explained in traditional linear concepts where effect preexists in the cause.

Third, the analytic approach of classical science, based on the assumption that reality could be understood by dissecting it into smaller and smaller pieces, that causes could be traced back in linear chains, bred acute specialization. As specialists, from geologists to neurologists, learned more and more about less and less, their disciplines became virtually air-tight—the specificity of their topics and terminology hindering communication with the uninitiates outside their narrow domains. While the need to understand the play of interdependence became increasingly urgent, specialization of inquiry blocked both the perception and the study of relationship. As Ervin Laszlo put it,

> We are drilling holes in the wall of mystery that we call nature and reality on many locations, and we carry out delicate analyses on each of these sites. But it is only now that we are beginning to realize the need for connecting the probes with one another and gaining some coherent insight into what is there.[7]

The Perception of Systems in the Life Sciences

General systems theory arose first in the science where the need to transcend an atomistic approach was perhaps the most obvious—biology. Here, in the work of von Bertalanffy, attention was directed not to parts, but to wholes and the way they function, not to substance but to organization. Referring to the early stages of his work in the 1920s, von Bertalanffy writes,

> [I] became puzzled about obvious lacunae in the research and theory of biology. The then prevalent mechanistic approach . . . appeared to neglect or actively deny just what is essential in the phenomena of life. [I] advocated an organismic conception of biology which emphasizes consideration of the organism as a whole or system, and see the main objective of biological sciences in the discovery of the principles of organization at its various levels.[8]

Such thinking was not isolated. A wholistic, process-oriented approach was in the air, with the appearance in that same period of Whitehead's philosophy of organic mechanism and physiologist Walter Cannon's work on homeostasis—a concept fundamental to systems thought.

Von Bertalanffy found that wholes, be they animal or vegetable, cell, organ, or organism, could best be described as systems. A system is less a thing than a pattern. It is a pattern of events, its existence and character deriving less from the nature of its components than from their organization. As such it consists of a dynamic flow of interactions. It is "non-summative" and irreducible; that is, the character of a system as a pattern of organization is altered with the addition, subtraction or modification of any piece. Hence it is more than the sum of its parts. This "more" is not something extra, like a vitalist principle or an *élan vital*, but a new level of operation which the interdependence of its parts permits. It is lost from view when a system's composite units are investigated independently.

Von Bertalanffy perceived that the organic interdependence that characterizes the internal functioning of a living system also typifies its relations with its environment. Whether it is an organism, cell or molecule, it functions and evolves within a larger system—in regard to whose character it is both dependent and indispensable. Systems enclose and are enclosed by other systems with which they are in constant communication, in a natural hierarchical order.[9]

The organized whole found in nature, then, is not only a system but an *open* system. It maintains and organizes itself by exchanging matter, energy, and information with its environment. These flow through the system and are transformed by it. These exchanges and transformations are the system's life and continuity, for no component of the system is permanent. The way they happen, that is, the principles by which a pattern of perpetually changing substance both retains its shape or identity and evolves its order, have been a central focus of systems inquiry. It was a major discovery by von Bertalanffy that the laws which govern these processes, or rather the invariances they display, are essentially the same whatever the nature of the system.

In maintaining and organizing itself, an open system is characterized by what von Bertalanffy termed *Fliess-Gleichgewicht*, which means "steady state", or, literally, "flux-balance." Flux is stressed because the system is in a continual state of inflow and outflow; never in chemical or thermodynamic equilibrium, its substance is continually altered by interacting events. Balance is stressed because the system maintains itself in tension between opposing forces—the building up and breaking down of its components. By importing and processing energy, it compensates for degeneration. It achieves and sustains a dynamic equilibrium between its own fantastically improbable state and the surrounding medium. While its elements are consumed, as in a flame, its pattern persists and can even grow in complexity. As such, its processes are anti-entropic, representing a maintenance and increase of order within the overall thermodynamic tendency toward randomness and disorganization. Its orderliness happens not just in spite of disintegrative forces but also by means of them—as a candle keeps its shape by burning.

Given the dialectical nature of this vision, it is not surprising to learn that von Bertalanffy admired and studied the work of Nicholas of Cusa. He was deeply interested in the thought of the fifteenth-century cardinal, in whom he saw a union of mystical intuition with mathematical rationality, and a precursor of sorts to the new systems science. In a treatise on Cusa's life and philosophy, von Bertalanffy writes, "The unity of opposites or *coincidentia oppositorum* is the central thought in Cusa's philosophy," and expounds on how this is reflected in Cusa's concept of God as infinite circle.[10] He notes that the image of the infinite circle, with its center everywhere, presents a view consonant with systems, that "any part of the world contains in a limited way, the infinite whole." Von Bertalanffy notes that Cusa is "reminiscent of Heraclitus, [in that] God as the animating principle of an organismic world is compared to fire, so that all becoming is due to modifications of fire or, as we would say today, transformations of energy."

The processes by which the system sustains and creates order in *Fliess-Gleichgewicht* are seen as twofold. One is homeostatic, whereby the continuity of structure or pattern is maintained. The other is self-organizing, whereby the structure is modified, its organization increased. In this complexification the system moves toward greater improbability and variety. This involves a decrease in structural stability: The system, more finely tuned, is more vulnerable to physical disorganization, but this in turn is counterbalanced by a greater flexibility and capacity to adapt, process information, and cope.

By both types of process the system constitutes a counter-movement to the mechanically and statistically demonstrable "running down" of the universe, which the Second Law of Thermodynamics represents. The open system becomes a pocket of negative entropy, where order and improbability are sustained and increased. Its conceptualization resolves the apparent contradiction between the law of dissipation in physics and the law of evolution in biology.

In a closed system, like a machine with no outside source of energy, entropy inevitably increases; but an open system, while it produces entropy, also imports energy from its environment and can increase its orderly differentiation. A closed system is an abstraction and does not exist in nature, unless the world as a whole is taken as one.[11] Even atoms, as enduring systems, interact with the surrounding medium from time to time, displaying the twofold processes of self-stabilization and self-organization.[12]

Cybernetics and the Concept of Feedback

The advent of communications theory and cybernetics provided concepts useful in understanding the processes by which systems stabilize and organize. These concepts sprang from work done during World War II. Nineteenth-century discoveries, such as homeostasis in the maintenance of the chemical balance of the blood and James Watt's invention of the governor on a steam engine, had already demonstrated processes of self-regulation. These now were further clarified by war-time work on self-guided missiles by such scientists as Norbert Wiener. To design these devices, cyberneticians directed their attention and research to the ways in which information is received, exchanged, and used to adjust to contingencies in the environment. Mechanisms were built that could monitor their own performance, correct for deviations and changing conditions, and even, within parameters, alter their goals. The process by which this is accomplished is called "feedback."

In feedback the output of a system, its behavior, is monitored back to its receptors, thereby signaling the degree of performance or nonperformance of an operation in relation to preestablished goals. This monitoring by means of feedback loops permits it to regulate its behavior in terms of these goals. Two types of feedback are distinguished, depending on the type of behavior each generates.

Negative feedback loops stabilize the system within its current trajectory. They reduce deviation between goal and performance, producing "homing-in" behavior and reestablishing the status quo. Positive feedback loops reinforce or amplify the deviations, each change adding to the next. Producing both novelty and instability, they can generate runaway growth or collapse unless stabilized anew within more inclusive negative feedback loops. When that happens, positive feedback conduces to modifying the goals of a given system. Note that these terms diverge from popular lay usage, where *negative feedback* connotes criticism and *positive* implies encouragement.

The feedback concept, while developed from work with artificial regulatory mechanisms, was immediately recognized as applicable to the functioning of natural open systems. In an organism the sensory report of the somatic result of a behavior—for example, a kinesthetic report indicating speed and extent of a movement, or the pain that follows touching a hot object—would constitute feedback. In social relations, it represents the direct perceptual report of the result of one's behavior on others—say, the perception of the return smile that greets one's own.[13] These cybernetic processes appeared to explain the transactional nature of the system's relationship with its environment and offered principles by which the system's extraordinary self-regulative capacity could be comprehended and analyzed.

As systems theory incorporated cybernetic concepts, the homeostasis of a system came to be seen as a function of negative feedback. In this view the system responds to perturbations in the environment in much the same way as a thermostat. It adjusts its performance (output) so as to minimize deviations between its perceptions or measurements of the environment (input) and its internal requirements, which are encoded in a control center (such as the autonomic nervous system). In this fashion it ensures the continuity of its pattern, it stabilizes itself.

The system's self-organization is understandable in terms of the changes incorporated through positive feedback loops. When perturbations in the environment persist and produce a continual mismatching between input and encoded norms, the system either becomes dysfunctional or hits on new behaviors which are adaptive to the new conditions. These are then stabilized at a new level of negative feedback. In the process the system has altered its norms and complexified its structure for greater adaptability. The novelty-producing feedback is called "deviation-amplifying"; the movement is toward differentiation and more improbable steady states.

Systems research shows that, starting anywhere except the thermodynamically most probable equilibrium, an open system will complexify in response to inputs from the environment.[14] This finding has led W. R. Ashby to say that in such a system "life and intelligence inevitably develop."[15]

Systemic Invariances and Hierarchies

To systems thinkers these processes are discernible in invariances evident throughout the observable cosmos. Similarities of behavior are perceived not only in biological systems, but in the sub- and supra-organic world as well—from atoms to social groups to the biosphere of our planet. Such invariances, once perceived, permit the entities or wholes to be seen as systems and to begin to reveal the logic of their behavior and interaction. They have also permitted theorists to formulate the inherent characteristics of a natural system.

These systemic properties are fourfold:

- The system is a nonsummative whole, that is, it cannot be reduced to its parts without altering their pattern. Aggregates, like a brick wall or a library or the contents of a shopping cart, where components can be added or subtracted without affecting the relations between other components, do not qualify.
- The system is homeostatic. It stabilizes itself through negative feedback; that is, the system adjusts its output to produce and sustain a match between the input it will receive and its internally coded requirements.

- The system is self-organizing. Where a mismatch between input and code persists, the system searches for and encodes a new pattern by which it can function. Incorporating positive feedback, differentiation and complexification of structure emerge.
- The system is not only a whole, but part within a larger whole. Whether a cell or organ, atom or animal, it comprises subsystems. It also is, itself, a subsystem within a wider system of whose character and in whose functioning it is an integral and co-determinative component. Open systems in interaction form more inclusive structures or patterns as a function of their mutual adaptations.

The system, then, is Janus-faced: as a whole it faces inward, as a subwhole it looks outward. As such, it is what system thinkers term a *holon*. Philosopher-novelist Arthur Koestler coined the term for this systemic property, adding to the Greek *holos* (whole) the suffix *on*, which, as in neut*ron* or prot*on*, suggests a particle or a part.[16]

Perceiving these progressive levels of systemic self-organization, systems theorists assert that the structure of observed reality is hierarchical. It is not a hierarchy of rank and authority, as in an army or church, nor is it a hierarchy of being and value, as in the thought of Plato and Plotinus. It is more like a set of nested boxes. Or it is a tree, an inverted tree—like that imaged in the Upaniṣads—where systems branch downward into subsystems.[17]

This important distinction from conventional notions of hierarchy has led to the coining of a new word—*holonarchy*—which some systems theorists substitute for the more problematic term in order to avoid confusion with notions of rank or unidirectional agency. For the movement of organization in natural systemic hierarchies flows in the reverse direction from that supposed in bureaucratic pyramids. Levels of higher or more inclusive integrity *emerge* from the interplay of their components; the organizing thrust is from the bottom up. Each new pattern builds on preceding patterns, which, as they integrate, produce new properties. The system never begins from scratch, and this permits stability, economy, and speed in the unfolding of new forms.[18] As seen in embryology, child development and evolution, growth is step-wise, based on the organization of preorganized components.

Like the shape of the inverted tree, or like pyramids, the natural systemic hierarchies narrow as they go up; the "higher" levels, since they comprise the "lower," are fewer in number. There are, for example, fewer molecules than the atoms that constitute them, fewer cells than the molecules of which they are composed, fewer organisms than cells, etc. Yet at the same time each new level of integrity, or self-organization, while displaying less quantity, reveals more variety. There are many more *kinds* of molecules than kinds of atoms, or organisms than cells.

This phenomenon has led Laszlo to graph natural hierarchies, from subatomic particles to solar systems, in not one but two pyramids. One, wide at the bottom and narrowing as it goes up, represents numerical quantity; the other, upside-down twin of the first, being narrow at the bottom and widening as it ascends, represents qualitative variety. These images reflect a key feature of the systems view of reality: the complementarity of integration and differentiation. As patterns interact, their interaction spawns new features, new properties.[19]

Natural hierarchies or holonarchies arise by virtue of constraint, as L. L. Whyte elaborates.[20] Their stepwise development is made possible by the definitions, or necessarily restricted structures, adopted by their components. Hence, Whyte says, hierarchical constraints are of a morphic nature. They channel energy to generate form. They filter or limit noise to disclose information. In the astronomic realm these restraints are gravitational; in the hierarchy from microphysics to organic life they represent electrochemical forces; in the social and cognitive hierarchies they function through the communication of symbols.

The morphic or form-generating nature of such constraints is reminiscent of terms we found in the early Buddhist teaching of causality: *nidāna*, and *upadhi*. Both terms, used interchangeably to denote the factors of causation, carry meanings of binding and restriction.

The production of novelty in the hierarchical self-organization of natural systems is a clear blow to reductionism. It represents, Maruyama asserts, a kind of creation *ex nihilo*. At each level, in each larger systemic pattern, features arise which cannot be traced back to features inherent in the components. As Laszlo points out, this view conflicts with monism in asserting the irreducibility of levels, and with dualism and pluralism in assigning generative relations between the levels.[21]

Systems Theory in the Social Sciences

Systems-cybernetic concepts rapidly spread beyond the natural and life sciences to the study of social institutions and behavior and to the study of psychological processes as well. More and more areas of life were seen as manifesting systemic properties and the "system," as a new way of seeing, was found applicable to the human being—not just as a biological phenomenon but as a social and cognitive entity. The notion of the system as internally dynamic and the recognition of the informational character of that which it processes break down dichotomies between subjective and objective data. The givens of inner experience, including feelings, cognitions, and perceptions of meaning, are no longer dismissed as nonempirical, but recognized, in the systems view, as relevant and accessible to scientific inquiry.

In social theory the systems view offered a resolution of the old nominalist versus realist controversy about the nature of society. For, while perceiving society as more than a collection of free agents (as in the theories of Rousseau and Locke), it avoids the problems of according it a reality or "entitivity" in its own right independent of the relations of its parts (as in some Marxian and National Socialist theories).[22] Methodologically, general systems theory gave rise to functionalism in contemporary sociology, permitting society to be approached in terms of the "interdependence of its parts," with "irreducible" properties of its own. In such terms Talcott Parsons stresses the dynamic wholeness of a social system. The self-regulatory processes of "equilibrium maintenance" and endogenous structural change, which he expounds, are similar in concept to negative and positive feedback.[23] Institutional structures from the familial to the federal level, their hierarchical mechanisms, and the way these function both to constrain and empower their members, are accessible to fruitful study from a systems perspective. Such a perspective illumines the reciprocally creative interaction of structures and mores, bureaucracies and behavior.

In similar ways the systems paradigm has been applied to economic systems and subsystems, whose transactional processes involve transfers of goods and money, as well as energy and information. Kenneth Boulding points to the relevance and importance of systems concepts in a number of areas. They underlie the equilibrium theory of the prices and outputs of commodities, clarify problems relating to organizational growth and stagnation, and can help explain economic cycles:

> If one is looking for an explanation of economic cycles, or fluctuations, either of particular speculative markets, such as the stock market, or in the economy in general, the feedback model is extremely useful. It is capable of explaining not only

regular fluctuations, in the case of equilibrating (negative) feedback, but is also capable of explaining disequilibrium processes, as in the case of destabilizing (positive) feedback. Yet there has been astonishingly little use of this model . . . perhaps as a result of the failure to take a significant intellectual tool simply because economists have not made it themselves.[24]

Political structure and process have been conceptualized and analyzed in terms of systems-cybernetic ideas by such theorists as Karl Deutsch. Viewing society as a communications network systemically processing information, Deutsch builds on analogies perceived between nerve systems, electronic circuits and societies. He points out that the application of the feedback model can help clarify social values and estimate the health of a political system. The model reveals the crucial role of communication and debate in ensuring adequate information about and response to changing conditions.

Learning nets and societies do not grow best by simplifying or rigidly subordinating their parts or members, but rather with the complexity and freedom of these members, so long as they succeed in maintaining or increasing mutual communication.[25]

As systems thinking has extended to the social sciences, it has been brought to the study of personality—to the understanding of the nature of mental health and of psychological development and disorder. The impact of systems theory on psychology and psychiatry is evident in the work of Gordon Allport, Karl Menninger, Viktor Frankl, Jerome Brunner, Jean Piaget, and Abraham Maslow among others, and is considered by psychiatrist William Gray as "perhaps the most important of von Bertalanffy's many great contributions . . . [showing] the way in which a humanistic psychology could be developed scientifically."[26]

The systemic principles von Bertalanffy discerned in biological process extended, he maintained, to the person *in toto* as a psychophysical entity. As such the person is an irreducible and dynamic whole, in open interaction with her world, sustaining and organizing herself through appropriation, transformation and differentiation of meanings and symbols. He vigorously took issue with the stimulus-response model basic to behaviorist psychology, which he termed "robot psychology" and "zoomorphic" to the extent it derives from observations of rats, pigeons, and other animals.

Behaviorism presents the person as motivated by tension reduction and primarily reactive; it postulates a homeostatic type of
equilibrium in which rest or inactivity is the goal. If this were
indeed the case, says von Bertalanffy, "life would never have progressed beyond the amoeba which, after all, is the best adapted
creature in the world . . . [and] Michelangelo should have followed
his father's request and gone in the wool trade, thus sparing himself lifelong anguish."[27] In contrast to the stimulus-response
(S-R) model, systems theory sees the individual as primarily active,
seeking not rest but that steady state maintained by the tension
of interaction, as evident in spontaneous, exploratory, and playful
behavior.

> In contrast to the model of the reactive organism expressed by
> the S-R schemes—behavior as gratification of needs, relaxation
> of tensions, reestablishment of homeostatic equilibrium, its
> utilitarian and environmentalist interpretations, etc.—we
> come rather to consider the psychological organism as a prima-
> rily active system. I think human activities cannot be consid-
> ered otherwise. . . . Man is not a passive receiver of stimuli
> coming from an external world, but in a very concrete sense
> *creates* his universe.[28]

Perceived as primarily active, the system is now seen as
possessed of purposefulness, a concept which had for centuries
smacked of nonscientific teleology and final causes. Now that cyberneticians had demonstrated goal pursuit and goal setting in feedback in machines, it became acceptable and respectable, even to
tough-minded psychologists, to ascribe purposefulness to humans
as well.[29] The reflex arc and conditioned reflex, which since the
work of Ivan Pavlov and John Watson had been taken for the basic
unit of human behavior, became replaced by the feedback loop. The
operation of feedback shows how an organism as an information
system moves toward a goal.

In therapy, the advent of the systems view has been heralded
as opening "a new era in psychiatry," representing a departure
from classical modes which emphasized stability at the expense of
growth.[30] It combines with insights from gestalt psychology (emphasis on wholeness of configuration), from classical psychoanal-
ysis (stress on the importance of spontaneous self-revelation), and
from archetypal psychology, (recognition of the self-differentiating
nature of personality). As the work of Maslow and Frankl attest, the

systems view centers attention on the personality's potential for creativity and definition of value.[31] Perceiving the personality holonically, as a system suspended in other systems with which it is interdeterminative, it treats disorders contextually, as in family therapy. By the same token, systems-oriented psychologists look not so much for original causes for a given complex but at its structure—how it hangs together. As systems psychologist Gordon Allport discerns, "motives may become functionally autonomous of their origins."[32] Therefore an etiological approach, seeking to trace and uncover early causes, has limited effectiveness. The systems approach is, as he puts it, more idiographic in outlook. "For now the vital question becomes 'what makes the system hang together in any one person?' "[33]

It has become evident in a multiplicity of fields of inquiry that suborganic, biological, electronic, social, and psychological systems can be treated nonreductively in terms of such constructs as totality, feedback, self-stabilization and differentiation, information flow, and transformation. These invariances are independent of the specific nature of the system's components and their degree of materiality. As a natural biological system is a pattern of externally observable physical events, the personality or cognitive system consists of internally experienced mental events. These events, be they perceptions, thoughts, or volitions, manifest a flow of information which both transforms and is transformed by the system's organization.

The Cognitive System

In the systems view, these subjective events cannot be reduced to or understood in terms of physical phenomena. The brain, which the neurologist observes, cannot be equated with the experience of mind to which its synaptic activity corresponds. No instrument, however delicate and precise, can render observable the sensations of the subject, for they are not on the same continuum. Laszlo affirms that they represent two distinct, but correlative perspectives on reality.[34] One is reality as it is observed from without (our external vision of a world of matter), and the other as it is experienced or felt from within. Neither is the product of the other, both are correlated. Thus, the world of inner subjective experience is accepted by systems theorists as a given that must be understood in its own right, and whose process can be made intelligible in terms of systemic self-regulation.

Experience, in the systems view, is conceptualized as a flow of perceptual data and information whereby the individual interacts with his environment. In this flow he extracts message from noise, meaning from percept, and responds in terms of the appropriateness of the message to his internal organization. As a transformer and transmitter of information, the cognitive system manifests the invariances analogous to those observed in physical systems. Communications theorist Lee Thayer compares the two:

> Just as the crucial component of physical metabolism is the conversion of raw environmental processes into energy forms consumable or processable by a particular living system, the crucial component of the communication process is the conversion of raw event-*data* into forms of *information* consumable or processable by that living system.[35]

These raw event-data are the input into the system; deriving from its environment they arrive in the form of percepts. The environment, however, is not perceived immaculately but rather is recognized and interpreted in terms of forms we have learned to see. Objects and ideas are registered in relation to patterns familiar and meaningful to us or, as Thayer put it, "converted into forms of information consumable or processable" by us. The shapes or gestalts by which we recognize objects, and the constructs by which we conceptualize, are evolved, or coded, in us by past experience. Whether the past experience is our own or our species', whether it is coded genetically or culturally, is not immediately relevant here, for in either case these codes provide the means by which we structure the stream of experience and, in either case, they are subject to modification through interaction with the surrounding world.

Where percepts match code, that is where the incoming data is meaningful in terms of the constructs by which we organize our experience, we respond in such a way as to perpetuate this match. This is, in effect, the operation of negative feedback, and by means of that the cognitive system stabilizes itself—the world makes sense. Of this negative feedback function, which is also termed "cybernetics I", Laszlo writes,

> Building and maintaining a milieu in the image of previous conceptions is a self-stabilizing activity, enabling the individual to live in the "assumed form-world" he evolved through his past experiences. . . . By this technique it brings about

conditions in its environment which confirm and correspond to its existing cognitive organization. All people build worlds around them which satisfy, to a greater or lesser degree, their conceptions of the world. When they command technological capacities, their purposely modified environment bears profound marks of their cognitive constructs, and serves to confirm and reinforce them.[36]

In negative feedback, the response of the cognitive system can be understood in terms of projection. The system acts on its environment in ways that seek to sustain the matching of percept and construct. In this sense the system's constructs can be said to be projected onto its environment—not only to ensure stability, but also to enjoy the transformation of subsequent percepts in terms of the given constructs. In this manner the scientist projects her hypothesis to prove it, or the artist his aesthetic conception to perceive it anew embodied in paint or music. Whether it is a melodic motif, on which to build fugues and variations, or a new idea, like systems, we project our constructs both to make life intelligible and also to enjoy the process of recognizing them in new forms and transforming our perceptions in their terms.

Changing conditions, however, can produce a persisting mismatch between percepts and constructs. In this event, experience becomes anomalous with respect to preconceptions. In order to make the new data meaningful and usable, new constructs are evolved. By these the system alters and refines its map of the world. The mismatch and the search for new constructs or codes are understood in terms of positive feedback, which corresponds to the process we call "learning." This represents a reorganization or self-(re)organization of the system, which fundamentally modifies its internal structure, as Laszlo, qualifying it as cybernetics II, explains:

Learning produces a reorganization of (the system's) essential parameters and becomes morphogenetic in character. . . . The fundamental reward in the feedback effect is intelligibility, attained by means of the input-construct match. Overt behavioral responses may not be produced at all if no reward is expected of them; intelligibility is the goal, and that will nevertheless have been gained. The motivation is assessed here as a striving toward meaning, rather than toward behaviorally obtained reinforcements.[37]

As a natural biological system self-stabilizes and self-organizes to adapt to changing conditions, so then does the cognitive system do so to make sense of its world. The process by which it extracts meaning both modifies the environment, through projection of its constructs, and changes the system itself, as it maps the environment in new ways.

Systems and Value

In all natural systems, self-organization into greater complexity represents a movement away from structural stability. As the system becomes internally more highly organized and externally interrelated with more factors, it becomes less stable and less predictable. At the same time and by the same token, by virtue of increasing the variety of its responses, it becomes more adaptable.

This gain in adaptability is won at the cost of structural stability and imperturbability, as the system becomes more open and susceptible to its environment. In order to register and respond to what is going on, the system becomes more vulnerable. This vulnerability in turn—and on ever more complex levels—enhances its capacity to cope, a capacity which systems thinkers call "cybernetic stability." It is the built-in goal or value to which all systems, by their inherent nature, tend.

For the cognitive system the ability to cope involves adaptation, not just to things as they are, but as they are coming to be. To ensure intelligibility as well as survival, the system seeks to comprehend not only the results of changes, but the factors of change in themselves. Like the tightrope walker who must raise her eyes to keep her balance, the system maintains its dynamic equilibrium by looking ahead. It keeps its balance not by standing still, subsiding into stasis, but by moving forward, projecting its constructs into the future. Such adaptation is a predictive and extrapolative activity, rather than an adjustment to present givens.[38]

Because it is the nature of a cognitive system to attempt to match percept with code, this adaptation represents value. So do those symbols and behaviors which enhance its capacity to take into account the most facets of experience. These symbols and behaviors, be they social, aesthetic, or religious, serve to reduce anomalies. They provide means by which one can derive more intelligibility from the known, more confidence in regard to the unknown.

Value then is not found apart from change or in the attempt to avoid change or in the positing of some permanent realm aloof from change. It is found rather in the way one incorporates and learns from change, "riding" it, the way a surfer rides the wave. For reality itself, in the systems view, is dynamic, flowing, ever breaking upon us like the waves of the living sea. And the cognitive system, the mind, rides it by the continual process of perceiving and elaborating meanings.

General systems theory itself is such a process. It extracts and elaborates principles by which change becomes intelligible, navigable. In contrast to the Greek view where, as von Bertalanffy says, "the world was static, things being considered to be a mirroring of eternal archetypes or ideas," systems theory sees "dynamic interaction [as] central in all fields of reality."[39] And this interaction reveals patterns and principles which attest in turn to the organized nature of reality itself. As he puts it:

> The unifying principle is that we find organization at all levels. The mechanistic world view, taking the play of physical particles as ultimate reality, found its expression in a civilization which glorifies physical technology that has led eventually to the catastrophes of our time. Possibly the model of the world as a great organization can help to reinforce the sense of reverence for the living which we have almost lost in the last sanguinary decades of human history.[40]

Organization is rather a cold and pallid term for a feature of the cosmos we are called to revere. Associating it with notions of administration, uniformity and control, we hardly greet it with a sense of wonder or gratitude, or find in it an epiphany, revealing a world alive with power and beauty. Yet intrinsically the word means no more or less than "arranged into a coherent unity, formed into a functioning whole."[41]

To see the universe so structured, exhibiting an order both embracing and transcending our separate selves, is of the nature of a religious perception and one in which we might find benediction. It means that we subsist in an overarching pattern of relationships, integral to our nature and "out of which we cannot fall."

These relationships are the stuff of the world, manifesting the order inherent in flux and permitting life forms to interact to create selves and societies. As such they are causal processes and, as discerned in many fields of inquiry from biology to psychiatry and physics, have a direct bearing on our understanding of causality. As we examine in greater detail in the following chapter, they attest to the dependent co-arising of phenomena, the mutual character of causality.

Notes

1. Bateson, *Steps to Ecology of Mind*, pp. 481–82.

2. Some thinkers, like Bateson and Varela, use the term *cybernetics* for the concepts we will discuss under the rubric *general systems theory*. Since the conceptualizations of von Bertalanffy and other pioneers in systems thinking are accepted and incorporated by those who call it cybernetics, and since general systems theory includes the perspectives furnished by cybernetics work, we will retain the term as the most inclusive for this body of thought. It should be noted that in popular thinking, *systems theory* is often identified with its applications in management and industry for purposes of efficiency and control. Its use toward goals that ignore the larger systemic context obscures the radical shift in world view that general systems theory entails, as well as its philosophic and moral implications.

3. von Bertalanffy, *General Systems Theory*, xxi.

4. Laszlo, *Systems View*, pp. 5, 6.

5. *Ibid.*, p. 34.

6. Bardwell, "Nonlinearity and Biological Sciences," p. 3.

7. Laszlo, *Systems View*, p. 4.

8. von Bertalanffy, *General Systems Theory*, p. 12.

9. The term hierarchical, as employed in systems thought, refers to larger and smaller (or more or less inclusive) units of organization rather than to higher and lower (or super- and subordinate) levels.

10. von Bertalanffy. *Perspectives on General Systems Theory*, pp. 60–66.

11. Kenneth Sayre observes, however, that "the universe cannot coherently be conceived as a closed system, since there is no coherent concept of what it could be closed to" (*Cybernetics and Philosophy of Mind*, p. 46).

12. Laszlo, *Introduction to Systems Philosophy*, pp. 62f, 205.

13. Milsum, *Positive Feedback*, p. 140.

14. Spyros Makridakis has generalized this principle as the "Second Law of Systems," which he says should be used to complement the Second Law of Thermodynamics, the latter being restricted in its application to closed systems. His "First Law of Systems," incidentally, is that the relation between organization and energy is nonlinear: more complex systems do not require more energy to self-organize and often much less. ("Second Law of Systems").

15. Ashby, "Principles of Self-Organizing System," p. 272.

16. Koestler, *Ghost in the Machine,* p. 48.

17. *Katha Upaniṣad,* in Hume, *Thirteen Principal Upanishads,* II, iii.1.

18. Simon, "Organization of Systems," p. 7.

19. Laszlo's pyramids illustrating this complementarity call to mind the two reversed and intersecting gyres which the poet W. B. Yeats beheld in his well-known vision. (Yeats, *A Vision*).

20. Whyte, "Structural Hierarchy," p. 275.

21. Laszlo, *Introduction to Systems Philosophy,* p. 179.

22. *Ibid.,* p. 98f.

23. *Ibid.,* pp. 100–9.

24. Boulding, "Economics and General Systems," p. 86.

25. Deutsch, "Toward a Cybernetic Model," p. 399.

26. Gray, "Bertalanffian Principles," p. 125.

27. von Bertalanffy, *General Systems Theory,* p. 192.

28. *Ibid.,* pp. 193, 4.

29. Kramer, "Man's Behavior Patterns," p. 141.

30. Jackson, "Individual and Larger Contexts," p. 387.

31. Frankl, "Beyond Pluralism," p. 943f.

32. Allport, "Open System in Personality Theory," p. 349.

33. *Ibid.*

34. Laszlo, *Introduction to Systems Philosophy,* pp. 151–55.

35. Thayer, "Communications," p. 52.

36. Laszlo, *Introduction to Systems Philosophy,* p. 128.

37. *Ibid.*, 129–31.

38. *Ibid.*, p. 264.

39. von Bertalanffy, *General Systems Theory*, p. 88.

40. *Ibid.*, p. 49.

41. *Webster's New Collegiate Dictionary.* Merriam-Webster, Inc., 1969.

5

Mutual Causality in General
Systems Theory

In the last resort, we must think in terms of systems of elements in mutual interaction.

—von Bertalanffy[1]

General systems theory grew out of the effort to understand phenomena displaying a multiplicity of variables—and to understand them not by analyzing the variables as separate entities but by attending to the interaction of these variables. Analysis of the components is useful, but limited in what it reveals about the whole, for in focusing on them features characteristic of the whole are lost to view. It appeared, then, appropriate and necessary to view life forms as organizations, or systems. As this perspective was adopted, it became evident that organizations in nature displayed comparable principles or invariances regardless of their material ingredients or external appearance.

How then, to comprehend these isomorphic, form-generating processes? Linear, one-way causal premises proved inadequate, for these can be applied only piecemeal to two variables at a time. As the pattern-building interactions of phenomena were studied, a different kind of causality came into view, one that is mutual, involving interdependence and reciprocity between causes and effects. Such a notion, which is an anomaly within the linear paradigm that has dominated Western culture, bears striking similarity to the Buddhist teaching of causality as we have studied it here.

It is to the specific nature of mutual causal processes as they appear in general systems theory that we turn in this chapter, to see more clearly their divergence from linear assumptions and the ways that phenomena arise interdependently and determine each other.

The Transformation of Causes within the System

The open system is dynamic. Its organization, however charted, does not represent an inert structure, but a pattern of events, the ongoing occurrence of exchanges and transformations within the system's parameters. By these transformations the system maintains and evolves its order in interaction with its environment. It processes that which it takes in through its receptors (the input) and extracts energy and information according to its needs or encoded norms. These codes represent how the system uses and responds to the input.

Matter, energy, or information do not flow through the system following a fixed pathway, triggering responses and producing behavior (output) directly. Rather they are subject to the dynamics of the system's internal structure. Incoming messages or inputs are sorted, sifted, evaluated, and recombined before they are transmitted to effectors and translated into action. The open system does not passively undergo the effect of external causes, but actively transforms them.

Such intrinsic activity on the part of the system does not fit the stimulus-response model of behavior, where input is seen as determinative of output in a direct linear fashion. The behaviorist notion is that stimuli could cause responses: Ring a bell; the dog salivates. The organism is assumed to be basically passive, a simple switchboard mechanism where messages are relayed and connections triggered. Change the signal and performance is altered. In the systems view, however, as von Bertalanffy affirms, "a stimulus does not *cause* a process in an otherwise inert system, it only modifies processes in an autonomously active system."[2] Neurologist Paul Weiss puts it this way: "The structure of the input does not produce the structure of the output, but merely modifies intrinsic nervous activities which have a structural organization of their own."[3]

In referring above to the active system, von Bertalanffy uses the term "autonomous." Systems theorists employ autonomy in its literal, etymological meaning of self-governing, but not in its associated sense of independent, for the system is certainly conditioned by the environment and by inputs from it. It is, however, self-governing in that inputs do not modify it directly but in their operation are subject to the system's organization. It is this internal structure which governs or determines its response.[4] Biologist-cybernetician Francisco Varela describes a systems autonomy in terms of "autopoesis." From this standpoint its structure is seen as recursive rather than behavioral.[5] A system, which is considered controlled, or behavioral, when viewed externally or from the standpoint of the environment, appears autonomous, or recursive, when the interaction of its component parts is brought into consideration. The recursive view is more useful because it takes more that is relevant into account.

In an open system, then, it is not the input that determines its action, but what *happens* to the input within the system: How it is registered and used in terms of the system's highly structured internal organization. As Laszlo affirms, "This is directly contrary to linear causality input-output systems."[6]

Such a view undermines the notion, inherent in the linear concept of causality, that similar conditions produce similar results and that different conditions will produce different results. This "sacred law of causality in classical philosophy," as Maruyama points out, has guided much research, leading scientists to seek the explanation for differences between phenomena in their initial conditions rather than in ongoing inter- and intrasystemic dynamics.[7] These dynamics, however, mitigate the influences, shape them in accordance with the system's codes and goals. In so doing, they can produce different results from the same initial inputs or similar results from differing inputs. Psychology yields many examples of the former, biology of the latter.

The great divergences individuals display in the way they respond to identical stimuli attest to the differences in their internal organization, whether these are attributed to environmental or genetic conditioning. Sensory impact on the optic nerves is probably the same in a meteorologist and in a poet as both view the sunset, but their responses are not likely to be. Nor are the responses of identical twins the same: Their cognitive structures, which have evolved in distinctive ways, process the same input differently.

As biologists have found, the same final state or goal may be reached from different initial conditions and by different pathways. For example, a normal organism of a given species can develop from each half of a divided ovum or from the fusion of two ova. Similarly an organism can attain growth normal to its species after adverse starting conditions; and after a critical disturbance it can resume its steady state processes unassisted, a capacity evident in the way organisms in nature can heal themselves. Because this kind of phenomena appears to contradict the classical laws of physics, lending to the organism an aura of independence from the external

operation of cause and effect, earlier biologists attributed it to a
soul-like vitalist factor. Von Bertalanffy, finding this kind of explanation inadequate and unnecessary, presented the phenomena as a
function of the dynamic organization of the system.[8] The system is
not solely subject to initial conditions or external forces, because its
component parts interact to stabilize and support each other.[9] As is
the case in such simple occurrences as shivering, shock, or fever,
these parts take on additional or emergency roles in order to supply
to the whole what the environment has removed or damaged. The
system's development is determined as much by this reciprocal interaction as by external causes.

Feedback as Causal Loop

The activity of the open system, then, as a transformer of energy and information in interaction with its environment, indicates
a causal process that is reciprocal or mutual. For a closer look at this
mutuality let us return in more detail to the notion of feedback.

Feedback represents the process by which a system receives
information about its own performance. Data about its previous actions, as part of the input it receives, is fed back so that the system
can monitor itself and direct its behavior. Just as the performance of
a motor or heating coil (the effectors) is monitored back to a radar
screen or a photoelectric cell (the receptors), so is that of a muscle to
a sense organ. In such fashion are percepts on the basis of which
performance is guided, altered by performance itself. The feedback
concept then is circular and self-referential by nature. Cause and
effect cannot be categorically isolated, but modify each other in a
continuous process whereby input and output, percepts and performance, interact. This interaction between perception and action is
basic to an organism's capacity to adapt and organize itself; it is evident in exploratory and learning behaviors, as it is in self-
stabilization.

Just as inputs and outputs interact in the operation of a given
system, so do they function between systems, data about performance coming back through others. The output from *A* modifies *B*,
whose response becomes part of the subsequent input received by
A. The way *B* responds to *A* is an aspect of *A*'s self-monitoring;
hence *B*'s response informs *A* about itself and its progress toward its
goals. In this information processing and exchange *A* functions for
B in the same way. Though they may perceive a given datum in

very different ways, depending on their internal codes, both are altered by their perceptions of their effect on each other.

The causal reciprocity involved is signaled by Laszlo, who calls
it interdetermination.[10]

> Now interdetermination implies a dual relation between cause
> and effect . . . A determines B and B determines A . . . The
> reciprocity of the causality connecting A and B consists in this:
> as a result of a cause emanating from A, B manifests a modifi-
> cation in its relations to A, which modification *itself* can be re-
> garded as the cause produced by B, acting on A, and resulting
> from the effect of the primal cause (A acting on B).

The feedback processes involved are like loops and indeed are
imaged as such. Linking the causal variables in a continuous flow
of information or energy, these loops, not unlike electrical circuits,
connect output with input, both within a given system and between
systems. They show that we are dealing with more than the general
notion of interaction, or the presence of influences in two directions. To function in terms of mutual causal loops, these influences,
as Maruyama points out, must influence each other.[11] A may effect
B in a way that is unrelated to B's influence on A (for example, A's
client relationship to B may be unaffected by B's patronage of A).
Only where A's effect on B is qualified by B's on A (or, where A is
modified by its effect on B), is there mutual causality.

The image of loop, or circle, tends to imply reversion to a pre-
existing state, an eternal return to the same point, precluding the
new. "We go around in circles and never get anywhere." But feedback processes in the systems view generate information and novelty. By their operation, elements of a system, be they members of a
family or cells in a body, become informed and differentiated.

In the early classic formulation of information theory, Shannon
held that information, or the ratio of nonrandom message to random noise, is transmitted; it must come from somewhere. Coming
from somewhere else, it can peter out. Revealing a carry-over of linear assumptions, it was held, therefore, that information can decrease (entropically, with the increase of random noise) but not be
generated *ex nihilo*.[12] Mutual causal processes, however, can produce novelty, generate message. An entity does not contain coded
within it from the start all the information required for it to evolve
into what it has or will become.[13] Its present and future do not pre-

exist in its past, nor are its patterns or potentialities precast. They derive rather from interaction.

These mutual causal processes are basic to a system's maintenance and evolution of order. Because they allow the system to stabilize itself in the face of the disintegrative tendency of entropy, and because they permit the flowering of variety, complexity, and improbability, thinkers like Kenneth and Elsie Boulding have called them "anti-entropic processes," "love principle," and "agape."[14]

In the maintenance and evolution of order two kinds of mutual causal processes are involved: those which stabilize the system around its preestablished norms (negative feedback) and those which trigger changes that can lead to new norms (positive feedback). Let us now view in turn these two kinds of loops and how they operate in the world. These terms, as we will use them technically, are reversed in their connotations from the way they have been adopted in popular idiom. In cybernetics, negative feedback does *not* mean "You are off target," but precisely the opposite (that the divergence of performance from set goals is negative). Nor does positive feedback connote approbation; rather it indicates positive need to change performance.

Negative Feedback Processes

The previous chapter explained that feedback is negative when percepts (input) match the code or present goals of the system. A negative feedback process occurs when, upon receiving a signal (input), the system adjusts its output to minimize the disparity between input and code. Its behaviors aim to affect the internal or external environment in ways that maintain the match between input and preestablished norm. This process is homeostatic, stabilizing the system in the face of changing conditions. It is known, therefore, as deviation-counteracting. These are cases where it can be said, "the more of one, the less of the other." In a thermostat this functions in the relation between temperature reading and furnace switch: the lower the temperature in the house the more the furnace comes on. Similarly in biological homeostasis, cold is counteracted by shivering: less warmth, more shivering. In each case the mutually affecting variables work to counteract or balance each other.

Within a social system such a causal relation can be seen, for example, between urban population and disease. As the number of people in a city increases, so does the amount of garbage per area and the resultant concentration of bacteria, which augments the incidence of disease. Since disease decreases the number of inhabitants, the feedback loop is negative, working toward a stabilization of the population. Fads and styles are often of this nature. As in the case of a newly discovered tropical beach, the greater the tourist response the less the appeal. Baseball's Yogi Berra once said about a popular nightclub, "the place is so crowded, nobody goes there any more."

Somewhat similarly, negative feedback can be seen as stabilizing the growth of organizations. Kenneth Boulding has pointed out that the greater the size of a firm, the longer and slower the communications route; increased delay and red tape produce inefficiencies, limit flexibility and profits. This in turn works toward a reduction in size. The causal loop, of course, continues, with reduced size improving communications and efficiency and leading consequently to renewed impetus toward growth.[15]

Another simplified example from the economic realm is the relation between government subsidies and revenue from employment. In the *Kūtadanta sutta*, the Buddha recommended to the king that instead of commanding ritual sacrifices, he devote the capital to creating jobs.[16] This, he argued, would stabilize the economy, establishing prosperous conditions that would in turn benefit the king more than any ritual. Here the relation between employment and royal expenditure is again one of negative feedback: more jobs, less need for subsidy and vice-versa.

Positive Feedback Processes

In contrast to the stabilizing effect of negative feedback, positive feedback *de*stabilizes. Positive feedback occurs when the signal indicating deviation (input) elicits a behavior (output) which increases the deviation. Instead of lessening the mismatch between percepts and preestablished codes, the response augments and accelerates it. In this kind of causal process the variables do not counteract, but abet and intensify each other's effect. Instead of "the more, the less," it functions as "the more, the more," like compound interest or an arms race or a snowball rolling downhill. Having a self-reinforcing and exponential character, positive feedback is termed "deviation-amplifying." It has also been dubbed the "second cybernetics," in recognition of its widespread and generative nature. For positive feedback systems are ubiquitous—operative in the accumulation of capital as well as the intensification of poverty, in the spread of both disease and new ideas.

Returning to our example of urban growth, we see such a process at work in cities around the world, in the relation between
modernization and immigration. Concentration of persons and
property leads to the modernization of facilities, which lures more
people from rural areas. These increase the city's drive to expand
housing and services, which in turn motivate more immigration in
an upward spiraling effect. Poverty and apathy interact similarly, as
do negative self-image and poor performance. The arms race is also
of this nature: An increment of weaponry on each side, perceived as
a threat by the other, motivates further military buildup, which in
turn stimulates more. In Buddhist thought such a positive feedback
relation exists between ignorance *(avijjā)* and craving *(tanhā)*. The delusion of separate selfhood produces anxiety and greed which further distort the view of reality, deepening the ignorance, which
aggravates in turn the disease of ego, and so on.

When unchecked and operating in isolation, positive feedback
processes lead to runaway growth or collapse. But in the evolution
or organisms and cultures their role is fundamental and constructive, promoting self-organization and differentiation into new forms
of adaptation and intelligence. This is because they trigger changes
in behavior that depart from preestablished norms. When and if
these novel behaviors become stabilized or nested in new, more inclusive negative feedback loops, they have generated something
adaptive and new. Much that is valued in nature and culture is the
fruit of this kind of mutual causality. Through positive feedback, biological, cognitive, and social systems complexify their organization, in apparent defiance of the Second Law of Thermodynamics—
breaking ground for the new and reaching toward greater variety,
interaction, and improbability.

The process of evolution is deviation-amplifying in a number
of ways, featuring positive feedback loops between mutations and
environment, within species, and between them. Taking an example from the last category, we can see how prey and predators interact to develop ever more refined features. The moths with more
effective camouflage survive better, as do their predators with
sharper detectors. In the course of generations the moths' camouflage becomes ever more cryptic, while the acuity of the hunters'
senses likewise increases.[17]

The growth of cultures presents a similar phenomenon, as
prized characteristics increase in frequency through cultural conditioning. This increase arises both through natural selection (features
like height and long legs being favored in American culture), and
through training and opportunity. A music-loving society, such as

eighteenth-century Germany, produces composers and audiences, players and patrons who train, stimulate and nourish each other in a dynamic, symbiotic relationship, a relationship which makes possible new skills and new forms. In a real way the audience creates the actor, the students the teacher—each brings forth the other. Such a symbiosis characterized early Buddhist society. The mutually enhancing roles of Sangha and laity encouraged, on the one hand, the scholarship and practice of the monks and, on the other, the erection of monasteries and the flowering of art, as an expression of lay support and devotion.

The operation of positive feedback is also discernible in the shift and generation of cultural paradigms. As thinkers, be they scientists or theologians, play ideas off each other, the freshly glimpsed perspective gains momentum, accelerates. Each thinker amplifies the intuitions, or deviations of the others, and frequently it is impossible to pinpoint the original originator of an idea. As in the case of an arms race or a marital feud, it is fruitless to try to determine who started it, because in mutual causation each party contributes to the spiral. Sometimes the initial kick that started the spiral can be historically determined, but it cannot be considered the cause in any definitive or responsible sense. Like the battle that was lost "for want of a nail" in the shoe of a horse, the results are out of all proportion to the initiating event. The real cause lies in the dynamics at play.

Recognition of these dynamics can be useful in showing where and how an initial kick can be given to set a desired mutual causal process in motion. In our economic system, for example, the effect of public health and welfare programs, taxation and education, is designed to be deviation-counteracting, since it tends to reduce the difference between the rich and the poor. In an economically underdeveloped society, however, as economist Gunnar Myrdal has convincingly shown, the rich get richer and the poor get poorer.[18] A deviation-amplifying process is in effect, as the privileged few use their wealth and power to accumulate more, while among the poor, disease, inefficiency and lack of education aggravate the poverty. Myrdal argues that such economies should not only be planned, but reinforced with an initial kick in an amount, direction, and duration sufficient to launch mutually enhancing causal processes. When these take over, he maintains, the resultant economic growth will far outweigh the initial investment.

The role of positive feedback loops in interpersonal relations has been increasingly appreciated by systems-oriented psychologists and psychiatrists. As attention is directed to interpersonal context, rather than individual histories, neurotic manifestations within a given family appear mutually causative and accessible to an approach that includes all parties. Individual testing and analysis frequently do not reveal or alleviate the deviation-amplifying dynamics at work. A couple having marital difficulties, for example, can be treated as if one or both of the individuals is disturbed and needs treatment. Or they can be viewed, as Jackson says, "as a mutual causative system, whose complementary communication reinforces the nature of their interaction."[19] Their respective behaviors trigger and intensify each other. In this case it does not matter how it all got started, nor is any alleviation of individual symptoms effective, unless the circle or game itself is interrupted. Jackson argues that more is involved here than a theory like "sadomasochistic symbiosis," which traditional psychiatry, recognizing the relational aspect, might come up with.

> I feel such a term is not useful because it reductionistically obscures the important elements of causality. Such a formulation implies that a sadist met a masochist and they lived happily ever after because they were "made for each other." On the contrary, we are constantly defining and *being defined by* the nature of our relationships.[20]

In this perspective, individual behaviors that are usually seen as symptomatic of personal ill health can be seen as functional, adaptive, and useful for the individual in the system within which he operates. Although they boomerang on the actor in ways she does not like, they testify to her basic strength and resourcefulness, wiliness even, rather than her weakness. Therapy that recognizes this respects her adaptability, the capacity to see and to change.

The current popular psychology that views neurotic behavior as "games people play" accords fairly well with the systems view, to the extent that in such a perspective all parties are seen as causally involved, co-determining each other's roles and goals.[21] Such mutual causation is perceptible as well in the dynamics of the relationship between therapist and patient. As Freud himself had noted, a patient tends to produce material that fits the theories of the analyst. Even dreams will generate appropriate symbols and styles, the Jungian analysand making Jungian dreams, the Freudian, Freudian, and so on. A positive feedback causal process is in effect here. Not only does the "good" patient satisfy the needs of the therapist by producing suitable material, but he intensifies in turn the therapist's efforts to treat him in terms of his pet theory. The process, as systems psychologist Ernest Kramer argues, perpetuates the treatment; it lies at the root of what he calls "the neverending course of psychotherapy":

> As patient and therapist feed each other in this manner . . . many years of talking and listening may thus pass together for this happy couple before an outside agency changes the system and interferes with the positive feedback loop.[22]

Seeing Causes

While the idea of mutual causal processes may jibe with some of our hunches and experiences, it runs counter to the logic to which we have been accustomed. In assigning responsibility and in locating the points at which we will bring pressure to effect change, we tend to look for single, isolable causes. This tendency slants not only our personal lives, but our social and scientific endeavors. It has led us, as sociologist Robert Dubin argues, to make stunted assessments, wrong predictions and futile efforts, whether we pursue individual happiness or social justice. The "causes" we hit on are rarely sufficient to permit us to solve our problems.

> We were predicting that better housing would "cause" alleviation of the curse of the slums (without being able to predict that the housing projects would be made into slums when slum culture was settled in); we were suggesting that desegregation of schools would provide better housing for Blacks (not considering the consequences resulting for Black education with the flight of the Whites from the central city); we were piously predicting the revolution spreading from our campuses (without giving even a careless thought to the resiliency of the body politic and its Establishment); we were certain that the "crime problem" was focused on the individual criminal (without even trying to see its far more central "Big Business" dimension); etc., etc. . . . Wedded to a causal format in our thinking we have proceeded to make our forthright, and usually wrong predictions about the social scene we studied, based on our limited two-variable analyses.[23]

The problem, as Dubin sees it, lies in our propensity to look for isolable one-way causes. This propensity is undermined to the

extent that there is awareness of reciprocity between variables. But
feedback processes can be hard to see, not only because attention is
not directed to them within the context of the linear perspective,
but also because, as W. J. Powers points out, they tend to be unno-
ticed by virtue of their very pervasiveness:

> Feedback is such an all-pervasive and fundamental aspect of
> behavior that it is an invisible as the air we breathe. Quite lit-
> erally it is behavior—we know nothing of our own behavior
> but the feedback effects of our own outputs. To behave is to
> control perception.[24]

Whether or not we find mutual causal processes easily discernible, their postulation presents a very different picture of the world
than that inherent in the linear view. They implicate us in new
ways in the events we behold and participate in, the problems we
would solve and the programs we mount. It is to such implications
of mutual causality that the next section of this book is devoted, and
their examination will draw on both Buddhist and systems views.

As stated in the introduction, this work attempts no direct
comparison between general systems theory and the Buddha
Dharma. Such a one-to-one comparison between human endeavors
as distinctive in nature as these would take us too far afield and
involve us in discussions irrelevant to our topic, mutual causality.
As we explore the epistemological, ontological, and ethical dimensions of mutual causality, similarities and divergencies between
these two bodies of thought will appear, but these, as such, are not
our focus. Our aim is to see how phenomena can be understood to
cause each other reciprocally, and to see what difference that might
make to our comprehension of this world and the way we live in it.

Notes

1. von Bertalanffy, *General Systems Theory,* p. 44.

2. Quoted in Laszlo, *Introduction to Systems Philosophy,* p. 251.

3. Weiss, "The Living System," 1969.

4. This distinction between self-governance and independence is a
helpful one in clarifying the meaning of autonomy in other contexts as
well—such as in political science or humanistic psychology, where the

amazon.com

Returns Are Easy! Most items can be refunded, exchanged, or replaced when returned in original and unopened condition. Visit http://www.amazon.com/returns to start your return, or http://www.amazon.com/help for more information on return policies.

SDmDNbFMZk

Your order of February 24, 2015 (Order ID 113-7094545-1029057)

Qty.	Item		Item Price	Total
1	**Mutual Causality in Buddhism and General Systems Theory: The Dharma** **of Natural Systems (Suny Series, Buddhist Studies)** Macy, Joanna --- Paperback (** P-1-Q38F71 **) 0791406377		$21.55	$21.55

This shipment completes your order.

	Subtotal	$21.55
	Order Total	$21.55
	Paid via credit/debit	$21.55
	Balance due	$0.00

Have feedback on how we packaged your order? Tell us at www.amazon.com/packaging.

0/DmDNbFMZk/-1 of 1-/UPS-CCHIL-D/second/9144630/0224-23:00/0224-12:46   **B2A**

search for greater autonomy is taken as a value. It suggests that what is sought is not a state impervious to the environment, but rather an internal structure that in its differentiated and complex interconnectedness commands a broader range of choices.

5. Varela and von Glasersfeld, "Problems of Knowledge"; and Varela and Goguen, "Systems and Distinctions."

6. Laszlo, *Introduction to Systems Philosophy*, p. 251.

7. Maruyama, "Mutual Causality," p. 306.

8. von Bertalanffy, *General Systems Theory*, p. 40.

9. *Equifinality* is the term von Bertalanffy coined for this principle by which open systems can reach the same goal from different starting conditions and in spite of differing perturbations (*General Systems Theory*, p. 132). The psychologist Sylvano Arieti defines *equifinality* this way: "This principle states that in contrast to equilibriums in closed systems, which are determined by initial conditions, the open system may attain a time-independent state which is independent of initial conditions and determined only by the system parameters" ("Toward a Unifying Theory of Cognition," p. 49).

10. Laszlo, *Introduction to Systems Philosophy*, p. 246.

11. Maruyama, "Mutual Causality," pp. 80–81.

12. Maruyama, "Paradigmatology," p. 252.

13. Genetics shows that body parts derive information from each other, and that each part does not contain within itself, or require, a pre-established blueprint for the organ it is destined to become. For example, if in an embryo tissue that would become an eye is transplanted at an appropriate stage of embryonic development into the part which would become skin, the eye-tissue becomes skin (Maruyama, "Mutual Causality," p. 310).

14. Quoted in Maruyama, "Symbiotization of Cultural Heterogeneity," p. 128.

15. Boulding, "Business and Economic Systems," pp. 104–7.

16. *Dīgha Nikāya*, I:127f.

17. Stephanie Hoppe, in a book about perceptions of animals, says that prey and predator "are both forming each other. To be the predator, one needs to be obsessed, one is totally formed in the direction of one's predation; on the other hand, to be prey is such an interesting existence". A turnabout in conventional notions about prey and predator, as well as about causality, is conveyed fancifully in the same book, in a story by Judy

Grahn: "Because of her habits of trembling without moving the mouse has taught the owl to do a great deal of sitting and dreaming it would not otherwise be doing. Because the mama mouse has habits of working at night the owl has been given plenty of night vision and silent, rapidly dropping flight in order to fall down on her from above. . . . For a mouse to have so many babies at a time as she loves to do she must have someone to give them over to and for this reason her kind have thought up the family of owls and dreamed them into existence."(*With a Fly's Eye, A Whale's Wit and a Woman's Heart*, edited by Theresa Corrigan and Stephanie Hoppe cited in *The New Settler Interview*, Willets, California, July 1989.)

18. Myrdal, *Economic Theory*, quoted in Maruyama, "Mutual Causality," p. 93.

19. Jackson, "Individual and Larger Contexts," p. 392.

20. *Ibid.*, pp. 393–94.

21. Berne, *Games People Play.*

22. Kramer, "Man's Behavior Patterns," p. 147.

23. Dubin, "Causality and Analysis," p. 112.

24. Powers, "Feedback," p. 351.

Part Three

Dimensions of Mutual Causality

6

Self as Process

Everything flows.

—Heraclitus

The perspective of mutual causality brings to view a world where "everything flows." To be interdependent and reciprocally affecting is to be in process. In this fluid state of affairs the self is no exception.

To think of our selves as changing patterns as fluid as water, as ephemeral as flame, runs counter to conventional assumptions. Language and society, indeed our very perceptions of a world "out there" distinct from a self "in here," encourage the notion that as selves we are separate and distinct individuals, anchored in separate and distinct bodies. If we conclude, as would be natural, that we exist independently in our own right with an identity that endures intact through time, then change can appear as a threat from which we need to protect ourselves. Such notions are undermined by the concept and perception of mutual causality, as is evident in both Buddhist and systems perspectives.

Everything Changes

Both early Buddhist teachings and systems theory emphasize that causation, as the interaction of mutually conditioning phenomena, entails the radical impermanence of these phenomena. Entities are ever-changing, because they participate in and are subject to relationships in a world constituted by relationships.

As the Buddhist scriptures repeat, *sabbe anicca*, all is impermanent. Indeed the Buddha stood in clear opposition both to Vedic and other non-Vedic thought in India when he ascribed reality, not to any substance, physical, psychic, or supernatural, but to change itself. Dependent co-arising, the Buddha's causal doctrine, is inseparable from this notion, as are the Four Noble Truths. One's grief arises from positing an enduring self where no self endures, from seeking to protect it from change when one's very law is change.

The things and substances which make up our world, *dhammā* and *saṇkhārā*, have process as their nature. Rendering these words as "order" and "formation," Oldenberg says, "Both include the idea that, not so much something ordered, a something formed, as rather a self-ordering, a self-forming, constitutes the subject-matter of the world."[1] Of such character is the very Teaching, or Law, which the Buddha revealed, the Dharma being not an eternal essence removed from or precedent to the realm of change, but intrinsic to it as law or invariance which process manifests.

Similarly is the systems view of mutual causality grounded in the assumption that all is in process. Von Bertalanffy stresses general systems theory's "recognition of the omnipresence and inevitability of change."[2] The universe is seen as made up not of things but of flows and relationships.[3] It is these relational patterns, not any "stuff," that abides. Therefore, Laszlo, in drawing out the metaphysical implications of general systems theory, is disinclined to posit any immutable essence aloof from time and change. "Platonic *ideas*, or Whiteheadian *eternal objects*, are rejected as uncalled for."[4] He argues that Whitehead's eternal objects enjoy "a one-way causal connection to actuality. . . . They are externally related to actuality, i.e. are themselves immutable and unqualified by their exemplifications in the actual world."[5] But in the causal interdetermination of the systems view, the "ordering is from within." Where all is mutually conditioned, "there are only internal relations" and no basis for positing an unaffected agent, external to the causal play of process.[6]

In the world seen in terms of relations, rather than substance, personal identity appears as emergent and contingent, defining and defined by interactions with the surrounding medium. Where all is process, so is the self, which by that token is neither categorically distinct from others nor endowed with any changeless essence. This is conveyed both in early Buddhist thought and in general systems theory, although it runs counter to both the conventional view of experience and to earlier philosophic tenets dominant in both India and the West. In contrast to the assumption that the self is an entity which has experiences, from which it is by nature distinct, the notion is put forth that the self is not separable from its experience, nor isolable as an agent from the thinking, saying, and doing we attribute to it.

The Illusion of Separate Selfhood

Integral to Buddhist teachings is the doctrine of *anattā* or no-selfness. Like *paṭicca samuppāda* and the four Noble Truths, it is presented as a teaching peculiar to the Buddhas.[7] It was greatly emphasized in an effort to counteract two types of "false views." One is the popular assumption of an enduring self, which derives in part from the conventional usage of "I" and "mine," and which leads to anxiety, attachment, and greed. The other is philosophic and speculative: the Upaniṣadic and Sāṃkhyan belief in a subtle metaphysical essence, be it *ātman, jiva,* or *puruṣa,* which resides at the core of each being as an immutable entity aloof from experience.

The early Buddhists called these notions *attadiṭṭhi* (view or heresy of self) and *sakkāyadiṭṭhi* (view of permanent self-being), and they presented them as the first fetter *(saṃyojanā)* that must be cast off in entering the path to enlightenment.[8] Belief in an enduring self *(attavāda)* is one of the four kinds of grasping *(upādāna)* which propel beings into suffering and rebirth. Final deliverance cannot be attained until the last remnant of the "I am" conceit, the last shred of the tenacious tendency to think of oneself as an enduring agent, is rooted out.[9]

Scholars like Edward Conze remind us that "the Buddha never taught that the self 'is not', but only that it cannot be apprehended."[10] To make such a categorical metaphysical denial (that self "is not") would have run counter to the Buddha's reliance on experience and would also have confused his teachings with that of the *ucchedavādins,* or annihilationists. He did not deny the subjectivity of experience, but rather the isolability of the subject. Every aspect of experience, every function we can assign to self, was remorselessly analyzed to show its transience. As Buddhaghosa pointed out, the teaching of the five *khaṇḍas,* or aggregates (body, mind, volition, perception, and feeling), was to demonstrate the absence of an enduring self. It is in ignorance of the composite nature of these *khaṇḍas* that we say "This is mine, this is I, this is my self."[11]

As the meditation which the Buddha taught reveals, no experiencer is separate from experience, no identity distinct from the flow of dharmas, no isolable self for whose protection or enhancement we need strive.[12] The "I" of agency is but a convenient abstraction, a convention of popular speech. As when we say "it rains," but do not mean that something external to the rain is raining, so it is with our doing. To ask *"who suffers?"* is not a fit question, as the Buddha told his disciples Kassapa and Timbaruka.[13] So thorough is the rejection of substantialism and reification, to which the conceit of enduring selfhood leads, that *anattā,* as a mark of existence, is made more universal than even *anicca.* Whereas all *saṇkhārās,* compounds or formations, are *anicca* and *dukkha,* all *dhammas* (and that would include *nibbāna* too) are *anatta,* devoid of independent and substantial self-existence, empty of own-being.[14]

No-selfness is then in Buddhism a characteristic of the universe as a whole and everything in it. This emptiness of own-being, which will be recognized in the Mahayana as an "absolute," the ultimate nature of reality, derives from dependent co-origination. Mutually conditioned, everything subsists in relationship and knows no independent self-existence. The individual "self," neither isolable nor fixed, is seen as a flowing stream, a stream of being, a stream of consciousness, *bhavasota, viññānasota.*[15] In constant interaction with its environment, consuming and constituted by its impressions, fueled by sights, sounds, touch, tastes, smells, mental objects, and driven by the wants that they awaken, the self-in-process is also like a fire. As the Buddha said in his first sermon at Gaya, "Everything, O Bhikkhus, is burning . . . the eye is burning, visible things are burning . . . the ear is burning, sounds are burning . . . the mind is burning, thoughts are burning. . . ." Such, until rebirth is ended, until "holiness is completed and duty fulfilled," is the nature of our existence.[16]

Arising interdependently, or "co-igniting," with what it perceives and on which it acts, the self cannot be considered apart from them—hence the incongruity of questions of survival. Whether the saint exists after death cannot then be answered, for either yes or no would imply an agency separate from action, an "I" distinct from its experience.[17]

No Clear Lines of Demarcation

In contrast to physicalist and behaviorist notions of the self, the systems view asserts the dynamic and irreducible nature of psychic activity. In so doing, it opens the realm of thought, feeling, and purpose to scientific inquiry in a new way—that is, without the idea that thought, feeling, and purpose can be equated with or understood solely in terms of externally observed phenomena. Yet while subjectivity is affirmed as a property of the system, as its internal or felt dimension, the subject—the who that is thinking and feeling—is not considered separable or abstractable as an agent.

The cognitive system is itself a series of mind-events, occurring in an ongoing pattern in interaction with its environment. In the web of relationships which form what we call the self there are

no clear lines of demarcation whereby it can be asserted, "This is I."
There is no homunculus in the brain to which we can attribute
agency, substance, or continuity. The systems view comes close to
the Buddhist in its radical suggestion that experience can be comprehended in the absence of an experiencer. It does "not see a categorical 'I' against a categorically distinct 'you' or 'it'," as Laszlo
expresses it:

> We must do away with the subject-object distinction in analyz-
> ing experience. This does not mean that we reject the concepts
> of organism and environment, as handed down to us by natu-
> ral science. It only means that we conceive of experience as
> linking organism and environment in a continuous chain of
> events, from which we cannot, without arbitrariness, abstract
> an entity called 'organism' and another called 'environment'.
> The organism is continuous with its environment, and its ex-
> perience refers to a series of transactions constituting the
> organism-environment continuum.[18]

By these transactions with the surrounding world the system
maintains its dynamic equilibrium in the interplay of opposing
forces. The physical identity of an individual does not consist so
much of the matter of which it is made, as of the metabolic processes by which food and air become flesh, again to break down
and pass out of the body. In similar manner does his psychic activity consist of a flow of mind events, as the cognitive system maps
the environment, adapts to changes, extracts information, evolves
and projects its interpretive constructs. As Buckminster Fuller says,
"I seem to be a verb."[19] Norbert Wiener writes,

> It is the pattern maintained by this homeostasis which is the
> touchstone of our personal identity. . . . We are but whirlpools
> in a river of everflowing water. We are not stuff that abides,
> but patterns that perpetuate themselves.[20]

As a pattern which keeps its shape although its substance continually changes, the system is like a flame. Wiener used this simile
for the body, but it is equally true for that which we call the self.
"The individuality of the body is that of a flame rather than that of
a stone, of a form rather than of a bit of substance."[21] Von Bertalanffy
used the image of the flame for the process nature of the system
early on. Noting how systems theory relates to Heraclitus's percep-

tion that *panta rhei*, everything flows, he says that from the Heraclitean and systems view, "structure is a result of function and the organism resembles a flame rather than a crystal."[22] Picking up the same image, systems theorist Leon Brillouin writes, "a living cell can be compared to a flame: here is matter going in and out and being burned. The entropy of a flame cannot be defined, since it is not a system in [rest] equilibrium."[23]

The flame burns because it is in constant interaction with its environment, because "matter is going in and out" in the process of combustion. In like manner the cognitive system is maintained by and consists of the continual exchange, processing, and transforming of information that flows through it, from and to the surrounding world.

In such a view it becomes difficult to locate the self as agent. Not only is the self always changing, but the very parameters of this change process are arbitrary, as Bateson makes clear. That which decides and does can no longer be neatly identified with the isolated subjectivity of the individual or even located within the confines of his skin. "The total self-corrective unit which processes information, or, as I say, 'thinks' and 'acts' and 'decides', is a *system* whose boundaries do not at all coincide with the boundaries either of the body or of what is popularly called the 'self' or 'consciousness'." Bateson provides some examples, which reveal some of cybernetics' implications for the notion of self.

Consider a man felling a tree with an axe. Each stroke of the axe is modified or corrected, according to the shape of the cut face of the tree left by the previous stroke. This self-corrective (i.e. mental) process is brought about by a total system, tree-eyes-brain-muscles-axe-stroke-tree; and it is this total system that has the characteristics of immanent mind. More correctly, we should spell the matter out as: (differences in tree)–(differences in retina)–(differences in brain)–(differences in muscles)–(differences in movement of axe)–(differences in tree), etc. What is transmitted around the circuit is transforms of differences. And a difference which makes a difference is an *idea* or unit of information.

But this is not how the average Occidental sees the event sequence of tree felling. He says, "*I* cut down the tree" and he even believes that there is a delimited agent, the "self," which performed a delimited "purposive" action upon a delimited object. . . .

If you ask anybody about the localization and boundaries of
the self, these confusions are immediately displayed. Or
consider a blind man with a stick. Where does the blind
man's self begin? At the tip of the stick? At the handle of
the stick? Or at some point halfway up the stick? These questions are nonsense, because the stick is a pathway along
which differences are transmitted under transformation, so
that to draw a delimiting line *across* this pathway is to cut off a
part of the systemic circuit which determines the blind man's
locomotion.[24]

Bateson recognizes the accuracy of religious intuitions that the
individual "self" is but an intrinsic part of a larger "self" of system.
This is how he understands the assertion, in twelve-step programs
such as Alcoholics Anonymous, that "there is a Power greater than
the self." And this is why that assertion is so effective, he says:

Cybernetics would go somewhat further and recognize that
the "self" as ordinarily understood is only a small part of a
much larger trial-and-error system which does the thinking,
acting, and deciding. This system includes all the informational pathways which are relevant at any given moment to
any given decision. The "self" is a false reification of an im-
properly delimited part of this much larger field of interlocking processes.[25]

One's notion of self then depends on the systemic parameters one
applies to any given situation or activity. It can include the wood-
cutter's axe and even the cut face of the tree, depending on their
role in the process taking place. The word *self*, in referring to the
continuity of an individual's physical or mental activity, is a useful
convention, but there is in actuality no enduring, delimited agent to
which it applies. Such a literal notion of "I" is a "false reification,"
as Bateson says.

Laszlo explains how we reify our gestalts and constructs in
this fashion, isolating the subject through an abstractive process
and then taking it as a given. In an effort to make sense of our
stream of experience and stabilize it, we differentiate our gestalts
and then project them onto our experience and assume that they
exist independent of our perceptions. Distinguishing self from nonself, or world, and abetted by the linguistic conventions, we draw
an ego-boundary, which divides objects "out there" from a self "in

here." "The scene is then set for the commonsensical spectator-spectacle view of the knowing process, with the subject gazing at the world of objects."[26]

The Lethal Mirage

Within the context of mutual causality, then, there is no separate individual self to be actualized. Popular psychological notions that set the goal of uncovering one's true identity, and affirming one's real self, are seen as misleading. As the systems-oriented theologian Ralph Wendell Burhoe writes,

> Our contemporary "doctrine of the soul" or "self" of man is illusory. . . . A comprehensive view reveals no such thing as personal self-actualization apart from a self's role or the self's niche in the larger ecosystem of civilization and the biosphere. The vision of an independent self to be fulfilled is a lethal mirage.[27]

Gordon Allport calls the mirage the "integumented view of personality." Our skin-encapsulated notion of the self is, he asserts, "the knottiest issue in contemporary social science. . . . [It] has prevented us from agreeing on the proper way to reconcile psychological and socio-cultural science."[28] These scholars suggest that the conventional notion of the self has narrowed the horizons, both of our cognition and our compassion. To quote Burhoe again, "Our civilization has failed the individual in failing to infuse him with an understanding of the larger dimensions of self as the servant of . . . a larger ecosystem."[29]

Such philosophical and ethical dimensions of mutual causality are developed more fully in later chapters. Basic to them all is the perception of the self as process: Mutual causality, as both Buddhist teachings and general systems theory attest, involves the perception that the subject of thought and action is in actuality a dynamic pattern of activity interacting with its environment and inseparable from experience.

Questions remain: How does the perceiver then know the world he perceives? How does present identity relate to past action, and in what does our continuity consist? How does mind relate to body? And what is at stake in this causal view in terms of ethics and value?

Notes

1. Oldenberg, *Buddha: Life, Doctrine, Order,* p. 250.

2. von Bertalanffy, "General Systems Overview," quoted in Gray *et al., General Systems Theory,* p. xx.

3. What flows through the causal circuits of systems, permitting maintenance and proliferation of forms, is not defined. Laszlo, on occasion, uses "energy" as a general term: "What flows is a mysterious non-individualized something we call energy" (*Systems View of World,* p. 80). Cyberneticians like Norbert Wiener, however, speak more in terms of information. That which is transmitted, "in a river of every-flowing water" (Wiener, *Human Use of Human Beings,* p. 130), permits messages and meanings to be extracted and patterns to perpetuate themselves.

4. Laszlo, *Introduction to Systems Philosophy,* p. 294.

5. *Ibid.,* p. 246.

6. *Ibid.,* p. 294.

7. *Majjhima Nikāya,* I:380.

8. *Ibid.,* I:380.

9. *Saṃyutta Nikāya,* III.131.

10. Conze, *Buddhist Thought,* p. 39.

11. *Saṃyutta Nikāya,* III.46f; *Majjhima Nikāya,* III.19.

12. The meditation practice attributed uniquely to the Buddha is described in the *Satipatthana Sutta* and known in English as "Mindfulness" or "Insight meditation." Considered to be the practice he pursued leading to his enlightenment, it contrasts with contemplations designed to center or tranquilize the mind.

13. *Saṃyutta Nikāya,* II.20f.

14. *Ibid.,* III.133; *Majjhima Nikāya,* I.288; *Aṇguttara Nikāya,* I.286.

15. *Saṃyutta Nikāya,* IV.128; *Dīgha Nikāya,* III.105.

16. *Vinaya, Mahāvagga,* I.21.

17. *Dīgha Nikāya,* I.1f.

18. Laszlo, *System, Structure, and Experience,* p. 21.

19. Fuller, *I Seem to be a Verb.*

20. Weiner, *Human Use of Human Beings*, p. 130.

21. *Ibid.*, p. 139.

22. von Bertalanffy, *Perspectives on Systems Theory*, p. 127.

23. Brillouin, "Life, Thermodynamics and Cybernetics," p. 153.

24. Bateson, *Steps to Ecology of Mind*, pp. 317–18.

25. *Ibid.*, p. 331.

26. Laszlo, *Introduction to Systems Philosophy*, p. 205.

27. Burhoe, "Civilization of the Future," pp. 171–73.

28. Allport, "Open System," p. 347.

29. Burhoe, "Civilization of the Future," p. 173.

7

The Co-Arising of
Knower and Known

If Lake Erie is driven insane, its insanity is incorporated in the larger system of *your* thought and experience.

—Gregory Bateson[1]

The mystery of the relation between mind, which we subjectively experience, and the world outside it, which we perceive, has teased humankind since first it reflected on the nature of things.[2] Walking the earth with a battery of senses, we see it, hear it, taste, touch, and smell it; we know the contours and colors of our world, its texture and topography. Yet at the same time it can appear to us, too, that we are locked in our heads, prisoners mocked by the solitude of that cell where we receive these impressions and reflect on them. It is there, what I see and touch, and as I see and touch it. Or is it? Am I making it up? How do I know? These eternal questions bemuse the mind of the growing child. They also, more formally, occasion among philosophers the pursuit of epistemology, the study of perception among scientists.

In confronting the riddle of the relation between perceiver and perceived, the linear causal paradigm has tended to put stress exclusively on the one or the other. Classical empiricists have held that the world is the cause of our perceptions. Taken incontrovertibly there, it registers its data on passive and neutral sense organs. These data, as T. S. Kuhn points out, are taken as given:

Is sensory experience fixed and neutral? Are theories simply [based on] given data? The epistemological viewpoint that has most often guided Western philosophy for three centuries dictates an immediate and unequivocal Yes![3]

In contradistinction, there are those thinkers and traditions who have said no. Sensing the power of mind and questioning the unilateral reality of the sensory world, subjective idealists have seen external phenomena as projection only. The cause is mind; therefore, knowledge can be independent of the data perceived.

Between these two positions, both expressive of linear thinking, there is no resolution; but the perspective of mutual causality opens a third alternative, as we can see in both Buddhist and systems thought. Seeing the perceiving subject as dependently co-arising with sensory impact, or as integral to a circuit through which information is exchanged and transformed, it offers a view in which the knower and the known appear as causally interdetermined.

Perception as Convergence of Factors

It was the Buddha's view that a clear understanding of the process of perception gives insight into the origin of suffering and the illusoriness of the self.[4] To this end he and his followers devoted attention to analyzing the way sensory impressions arise and how they relate to other cognitive and affective activities. These perceptions represent the function, not only of the five sensory faculties we recognize in the West, but also of thought. In the Indian perspective (Hindu as well as Buddhist) the senses are six, and include the perception of mental objects as well.

Discarding belief in the existence of an enduring soul or *attā* (Sanskrit: *ātman*), the early Buddhists accounted for the causes of sensory perception in a manner very different from Vedic thought. The Upaniṣads tend to interpret sensory functions in a linear, unidirectional perspective, seeing them as representing in the last analysis the activity of the *ātman*. As prime agent it is the *ātman* that sees through our eyes, hears through our ears. It is that by virtue of which we perceive the world, for "there is no other seer than he, no other hearer than he. . . . "[5] In Sāṃkhya it is the intellect *(buddhi)* that takes in the form of a sense object and casts its reflection upon the transcendental self, the passive *puruṣa*. Both *ātman* and *puruṣa* represent the silent witness, the imperturbable rider of the chariot, spectator of all events.

In contrast to these notions, the early Buddhists represent perception as produced by a convergence of factors. Here sensory perception does not reside in the power of a single agent, but rather in the interaction of three conditions: (1) an unimpaired internal sense organ, (2) a sense object coming within its range, and (3) impact or an appropriate act of attention, be it automatic or deliberate. All conditions must be present for sensory cognition to occur. If condition (1) is satisfied, but not (2) or (3), or if (1) and (2) are met but not (3), the result will not take place.[6] In such a view, as Jayatilleke acknowledges, "there is recognition of mutual causal dependence of sensible objects and their respective cognitions."[7]

This mutual dependence of sensory factors is made clear in the *nidāna* series. There the components of perception are represented by *saḷ'āyatana*, the "six gateways," corresponding to the six senses, which arise conditioned by name-and-form. That is, the prerequisites for perception are present when a psycho-physical entity happens, when *nāmarūpa* constellates. Now the *āyatanas*, interestingly enough, denote both sense organ *and* sense object; they represent the sensory "sphere" (another translation of *āyatana*), which includes them both. The convergence of organ and object within this sphere, or the impact between them, is represented by *phassa*, contact (*phassa* then figures as the next factor in the series). If one views the series consecutively, it may appear odd that it follows that to which it is integral, the conjunction of whose elements it represents. Viewed idiographically, however, this setting apart of *phassa* underscores and dramatizes the relational, convergent nature of the perception event. By isolating *phassa*, impact itself, the teachings render it very difficult to assign causal priority to either sense organ or sense object. *Phassa*, as pure contact, is inserted as if to block our tendency to make either perceiver or perceived solely determinative. It is their encounter which occasions perception.

Consciousness: Conditioned and Transitive

In the causal series, *phassa* conditions feeling, and from feeling arises craving, etc. In other passages *phassa* is presented as that from which consciousness itself arises. Although consciousness or cognition (*viññāna*) is accorded in the series a position precedent to sensory activity, it is elsewhere specified as its product also. It appears as occasioned and shaped by the perceived object.

> It is because, monks, an appropriate condition arises that consciousness is known by this or that name: if consciousness arises because of eye and material shapes, it is known as visual consciousness; if consciousness arises because of ear and sounds, it is known as auditory consciousness, [etc.]. . . .

Monks, as if a fire burns because of this or that appropriate
condition, by that it is known: if a fire burns because of sticks,
it is known as a stick-fire . . . and if a fire burns because of
grass, it is known as a grass-fire. . . . Even so, monks, when
consciousness arises because of eye and material shapes it is
known as visual consciousness . . . when consciousness arises
because of mind and mental objects, it is known as mental
consciousness.[8]

Encounter with the world through the six senses is, then, generative of consciousness, and consciousness arises in terms of what
is apprehended, be it factual or symbolic. Co-arising with sensory
activity, consciousness includes both perceptual interpretation and
cognition ("it is with *viññāna* that one understands something").[9] It
reveals itself as it functions, processing data. It does not exist prior
to or independently of its environment, but is called into being and
conditioned by that which in turn becomes its object. It is always
consciousness *of* something. For "apart from condition there is no
origination of consciousness."[10]

By the same token, the Buddha, as Jayatilleke documents, rejected the independent validity of *a priori* reasoning.[11] *Takka*, as pure
logic, was distinguished from *anumāna*, inferential or empirical reasoning, and seen as both controversial and unreliable. First of all, it
derives from perception; there is no self-justifying realm of pure
reason aloof from or unconditioned by the sensory world.

There exists no divers truth which in the world are eternal,
apart from perception. Having formulated theories in accordance with logic, they have arrived at the two-fold categories
called the "true" and the "false."

Reckonings characterized by conceptual proliferation have perception as their source.[12]

Consequently the fruits of *takka*, if taken independently, are
suspect.

Even that which is well reasoned (*suparivitakkitam*) is liable to
be baseless, unfounded and false, while that which is not well
reasoned or well thought out may turn out to be true, factual
and not false.[13]

Views arrived at and defended in terms of *takka* alone are suspect in the Buddhist view, because knowing is conditioned by habit and vested interests. As a *khanda*, the faculty of knowing is one of the five components of human activity (along with body, sensation, perception, and volitions) and it is interdependent with these other four. The recorded statements of the Buddha make this clear.

> Were a man to say: I shall show the coming, the going, the passing away, the arising, the growth, the increase or development of consciousness apart from body, sensation, perception and volitional formations, he would be speaking about something which does not exist.[14]

As is set forth in the causal series, volitional formations *(saṅkhārā)*, which represent the persisting tendencies that acts engender (be they acts of mind, body, or speech), condition consciousness. In other words, the habits and impulses to which mental activity gives rise, come in turn to modify it, and thereby to interpret the external world and impose fabrications upon it.

The process by which this fabrication occurs is described in the *Madhupindika Sutta:*

> Depending on eye and visible form arises visual consciousness; meeting together of the three is contact *(phassa);* because of contact arises feeling or sensation *(vedanā);* what one feels, one perceives *(sañjānāti);* what one perceives, one reasons about *(vitakketi);* what one reasons about, one proliferates conceptually *(papanceti);* what one proliferates conceptually, due to that, concepts characterized by such obsessed perceptions *(papañcasaññasankhā)* assail him in regard to visible form cognisable by the eye, belonging to the past, the future and the present.[15]

Here one's reasoning *(vitakketi)* about what is perceived produces a proliferation and objectification of concepts, which then act on the perceiver, "assailing" her and shaping her perceptions.

Bhikkhu Ñāṇananda, offering a commentary on this passage, interprets the nature of this circular process. He distinguishes three stages in the perceptual events which this section of the *Madhupindika Sutta* delineates. The first stage, he notes, is presented in the style of the general formulations of *paṭicca samuppāda*—"depending on . . . arises . . . "—and deals with impersonalized functions.

With *vedanā* (feeling), however, the impersonal style ends and sub-sequent actions are conveyed in the active third-person verb form. A subject is thereby implied, he says, the intrusion of ego-consciousness, as painful or pleasant feelings give rise to judgment and avoidance or attraction. In the third stage, with proliferation of concepts, the subject becomes "assailed" by them. As Ñāṇananda puts it, "He who has hitherto been the subject now becomes the hapless object." Summarizing the development, Ñāṇananda says,

> the latent illusion of ego wakens at the stage of *vedanā* and thereafter the vicious duality is maintained until it is fully crystallized and justified at the conceptual level. Thus what has been a complex, conditionally arisen process, tends to be resolved into a direct relationship between the ego and the non-ego.[16]

For this development he offers a vivid image. "Like the legendary resurrected tiger which devoured the magician who restored it to life out of its skeletal bones, the concepts and linguistic conventions overwhelm the worldling who evolved them."[17]

Perception, then, in the view of the Nikāyas, is a highly inter-pretive process. It represents the interaction of perceiver and per-ceived, as sensory stimuli are screened and appraised in terms of the projects and preconceptions of the ego. As Streng says, *paṭicca samuppāda* recognizes that "thinking itself is a contributing factor in the rising of phenomena."[18]

We create our worlds, but we do not do so unilaterally, for consciousness is colored by that on which it feeds, subject and ob-ject are interdependent. The Nikāyas, denying neither the "there-ness" of the sense objects nor the projective tendencies of the mind, see the process as a two-way street. Sensory experience shapes us and we in turn shape it. The conditioning is mutual.[19] Never is the world presented as independent of the viewer, nor the viewer as independent of perception, for cognition is transitive, *viññāna* takes an object.

Modern experiments with sensory deprivation offer results supportive of this view. The removal or even interruption of exter-nal stimuli occasions disturbances, such as visual and aural hallu-cinations, and indicates the organisms's dependence on their flow for the maintenance of inner stability.[20] Similarly, as research has revealed, an image stabilized on the retina disintegrates into darkness. Just as one ceases to hear a steady sound, or as an immobilized hand no longer feels contact but must move its fingers to ascertain its touch, movement and change of stimulus is requisite to perception. Eyes or object must move, even the faintest flicker, for vision to occur.[21] Such examples support the Buddhist notion that perceiving and knowing is an active encounter, triggered by impact, ignited by friction between subject and object.

> Just as, monks, from the coming together of two sticks by way of friction, there arises heat and fire is produced . . . even so, monks, feelings are born of contact, rooted in contact, arisen out of contact, dependent on contact.[22]

Because we are believed to co-create our minds and our worlds, it is important, in the Buddhist view, to understand how we do so. Careful attention to sensory data, the arising and ceasing of psychophysical events (dharmas), constitutes the basis of the meditation that the Buddha taught in the *Satipaṭṭhāna Sutta*. Its purpose is not so much tranquility of mind, as insight into the mental processes which give rise to objects and egos. The awareness this meditation breeds is carried into all activities as mindfulness, a requirement of the Eightfold Path. Together they build the capacity to see existence "as it is" (*yathābūtham*). Given the views of perception and cognition the scriptures express, this seeing *yathābūtham* would not represent an assumption of naive realism, that we can see the world naked of interpretation; it would mean rather a clarification of the interactive processes by which we construct our world. As Ñāṇananda puts it, seeing *yathābūtham* "analyzes and lays bare the very structure of experience." This structure, "as it is," represents a dynamic mutual relation between world and viewer.

Information Circuits

This mutual relation is recognized today by general systems theory. Viewed as a circuit along which information flows and is transformed, perceptual and cognitive activity is seen as embracing both that which is perceived and that which is perceiving. Just as self and nonself cannot be categorically isolated in this information flow, neither can knower and known. These terms are relative and dependent on perspective. For, as in Buddhist thought, we are dealing here with process not substance, acts rather than actors.

In the systems view, as we saw, information input from the environment arrives in the form of percepts, and these percepts are interpreted in terms of the system's gestalts and constructs. We do not see objects so much as our ideas of them. Laszlo puts it this way:

> Would we see the perceptually signaled objects themselves, seeing would be a simple matter—and it would be utterly confusing. For in each instance we would see what our eyes tell us, and they never tell us the same thing twice. But seeing (hearing, touching, etc.) is not a simple matter, and it is not (at least not usually) confusing. This is because we immediately refer our sensory information to our established gestalten and it is these gestalten that we apprehend clothed, as it were, in the sensuous material of actual perceptions. We see our sensory data *as* the familiar objects of our environing world, rather than seeing the data themselves.[23]

Our gestalts screen the data we register with our senses (so do our conceptual constructs) and filter the ideas we encounter. Prior assumptions and constructs shape the direction and content of scientific research, as T. S. Kuhn has demonstrated. With notions as well as objects, perception is shaped by prior knowledge or, as Hanson puts it, "seeing is a theory-laden understanding." "How should we regard," he asks, "a man's report that he sees x if we know him to be ignorant of all x-ish things? Precisely as we would regard a four-year old's report that he sees a meson shower."[24]

The gestalts and constructs by which the world is interpreted are understood, in the systems view, to be coded by past experience. As such, they are functionally equivalent to the Buddhist notion of *saṇkhārā*, the volitional formations constellated through earlier activity, which co-condition the content of perception and cognition. As "accumulated sense experience fermented by ignorance," these constitute, in Ñāṇananda's words, "the ruts and grooves of our mental terrain," and "influence every moment of [our] living experience."[25] The perceptions we take for granted as given turn out, under examination, to be synthetic and composite, *saṇkhata*. While the Buddhist view highlights, in a way that systems does not, the role of attachment in the perpetuation of these formations, both bodies of thought recognize their significance for perception, and both see them as subject to alteration. Formed by experience, these codes are modified by experience.

Stimuli, then, do not impose their meaning, rather we read meaning into them by referring them to the familiar forms by which we gauge present needs, past behavior, and future projects. As Laszlo reiterates, cognition presupposes recognition. "Absence of reference presents us with an enigma," he points out; "complete novelty excludes understanding."[26] "With some exaggeration one can say that we perceive what we know rather than know what we perceive."[27] Even systemic "organization" is, as Ashby says, "partly in the eye of the beholder."[28] Given the same perceptual data, we can see a society, a family, a beehive, either as a collection of individuals interacting, or as an organized system with its own dynamics and trajectory. We cannot count the bats in an inkblot, Bateson said, because there are none, "and yet a man—if he be 'bat-minded'—may 'see' several."[29] In other words, we see by interpreting and live, each of us, in our own assumed form-world. Such assumptions are necessary, both in ordinary perceptions and in scientific thinking, for both are deductive, requiring a leap beyond the plane of percepts and the interpretation of reality in terms of postulations and hypotheses.[30]

Von Glasersfeld and Varela, bringing to this new epistemology the ideas of G. Spencer Brown (*Laws of Form*, 1969), show how any act of perception and cognition involves the value-laden making of distinctions or cuts, separating figure from ground, which are in the last analysis self-referential in nature. They also point out how Piaget's studies (*La construction du réel chez l'enfant*, 1937) reveal how the objects of our world emerge through the gradual coordination of such perceptual and conceptual distinctions. "That peculiar elusive relationship between the subject and the object of the act of cognition [is one of] . . . total interdependence in which relative stability is achieved and maintained through the circularity of interaction."[31]

Shaping the World through Projection

In this "total interdependence" our preconceptions not only shape our interpretations of the world, but impinge on the world itself. For the feedback loop circles through the environment "out there," extending beyond the subjective realm and the selective interpretation of sensory data. This is so because we rely on this causal loop—the operation of feedback—to ensure meaning, the maintenance of intelligibility. The cognitive system finds satisfaction and value in the distillation of meaning, in extracting message from noise and making sense of the world. Where it succeeds in interpreting percepts in terms of internal codes, it seeks (in negative feedback process) to perpetuate this match. It acts upon the environment in such a way as to confirm these interpreted percepts and produce more of them.

In this way the cognitive system can be said to "project" its codes upon the environment so that it can continue to transform perceptions in their terms. By such projection the scientist shapes his research and the kind of data it can render to fit his concepts, and the architect gives body to his dreams. To perpetuate the match between cognition and perception we impose shapes on our world which then reflects them back. In excavated gardens or fortifications we can read something of the character of an ancient city, for in them its meanings, gestalts, and constructs, took form: notions incarnate. And when we possess a powerful technology, this incarnational capacity is fearsome. Our imaginations erect Pentagons and Disneylands, and even the land itself mirrors back our fantasies, as, gouged and paved over, it testifies to our search for mastery and our fear of what we cannot control. In the world we create we encounter ourselves.

Learning as Self Reorganization

According to systems theory, codes are altered when anomalies develop and persist. That is, when changing conditions and circumstances render them no longer appropriate to interpret incoming percepts, or when data no longer yield meaning in terms of these codes. In positive feedback, when codes reveal their inadequacy to process the stream of experience, the cognitive system searches for new ones by which novel and confusing percepts can be made intelligible. This exploratory self-organization continues until constructs are evolved which can deal with the new data. This positive feedback process represents learning; it also represents the way in which the world shapes the system. While in negative feedback the knower modified the known through projection, in positive feedback the world in turn affects the viewer, mapping itself in new ways in the internal organization of the system. This learning is not something added, rather it represents a fundamental reorganization of the system. New nets and assemblies occur, loops form, alternate pathways develop. The viewed world is different, and so is the viewer.

Implicit is such a view is the recognition of the creative function of cognitive crisis. When old, habitual modes of interpretation become dysfunctional, confusion can be fruitful. The experience of anomaly then motivates the system to achieve a higher level of organization, one which embraces and integrates data of which it had been previously unconscious.

The recognition that learning represents a reorganization of the system and its components, rather than the mere addition of data, is also present in the Buddhist view. Here organization is understood in terms of the *khandas* or components of experience, which, as the *Mahaṭṭhipadopama Sutta* maintains in its analysis of perception, represent five ways of grasping or apprehending the world. In this apprehension "there comes to be inclusion, collecting together and coming together of these five forms of grasping."[32]

The Buddha was not interested in conveying theories so much as in motivating his followers to reorganize their experience by attending to its very process. The Zen master, approached for teachings, filled his caller's teacup till it overflowed—showing in this manner that the new could not be perceived until one has emptied oneself of preconceived notions. Neither did the Buddha "pour" precepts into his followers' heads, so much as invite them to free themselves of habitual ways of seeing. That this involved a dismantling of old interpretive constructs is evident in the meditation which he taught.

Seen in systems terms, the practice of *vipassanā*, with its bare attention to the rising and ceasing of dharmas, represents a short-circuiting of the codes we impose on reality. These are undercut and disempowered as the mind trains to register percepts without editorial comment or discursive thought. By remaining aloof from conceptualization, which tends to function within preestablished constructs, the practitioner refrains from perpetuating their validity. Rather than processing noise to extract message, she, in effect, switches off the message in order to receive more of the noise. The exercise amounts to a deliberate mismatching and production of positive feedback, as awareness widens to the rush of impersonal psycho-physical events, wherein no permanent "I" is evident. The cybernetic circuit, experienced in this way, is particularly suitable to validation of the Buddha's teachings about self, since, as Laszlo points out, "in such analysis (of experience) we do not see a categorical 'I' against a categorically distinct 'you' or 'it'."[33]

Such use of mismatch and positive feedback deliberately to dismantle old constructs is evident in a variety of religious and aesthetic efforts. An example of unhingeing old habits of interpreting the world is Don Juan teaching Carlos Castaneda how to see by trying to define visual perceptions in terms of shadow or space instead of the solid form. Some motivations and consequences of drug experience are, likewise, of this type. Rimbaud's "dérèglement des sens" is a similar case. The French poet sought to open himself to new vision, in spite of the painfulness of the initially resulting disorientation (though what he actually "derailed" was not his senses but his gestalts and constructs). In all of these instances, the world maps itself in the system in new ways.

The two types of feedback, then, involving respectively, projection and mapping, represent complementary ways in which viewer and world, knower and known, interact in mutual determination. Expressing this reciprocity in what he calls systems' "brain-language," Laszlo writes,

> Although it may be put to purely cognitive uses, perception . . . is nevertheless the interaction of organism and relevant environment; a process whereby the states of the latter are mapped by the higher nervous centers of the former, and his correlated motor responses impose states on the environment which correspond with the preestablished mappings.[34]

The consequent mutuality between knower and known is dramatized by systems theorists' new use of quite ordinary words. Robert Rosen, in discussing how the observer-related nature of complexity can be measured, employs the word *measure* interchangeably with the word *interact*.[35]

The Limits of Cognition

If knowing is interactive, it becomes difficult to claim and impossible to prove an ultimate truth. For knowing is not only relative to the perspective of the knower, but conditioned by his past and present experiencing, and colored by the gestalts and constructs he imposes on perceptual data.

In systems thinking these limits to cognition are recognized in a variety of ways. One is implicit in the self-referential character of feedback. By virtue of the causal loops that interconnect the observer with his environment, all percepts and concepts, as we have seen, are modified by past experience and, therefore, interpretive. Furthermore, these circuits are such that only "short arcs," or portions of the factors they link, are discernible by the conscious knower. As Bateson points out, "life depends upon interlocking *circuits* of contingency, while consciousness can only see such short arcs as human purpose may direct." He takes this as grounds for arguing that "purposive rationality" is pathogenic to the extent that it is "unaided by such phenomena as art, religion, dream, and the like."[36]

Because systems, furthermore, are irreducible, a subsystem within a larger system is not interchangeable with others—it has its own particular role and perspective, as Bateson observes elsewhere.

> Cybernetically speaking, "my" relationship to any larger system around me and including other things and persons will be different from "your" relation to some similar system around you. The relation "part of" must necessarily and logically always be complementary but the meaning of the phrase "part of" will be different for every person.[37]

Von Bertalanffy called attention to an additional limit to cognition: the dialectical nature of existence itself. The open system, as he points out, is made possible by the interplay of opposites, the building up and breaking down of its very substance; he saw this creative tension as characterizing "reality" as a whole. While the play of polarities can be intuited, any statement *about* it can be only partial. This recognition leads von Bertalanffy to affirm the logical necessity of antithetical statements.

> All our knowledge, even if de-anthropomorphized, only mirrors certain aspects of reality. If what had been said [about systems] is true, reality is what Nicholas da Cusa called *coincidentia oppositorum*. Discursive thinking always represents only one aspect of ultimate reality, called God in Cusa's terminology; it can never exhaust its infinite manifoldness. Hence ultimate reality is a unity of opposites; any statement holds from a certain viewpoint only, has only relative validity, and must be supplemented by antithetical statements from opposite points of view.[38]

Given its doctrine of dependent co-arising, the early Buddhist view also sets limits to that which can be ascertained and asserted. Gotama was unique among teachers of his time in refraining from establishing a definitive metaphysic. To the puzzlement and exasperation of many of his followers, he refused to define in ultimate terms the way things are "out there" in objective reality indepen-

dent of the knower. Gotama was suspicious of theories that define
the ultimate source and status of things because they are necessarily partial and also because they become objects of attachment. Instead he directed his attention and that of his followers to the
processes by which the beholding mind itself shapes its world.
Speculative views that claimed exclusive and final accuracy were
shunned, dismissed with barely disguised contempt.

> Whatever is seen, heard, sensed or clung to, is esteemed as
> truth by other folk. Amidst those who are entrenched in their
> own views, . . . I hold none as true or false. This barb I beheld
> well in advance, whereon mankind is hooked, impaled: "I
> know, I see 'tis verily so"—no such clinging for the
> Tathagatas.[39]

The phrase "I know, I see 'tis verily so" (*jānāmi passāmi tatheva etam*)
is often cited in the texts to represent the dogmatism the Buddha
decried, as is also the doctrinaire assertion, "This alone is true, all
else is false" (*idameva saccam moghannam*).

From the viewpoint of mutual causality, the impossibility of
arriving at ultimate definitions and formulations of reality does not
represent a defeat for the inquiring mind. It is only final assertions
that are suspect, not the process of knowing itself. It is the illusion
that knower is separate from and unconditioned by the world she
would know that drives her into error and derails her pursuit of
truth. When the dependent co-arising nature of her mental processes is acknowledged, then her knowing enhances her conscious
connection with and participation in the reality of which she is a
part.

From a systems view, this participation is enhanced by the ongoing creation of new meanings, symbols, and patterns of order
which take more into account, embrace wider ranges of data and
experience. While no symbol or construct can be the last word, each
is past of a vaster enterprise. For the knowing we engage in is not
co-terminous with our separate identities, but extends beyond us in
information flows integral to the self-organization of other systems
as well.

From the early Buddhist standpoint, the recognition of the
contingent nature of knowing is more emphatically stressed as a
value. It is intrinsic to *paticca samuppāda* and therefore basic to wisdom (*paññā*) itself, and a necessary precondition to enlightenment.
It helps free the individual from the opinions, judgments, and

points of view to which he clings. For the false notion of his independence as a knower from that which he knows leads to the delusion of ego.

Objectless Knowing

If perception and cognition are interactive with world, what do we make of those experiences where world and senses fall away? In our discussion so far, the act of knowing has been seen as transitive, implying an object, be it thing or idea. Can the paradigm of mutual causality accommodate the experience of objectless knowing or pure consciousness? To pursue this question, let us see how such experience can be viewed and interpreted in systems and early Buddhist terms.

In the systems view of things, organized forms of life arise and evolve as their parts interact to permit internal self-regulating functions. These functions operate automatically up to levels of complexity which require the weighing of alternatives; self-reflexive consciousness appears with choice-making. At this point learning, the system's adaptive self-organization, necessitates intracerebral evaluation: thinking not only about perceived data but about the constructs by which they are interpreted. Deutsch refers to this self-reflexive consciousness as dealing with "secondary messages," the guide cards and index tabs by which the system orders the information flowing through and stored within it.[40] By appraisal and manipulation of these symbols the interaction between system and environment can itself be analyzed. Higher level feedback loops are instituted; a hierarchical cognitive structure evolves in which each level completes the one below it in some essential respect. Since each, as a creative synthesis, involves nonsummative organization, these levels are nonreducible. In this manner second-order thinking develops, at a remove from empirical problems and results, both in the individual and the culture. As systems explore dimensions of meaning, this activity becomes autonomous and self-validating, serving ends of its own far beyond fulfillment of biological needs and even at their expense.[41]

This circular reflexivity, by which cognitive circuits themselves can be known, is not limited to model-building or the evaluation of ideas. There is no inherent reason why it cannot go beyond the manipulation of symbols to the experience of the knowing itself. In such an experience, all connections with empirical cognitions are severed, as scientist Harley Shands describes.

There is an intense feeling of *knowing*, but a total denial of *object*. When the mystic finds himself knowing *something*, the moment of intensity has passed. The ecstasy is in knowing— but in this sense knowing becomes an intransitive verb, since it does not take an object—or, if one wants to put it the other way around, it is knowing knowing.[42]

This view affirms what mystics have maintained, the noetic character of the experience. Roland Fischer has sought to explain the nondual nature of this consciousness, including the oneness experienced in *samādhi* (meditative absorption), in terms of the integration of cortical and subcortical activity in the nervous system.[43] Laszlo, approaching the question in "mind" rather than "brain" terms, sees it as a higher level awareness of the system's own capacity to know. "Thus," he says, "we trace the gradual stepwise progression from survival to knowing, to knowing knowing, and ultimately to knowing the knowing knowing itself."[44] Boundaries between subject and object are dissolved, because, as Bateson points out, the mentality of the system "is immanent, not in some part, but in the system as a whole," and the "system as a whole" includes both the "agent" and the larger system with which he is in interaction.[45]

The early Buddhist scriptures do not specify a term for pure awareness or objectless consciousness, as the Mahayanists do with *cittamatra* and *ālayavijñāna*. Yet they make it clear that the polarity between subject and object, common to conventional perception and cognition, can be transcended, and that a consciousness can arise which is removed from sensory stimuli and concepts.

Consciousness which is non-manifestative, infinite and lustrous all round: It does not partake of the solidity of earth, the cohesiveness of water, the hotness of fire, the movement of air, the creaturehood of creatures, the devahood of devas, the Pajāpatihood of Pajāpati, the Brahmāhood of Brahmā . . . the Overlordship of the Overlord and the Allness of the all.[46]

The verb "does not partake of" is sometimes also translated as "cannot be reached by." (For example, Ñāṇananda uses the former, I. B. Horner the latter.) This infinite consciousness, then, is not imbued with or attainable through sensory data. Significantly, it is also stressed that infinite consciousness is similarly unconnected with and nonmanifestive of a supernatural ontological realm, "the

Brahmāhood of Brahmā" or even the "Allness of the all." Perhaps this stress is to distinguish infinite consciousness from interpretations which Vedic thought would place upon it.

The nature of such consciousness has puzzled many a disciple. "Could there be such an attainment of concentration," asks Ānanda, "that the monk will not be conscious of earth in earth, nor of water in water, (etc.) . . . and yet he will be conscious?" The Buddha answered,

> Herein, Ānanda, a monk is thus conscious: 'this is peace, this is excellent, namely, the calming down of all formations . . . destruction of craving, detachment, cessation, nibbāna'.[47]

This reply suggests that there is still an object of knowing, consisting of the peace which arises with the cessation of craving and suffering. Ñāṇananda, in commenting on this passage, calls it a "quasi-object," for he sees this experience as one which deprives all percepts and concepts of their object-status.

> 'Objects' play no part in this 'perception' precisely for the reason that the 'subject' is missing. This experience of the cessation of existence (bhavanirodho) which is none other than 'Nibbāna here-and-now', is the outcome of the eradication of the conceit 'I am'.[48]

The question which Ānanda asked above is then put by him to Śariputra. This eminent and enlightened senior disciple then answers,

> 'Cessation of becoming is nibbāna'; 'cessation of becoming is nibbāna': thus, friend, one perception arises in me, another perception fades out in me. Just as, friend, when a faggot-fire is blazing one flame arises and another flames fades out, even so, friend, one perception arises in me: 'Cessation of becoming is nibbāna' and another perception fades out in me: 'Cessation of becoming is nibbāna.' At that time, friend, I was conscious of this: 'Cessation of becoming is nibbāna'.[49]

Śariputra's reply would indicate that this consciousness is still a series of momentary events or *dharmas*, that it partakes of the world of flux, and is transitive in the sense that the very cessation of usual perceptual cognition becomes in turn that of which one is conscious.

As we see, this kind of consciousness about which Ānanda asked need not be seen as a breach of dependent co-arising, but can be interpreted within the context of that causal doctrine. It can either be seen as still transitive (peace or cessation of suffering remaining as objects of cognition) or, if taken intransitively, as a direct experiential validation of the interdependence of subject and object (where the "I" is no longer experienced, neither is the object).

A variant on these interpretations, consonant with mutual causality and its radical relativity, is analogous to that which Shands and Laszlo suggest—knowing the knowing of knowing. While Laszlo conceptualizes it as a metalevel of reflexive consciousness, it could also be taken as immanent and intrinsic to all mentality, as the very means, capacity, or invariant by which we know and interact with the world. As such it would be always present, without beginnings or ending; it would transcend sensory experience, going beyond all the distinctions by which it permits, in our interaction with the world, the registering and ordering of phenomena.

Early Buddhist scripture offers grounds for such an interpretation. This nondiscriminatory awareness is referred to as *saḷāyatana nirodha*, the cessation of the six sense spheres or six sensory ways of perceiving.[50] Yet it still is referred to as a mode of perception, rather than an object of it, as in the celebrated passage from *Udāna* 80:

> There is, monks, that sphere wherein there is neither earth, nor water, nor fire, nor air; wherein is neither this world nor a world beyond, nor moon nor sun. There, monks, I declare, is no coming, no going, no stopping, no passing-away and no arising. It is not established, it continues not, it has no object. This indeed is the end of suffering. . . . Monks, there is a not-born, a not-become, a not-made, a not-compounded. Monks, if [there were not], there would be no stepping out here, from what is born, become, made, compounded.[51]

It is significant that the term, translated here as "sphere," is *āyatana*, the "gateway," or faculty that permits the occurrence of perception, as in its use in the *nidāna* series in *saḷāyatana*, the sixfold spheres of perception. It is reasonable, then, to accord it such a meaning in this passage, that is to take it to represent the means by which we perceive, or the way in which we perceive, rather than an objective self-existent, supernatural essence or realm. The use of the term *āyatana*, rather than any term denotative of object, place, or entity, suggests that such a meaning was intended.

In that case, the knower, while out of touch with the environment (in that the six senses are transcended), would be very much *in* touch with what permits her interaction with the environment. She would be conscious of that by which she knows it and, therefore, by which she can "step out," to use the phrase employed, from the fabrications she imposes upon it.

Misconstructions of *asaṅkhata* (as "unconditioned" instead of its literal meaning of "uncompounded") and of *āyatana* (as "essence" or "realm" instead of "perceptual mode") have led many to read *Udāna* 80 as referring to a metaphysical, self-existent absolute. The interpretation we suggest here permits the passage to be construed in a fashion consonant with the Buddha's doctrine of causality, wherein all dharmas are *anattā*, and reality perceived not in terms of substance but relation. It is pertinent to note that while *Udāna* 80 seems to identify this "sphere" with enlightenment (saying, "This indeed is the end of suffering"), the early texts as a whole do not equate nondiscriminatory awareness with enlightenment. Kalupahana points this out.[52] Often termed *nirodhasamāpatti* or *saññāvedayitanirodha*, the "cessation of perception and feeling" is equivalent to the *samādhi* attained by advanced yogis of the time. Learned by Gotama well before he sat under the *bodhi* tree, it was used to attain rest and release from pain and considered helpful in developing the concentration requisite to insight. But it is distinct from insight—that recognition of the dependently co-arising nature of existence, that is seen as integral to the enlightenment of the Buddhas and all beings.[53]

Who is Knowing?

Mutual causality presents reality as so structured that knower and known do not exist independently. Its epistemology suggests that a process is going on wherein such categories are, in the last analysis, insubstantial and arbitrary. Consciousness in and of such a world is hampered to the extent that the distinctions between knower and known are reified.

Such a conclusion is implicit in systems-cybernetics. The cognitive system enhances its capacity to cope and to extract meanings by learning how to take more into account. This involves constantly revamping its codes, codes which include self-definitions. In learning how to process more information, old constructs of who is doing the knowing are jettisoned, altered, expanded. The knower appears then as a shifting construct, subject to the very process by which it would know.

Von Glasersfeld and Varela argue that "the self we do experience and incorporate into our cognitive structure, by that very act of construction, ceases to be the self that does the experiencing"—or, we can add, knowing.[54] Who, then, is knowing? It is no isolable entity, for as soon as distinguished, it is the known, not the knower. So, unable to locate an agent, we are driven, in the last resort, to accord that function to the intra- and intersystemic invariances which permit cognition to occur—or indeed, to the universe itself, which appears, as G. Spencer Brown concludes, so constructed as to be able to observe and know itself.[55]

Both the need to transcend dichotomies between knower and known and the possibility of doing so are explicit in early Buddhist teachings. There the mental distortions which obscure to us the nature of our being in the world are viewed in a merciless light. Yet, at the same time, the idea that we can eradicate and break free from them is proclaimed. Not only is this possibility affirmed but methods are set forth by which it can be achieved.

In *vipassanā* training this is done by directing attention not to the things we see but to how we see them, the dependently co-arising nature of feelings, thoughts, and perceptions. Thus can be gained the "eye of wisdom" *(paññācakkhu)*, that dissolves the hatred and greed we project upon the world. The knower, seeing with the "eye of wisdom," does not seek to extricate herself from the objects of her knowing, so much as to free them from the fabrications she imposes upon them. As the object of knowing seemed to disappear in the experience of *saḷāyatana nirodha*, so now, with insight or *vipassanā* practice, does the subject seem to evaporate.

> Then, Bahiya, thus must you train yourself: In the seen, there will be just the seen; in the heard, just the heard; in the sensed, just the sensed; in the known, just the known. That is how, Bahiya, you must train yourself. Now, when, Bahiya, in the seen there will be to you just the seen; in the heard, just the heard; in the sensed, just the sensed; in the known, just the known, then Bahiya . . . you will not be in it. And when, Bahiya, you will not be in it, then, Bahiya, you will not be 'here' nor 'there' nor 'midway-between.' This itself is the end of suffering.[56]

In the epistemology of mutual causality, both the what that is known and the who that is knower are elusive. Neither can be fixed or pinpointed as static, self-existent entities. Shifting and dancing out of reach as we seek to grasp them, they suggest, in mockery of this chapter's title, that there is not knower or known so much as "just knowing."

Notes

1. Bateson, *Steps to Ecology of Mind*, p. 484.

2. *Mind* here is used in its conventional sense and without metaphysical connotations, that is to represent the subjectivity of experience or that in an individual which "feels, observes, perceives, thinks, wills and reasons" (Webster's New Collegiate Dictionary. Merriam-Webster, Inc., 1969).

3. Kuhn, *Structure of Scientific Revolutions*, p. 126.

4. *Saṃyutta Nikāya*, IV.138.

5. *Brihad-Araṇyaka Upaniṣad*, in Hume, *Thirteen Upanishads*, III,7, 16–23.

6. *Majjhima Nikāya*, I.190f.

7. Jayatilleke, *Early Buddhist Theory*, p. 434. Sarathchandra gives a comparable analysis in his *Buddhist Psychology of Perception*, p. 9.

8. *Majjhima Nikāya*, I.259–60.

9. *Ibid.*, III.242.

10. *Ibid.*, I.257.

11. Jayatilleke, *Early Buddhist Theory*, p. 270f.

12. *Sutta Nipāta*, V.886, V.874.

13. *Majjhima Nikāya*, I.171.

14. *Saṃyutta Nikāya*, III.57.

15. *Majjhima Nikāya*, I.111, translated by Ñāṇananda in *Concept and Reality*, p. 516.

16. Ñāṇananda, *Concept and Reality*, p. 10.

17. *Ibid.*, p. 6.

18. Streng, "Reflections," p. 78.

19. Mizuno, in describing early Buddhist teachings, writes that the individual "incessantly receives stimulus and influence from the outside world and at the same time influences the outside world . . . [there is] mutual influencing . . . we exist by what surrounds us" (Mizuno, *Primitive Buddhism*, pp. 126–27).

20. Allport, "Open System in Personality Theory," p. 347.

21. Koestler, *Beyond Reductionism*, p. 297.

22. *Saṃyutta Nikāya*, IV.215.

23. Laszlo, *System, Structure, Experience*, p. 43.

24. *Ibid.*, p. 102.

25. Ñāṇananda, *Magic of the Mind*, pp. 41–43.

26. Laszlo, *System, Structure, Experience*, p. 43.

27. Laszlo, *Introduction to Systems Philosophy*, p. 199.

28. Ashby, *Principles of Self-Organizing System*, p. 110.

29. Bateson, *Steps to Ecology of Mind*, p. 272.

30. Laszlo, *Introduction to Systems Philosophy*, pp. 208–10.

31. von Glasersfeld and Varela, "Problems of Knowledge."

32. *Majjhima Nikāya*, I.190.

33. Laszlo, *System, Structure, Experience*, p. 21.

34. Laszlo, *Introduction to Systems Philosophy*, p. 185.

35. Rosen, "Complexity as a System Property," p. 228f.

36. Bateson, quoted in Brand, *Cybernetic Frontiers*, p. 10.

37. Bateson, *Steps to Ecology of Mind*, p. 332.

38. von Bertalanffy, *General Systems Theory*, p. 248.

39. *Aṅguttara Nikāya*, II.24.

40. Deutsch, "Toward a Cybernetic Model," p. 394f.

41. Laszlo, *Introduction to Systems Philosophy*, pp. 193–96.

42. *Ibid.*, p. 195.

43. Fischer, "Cartography of the Ecstatic," pp. 897–904.

44. Laszlo, *Introduction to Systems Philosophy*, p. 195.

45. Bateson, pp. 315–16.

46. *Majjhima Nikāya*, I.329f.

47. *Aṅguttara Nikāya*, V.7f.

48. Ñāṇananda, *Magic of Mind*, pp. 54–55.

49. *Aṅguttara Nikāya*, V.9f.

50. *Saṃyutta Nikāya*, IV.2.

51. *Udāna*, 80–81

52. Kalupahana, *Causality*, pp. 180–81.

53. *Dīgha Nikāya*, I.83.

54. von Glasersfeld and Varela, *Problems of Knowledge*, p. 18.

55. Brown, *The Laws of Form*, App. I.

56. *Udāna*, p. 8.

8

The Co-Arising of Body and Mind

The transient Here seems to need and concern us strangely.

—Rilke, Ninth Duino Elegy

The mind-body riddle—the relation between consciousness and matter, or between spirit and flesh—has been a perennial source of philosophic speculation. These speculations are rarely idle and seldom without consequence, for the perspectives they yield determine the relative reality, and hence the value, that people and cultures attach to these dimensions of life. The ontological status accorded them deeply affects assumptions about the power and scope of the mental and imaginal world, about the dignity and the claims of body and nature.

Of the many connotations of mind and the ways in which it has appeared different from matter, it is useful here to distinguish two. On one hand, mind represents the subjective: the awareness, sensation, and cognition which constitute internal experience. It is in that sense that we will discuss its relation to body and matter. On the other hand, mind, whether human or divine, has also been seen as that which orders, shapes and works its purpose on the material components of life. From the standpoint of mutual causality this connotation is no longer easily distinguishable from the physical domain of nature. Whether viewed in terms of self-organizing open systems, or in terms of dependently co-arising factors of existence, the natural realm appears as a dynamic coherent process. It displays the orderly and ordering character that has been, in linear causal views, assigned to human or divine intellect and taken as distinct from the mindless, inert realm of matter.

But what of subjective consciousness? Is it the product of the body, an excretion of the glands? Or is it essentially independent, more real and more trustworthy than this self-reproducing contraption for the processing of matter? Let us look at some customary assumptions.

Linear Views

In addressing the riddle of consciousness and matter, the linear causal paradigm has afforded various approaches; these appear in comparable form in both Western and Hindu traditions. Assuming that phenomena can be traced back in linear chains and understood in terms of initial causes, the paradigm has either explained one in terms of of the other (reducing mind to matter or matter to mind) or bifurcated them into two discontinuous realms. Either solution presents problems.

The materialists of ancient India and classical Western science, seeing the psychic as derivative of the physical, appear to deny the autonomous reality we experience in introspection, and the power of ideas and feelings that we can observe around us. The idealist stance reverses the order, seeing mind as more real than matter. Springing from Vedic and Platonic traditions and coloring Hindu and Western religious thought, it has, as we increasingly experience, devalued the physical, and deafened us to body and nature. These opposing views are basic to the "two cultures" that have in recent centuries split the modern world.

A dualistic perspective according separate but equal ontological status to each realm, as in Sāṃkhyan and Cartesian thought, offers no remedy, for it perpetuates rather than heals the bifurcation of value. In Sāṃkhya, the division postulated between *puruṣa* and *prakṛti* (spirit and nature) functioned to devalue the latter, while in the West the Cartesian dichotomy, operating within the context of classical empiricism, rendered subjectivity irrelevant to the knowledge of external reality.

The mutual causal paradigm offers a perspective on the mind-matter relation that is distinct from the above approaches. In the last chapter, we saw that its epistemology involves a reciprocal interaction between the perceiving, knowing mind and the world which it perceives and knows. It is, therefore, not surprising that its ontology entails neither the dichotomization of the psychic and physical realms, nor the reduction of one to the other.

"Like Two Sheaves of Reeds"

The early Buddhist texts made a clear break with previous metaphysics in their view of the body. In contrast to the materialists of the time (the Lokāyatas and Cārvākas, who held consciousness to be epiphenomenal to matter), the Buddha's teachings affirm the ir-reducibility of mind. Furthermore, in contrast to the idealist and du-alist postures of Upaniṣadic and Sāṃkhyan thought, the doctrine of *paṭicca samuppāda* breached the dichotomy between mind and mat-ter, and revalorized the physical by placing it in an interdependent relation with the mental.

Given the strong ascetic flavor of the Pali Canon, the thesis that the Dharma revalorized the body may appear startling. Is not body called as insubstantial and illusory as a "mass of foam," and the world a "mirage," a "bubble"?[1] Are the monks of the Sangha not counseled repeatedly to avoid temptations of the flesh, to feel revulsion for the body? Indeed, to this end meditative guides are provided in the scriptures, the monk being urged to develop aver-sion by seeing the body in terms of "kidneys, heart, liver, pleura, spleen, lungs, intestines, mesentery, gorge, faeces, bile, phlegm, pus, blood, sweat, solid fat, saliva, mucus, synovic fluid, urine."[2]

Such passages, as well as the ascetic, even prudish tone of many early Buddhist texts, must be seen within context. First, re-nunciation and sexual abstinence were the norm for all *samana* (wandering religious) movements of the time. The Sangha as a mo-nastic order in India had a stake in helping its adherents maintain celibacy. Given that the scriptures of the Pali Canon represent the views of the most narrowly monastic of the early Buddhist schools, it is not surprising that they feature attitudes which facilitate self-denial and celibacy. Furthermore, and the essential point, these re-flections on phlegm, pus, mucus, and so on, did not degrade the body to exalt any higher function or faculty.

The body, although viewed as mercilessly as by any first-year medical student, was not dismissed as less real or less valuable than consciousness, reason, intellect. As the monk was to meditate on the impermanent and composite nature of the body, so was he also to meditate on the composite and transient nature of the mind. Mind, too, was dissected and viewed in terms of the passing flux of thoughts, notions, sensations of which it is constituted. For reality in the Buddhist view is process, and no substance—mental, psy-chic, or supernatural—is aloof from it. Like all dharmas, both con-sciousness and body are conditioned and transient. No essence is held up as inherently nobler or purer or more real than this bag of decaying flesh. The monk's goal, in reflecting on the body, is to become more mindful of it, not to withdraw from it or to alter it. This represents a subtle but important difference from Vedic-style *tapas* (austerities).

The Buddha's nondichotomous view of mind and body is evident in his central teaching, *paṭicca samuppāda*. In the *nidāna* series, the factors of *viññāna* (consciousness and cognition) and *nāmarūpa* (name-and-form) are presented as co-arising. *Nāmarūpa* represents the only factor explicitly identified with physicality, and it is at this point in the series that many of the texts stop and circle, so to speak. After stating that name-and-form is conditioned by consciousness, they take care, before going on, to reverse the order and state that consciousness itself arises conditioned by name-and-form. Here the interdependence and reciprocality that is implicit between all the factors, as we demonstrated earlier, is made explicit, perhaps to counter the Vedic tendency to absolutize consciousness. As we recall, Sāriputra likens these two *nidānas* to "two sheaves of reeds leaning on each other. . . . So also, my friend, consciousness grows out of name-and-form, and name-and-form out of consciousness."[3]

Ñāṇananda offers, in addition to the simile of the two sheaves, that of a vortex. "Perpetually supporting each other and revitalizing each other as they go round and round, 'consciousness' and 'name and form' make up the samsaric vortex which is the rallying point of all existence."[4] The dualistic illusion of subject and object, mind and matter, then sustains and is sustained by the rest of the *nidāna* series.

> The trends that set in with the vortical interplay between consciousness and name-and-form continue through the subsequent links of the formula of Dependent Arising. The six sense-spheres bifurcate themselves precipitating a dichotomy of an 'internal' and an 'external' with its concomitant notions of a 'here' and a 'there,'

and feelings, cravings, etc., perpetuate the bind, giving rise to ego and the suffering it engenders.[5]

When consciousness was construed by one of his monks to be a self-existent, enduring essence, aloof from materiality, the Buddha responded with unaccustomed asperity.

> But to whom, foolish man, do you understand that *dhamma* was taught by me thus? Foolish man, has not consciousness generated by conditions been spoken of in many a figure by me, saying: Apart from conditions there is no origination of consciousness? But now you, foolish man, not only misrepresent me because of your own wrong grasp, but you also injure

yourself and give rise to much demerit which, foolish man, will be for your woe and sorrow for a long time.[6]

As the two sheaves of Śariputra and Ñāṇananda's vortex illustrate, that which we call mind and matter are interdependent. In the early Buddhist view, consciousness is not a pure substance antecedent to matter as the Upaniṣads hold, and it is not in opposition to matter as Sāṃkhya teaches, nor is mind a byproduct of matter, as the materialists of the time maintained. The view of dependent coorigination is clear: they arise in conjunction and cannot be known or posited apart from each other. The body, requiring constant nourishment and subject to decay, appears exceedingly transient, but consciousness is, for that matter, no less dependent on it, as the *Samaññaphala Sutta* emphasizes.[7]

This body of mine has form, it is built up of the four elements, it springs from father and mother, it is continually renewed by so much boiled rice and juicy foods, its very nature is impermanence, it is subject to erosion, abrasion, dissolution and disintegration; and therein is this consciousness of mind, too, bound up, on that does it depend.

The text goes on to employ, for the interconnection of consciousness and body, the simile of a gem, translucent and flawless, through which a string is threaded. "If a man, who had eyes to see, were to take it in his hand, he would clearly perceive how the one is bound up with the other."[8]

Therefore, the ascetic flavor of the early Buddhist texts should not mislead us, for the evidence is consistent. Never is matter presented as less real than consciousness, or as inherently dangerous. Pleasures of the flesh that stimulate our craving are to be shunned, but so are tendentious views and judgments. Anything which deludes us into thinking that substance, be it thing or theory, can satisfy, is to be shunned. For it cannot; hence, our pain. It cannot, because the world is not substance, but process.

The body appears to be seen as more innocent, less perilous, less stimulative of our clinging attachments, than are our conceptual reifications. Grasping *(upādāna)* is explained in the *Mahānidāna Sutta* in terms of four kinds of grasping "at things of sense . . . through speculative opinions . . . after rule and ritual . . . through theories of the soul."[9] Of the four kinds of clinging, only one is physical.

In the *Saṃyutta Nikāya* the Buddha says, "The untaught many-folk, brethren, might well be repelled by this body, child of the four great elements, might cease to fancy it and wish to be free from it, (seeing its) growth and decay." Yet the manyfolk are not repelled by consciousness; they cling to it, thinking, "This is mine, this I am, this is my spirit." But the body persists for years—ten, thirty, fifty, a hundred or longer—whereas consciousness changes ceaselessly. "Just as a monkey, brethren, faring through the woods . . . catches hold of a bough, letting it go seizes another, even so that which we call thought, mind, consciousness, that arises as one thing, ceases as another, both by night and by day." Those who are repelled by what is transient should hardly prefer mind to matter, he suggests as he concludes: "Therefore, it were better, brethren, if the un-taught manyfolk approached this body, child of the four great ele-ments, as the self rather than the mind."[10]

Yet he did not, of course, teach that the body was the self. He did not present it as more real than mind, or as less. His teaching of the *khaṇḍas,* that compose our psychophysical personality, and of meditation clearly acknowledge and distinguish these aspects of ex-perience, but he refused to make metaphysical statements about their respective status. He declined either to identify them or sepa-rate them ontologically; in the perspective of *paṭicca samuppāda* they represent two interdependent dimensions of life.

> Where, brother, there is the view: 'soul and body are one and the same,' or the view 'soul and body are different things,' there there is no divine living. The Tathāgata teaches neither of these two extremes; he teaches a Middle Way . . . [11]

Here follows in the text the exposition of *paṭicca samuppāda* in the *nidāna* series, where factors that are both mental and physical inter-act causally and where no separate agent, body or soul, is set apart from the co-arising process itself.

The Buddha himself was scorned by his early ascetic compan-ions for having, in his pursuit of enlightenment, indulged the flesh rather than punished it. After grueling and fruitless austerities, and before seating himself in meditation under the *bodhi* tree, he took rice and milk. When he did, the yogis, he reported, "turned on me in disgust, saying the recluse Gotama . . . has reverted to a life of abundance."[12] When after his enlightenment he went to preach to them, they initially said, "Here comes the recluse Gotama who lives in abundance . . . let us not salute him."[13] But the woman who fed him is honored in carvings throughout much of the Buddhist world. Kneeling with her bowl beneath the lotus throne, she can be interpreted as a symbol of the recognition that the body is not to be despised as less real or less worthy than the mind.

Because the body does not appear as an inherent obstacle to holiness and wisdom, it is not seen as an object to be overcome or punished. Such mortification of the flesh had been practiced by Gotama before his enlightenment, and the hunger, filth, exhaustion, and emaciation be inflicted on himself has been vividly portrayed. What a contrast this is in the *Samaññaphala Sutta*, where, in the descriptions of higher states of consciousness, the body itself participates in the sense of well-being they afford. As the meditator progressively enters the first four *jhānas*, "his very body does he so pervade, drench, permeate, and suffuse with the joy and ease born of detachment, that there is no spot in his whole frame not suffused therewith."[14] For such gladness of the body a variety of analogies is provided: it is like being massaged with a perfumed ball of lather by a skilled bathman; it is like a deep pool pervaded with cool spring waters; it is like being wrapped head to foot in a fresh, clean white robe.[15]

Beyond these levels of *jhāna* or trance, there are those qualified as *arūpa*, formless, as well as the "higher knowledges" *(abhiññā)*, such as telepathy, clairvoyance, and the recall of former lives. These possibilities are recognized as achievable when, in concentration, the mind is tranquil and pliable.[16] It is noteworthy that these paranormal types of psychic experience are not interpreted as spiritual realms ontologically divorced from matter. Neither these categories of experience, nor belief in other planes of existence, such as the *deva* worlds or those of the hungry spirits, are taken to suggest that *viññāna* is ultimately independent of materiality. Indeed, the higher knowledges, as the texts declare, let the mind observe introspectively and directly the association of consciousness with body.[17] They are not considered beyond the senses, or extrasensory, so much as they represent a more concentrated use of the senses and an extension of their normal range through mental discipline. The *abhiññā* open the concentrated mind to broader reaches of memory and a wider spectrum of mental, visual, and auditory data. They are not presented as aloof from cause and effect or as previsionary in revealing the future.[18] Trances and paranormal powers do not appear to persuade the early Buddhists that consciousness is exempt from dependent co-origination, or that mental and cognitive experience can be dissociated from matter.[19]

Two Sides of a Coin

The general systems view is comparable to the Buddhist view in refusing to dichotomize or identify mind and body, or to reduce one to the other. It does so, not because it can behold their interaction, but precisely because it cannot. In this view, mind and body emerge, on the one hand, as inseparable, and on the other as so distinct in experience and observation that no causal relation can be posited between them or can permit us to explain one in terms of the other.

As we noted in Chapters 4 and 5, a person can be seen as a biological system or as a cognitive system, a patterned series of mind events. Which of these one sees depends on the perspective and data employed. Where one's data are physical, say neural activity in the cortex, then one is seeing a physical system, that of the brain. But synaptic connections, however closely observed, cannot yield the inner experience of sensation or ideation to which they correspond. That requires an internal perspective, that of the cognitive system itself. The only cognitive system we know first-hand is our own. We infer that others exist, in our husband or child, president or postman, only because it makes sense, because there is no *a priori* reason not to, and because we might go mad if we did not. When we see them and deal with them as cognitive systems possessed of their own subjectivity, we do so by inference and reliance on symbolic communication. We have no direct access to their raw experience because that immediacy is restricted to the privacy of the cognitive system in question, and it is not available to external observation.

Because a difference in perspective is involved, we cannot observe causal interaction between mind and matter. At no point do these two dimensions coincide, for they are not on the same continuum. We can see where perceptions of material phenomena alter mental attitudes, but there we are dealing with a cognitive system, the perceptions themselves being mental. If the reader objects and says that perceptions are physical because we can, with instruments, observe the neural connections in the retina of the eye and in the ocular portions of the brain, then let her be reminded that all consequent activity can also be described physically—from the synaptic signals in the brain to motor responses. One is dealing then with a physical system. The two realms, or rather perspectives, are isomorphic but distinct. Like the two sides of a coin, or the inside and outside of a house, they correspond and are inseparable, but they never meet. This fact led systems thinkers Arturo Rosenblueth and Ervin Laszlo to suggest that a "non-causal correlation" is involved.[20]

In the systems view, therefore, both dichotomous and reductionistic resolutions of the mind-body riddle are inadequate and entail a suppression of evidence. Dualism is unwarranted because of the inseparability of the phenomena involved, and reductionism (either mind to body or body to mind) is fallacious because of their distinctiveness. The notion that emerges to qualify their relation has been called "brain-mind correlation" by Rosenblueth and "binomial psycho-physical parallelism" by neurologist K. E. Rothschuh. Rothschuh sees psychic experience as "coordinated" with nervous processes as their "inner side," and both types of experience are "running parallel to each other."[21] With more economy of language, Laszlo has coined the term *biperspectivism*.

This term conveys the complementarity and irreducibility of the mental and the physical, which systems thought affirms. "Whether a system is physical or mental," writes Laszlo, "depends on the viewpoint of observation. The operation of passing from the one to the other viewpoint permits the alternate inspection of the complementary (but not simultaneously appearing) aspects."[22] Physicality and mentality represent, then, aspects of the same reality. As von Bertalanffy's work led him to affirm, "matter and mind, body and consciousness are not ultimate realities. Rather they are conceptualizations to bring order . . . into experience, [having] no rigid metaphysical boundaries."[23] For similar reasons, the Buddha refused to make metaphysical statements about either the identity or difference of body and soul. As a conceptualization or metaphor, biperspectivism permits us to deal with both sides of experience without reifying consciousness or matter or both into ultimate essences.

Theologian William W. Everett writes that in the mind-body model that cybernetics provides, "the self appears under two aspects. On the one hand, it is *totally mind*," in that it is an elaborate system of communication. "On the other hand, it is *entirely body*," for its organization of information is represented and observable in "material" structures, from its genes and chromosomes to its cerebrum (emphasis added).[24]

The Internality of All Systems

While the parallelism of mental and physical experience is affirmed by systems theorists in general, we find its philosophic rationale and implications elaborated in Laszlo's systems philosophy.

Pointing out that variations of the principle of psycho-physical co-extension have been offered before in the thought of Spinoza, Bergson, Whitehead, and Teilhard de Chardin, he develops the principle in terms of the discoveries and concepts of general systems theory.[25] In these terms, self-reflexive consciousness, as explained in Chapters 4 and 7, appears as a function of the self-monitoring of the open system, deriving from the internal requirements of increasing organization. In interaction with its environment the system elaborates the means to monitor, evaluate and complexify its performance—from measuring chemical balance to manipulating symbols. At each level of complexity and flexibility, these evaluative capacities become autonomous, that is, irreducible to more primitive forms of organization. Consciousness as it evolves, then, represents the internal experience of the system's organization.

> The phenomenon of mind is neither an intrusion into the cosmos from some outside agency, nor the emergence of something out of nothing. Mind is but the internal aspect of the connectivity of systems within the matrix. It is there as a possibility within the undifferentiated continuum, and evolves into more explicit forms as the matrix differentiates into relatively discrete, self-maintaining systems. The mind as knower is continuous with the rest of the universe as known. Hence in this metaphysics there is no gap between subject and object . . . these terms refer to arbitrarily abstracted entities.[26]

As the interiority, or "lived" dimension of the system, mind is correlative to matter, its external and observable dimension.

There is, Laszlo argues, no reason to restrict this interiority to the human phenomenon alone. We infer it in other people and higher mammals by analogy with our experience, because theirs appears similar, and we tend to place other phenomena in the category of things and objects. If, however, systemic properties serve as criteria for the attribution of interiority, then there is no basis for drawing a line below which to deny an introspective viewpoint. No intrinsic reason exists for denying subjectivity to animals, plants or even suborganic systems. Although the givens of their internal experience would be very different from the human, they represent mind-events nonetheless.

If we remember that some 10^{11} neurons form the complex cerebral nets (physical events) which correlate with human mind-events, we must beware of attributing anything resembling human mind-events to lesser systems, such as atoms and molecules. Their mind-events must be entirely different in "feel" from ours, yet they can be mind-events nevertheless, i.e. types of sensations, correlated with, but different from physical processes.[27]

It is through the interiority of systems, progressively organized through their interdependent transactions, that the world experiences itself. Not only do suborganic and organic systems have innerness, but, by the logic of biperspectivism, so do social or supra-organic systems as well. Collective forms of consciousness, "group heads" in a family, sect, or society, are evident in our experience. They can display a character and dynamic that are not reducible to the individuals that comprise them and can even appear autonomous. Being loosely organized in comparison with the intricacy and coherence of a human cognitive system, these social bodies display proportionately weaker form of consciousness.

The organization of the hundred billion neurons which constitute the human brain, and which permit the complex functions to which the human mind is correlated, is characterized by both integration and differentiation. As in any open system complexity and versatility are dependent not only on the coherent and cohesive interrelationship of components, but also on their heterogeneity. As the complexity of systemic organization is commensurate with both the unity and diversity of components, so also is the correlative level of mentation. Although a molecule is highly integrated, its differentiation is relatively low. While a social system includes more diversity than a molecule, it is still relatively undifferentiated in comparison with a biological system, and far less integrated. Therefore, while biperspectivism attributes consciousness to social bodies and groups, their mental events would be simple and incoherent relative to the cognitive system afforded by our own mind/brain.

Mentality, then, is seen as correlative to the physical organization of an open system, as its interior, or "lived," dimension. Mental events would be present as well in an artificial system, if a machine could display all the characteristics of an open system, that is if it is self-organizing, a prospect which cyberneticians consider feasible in principle. Since it is unlikely that any computer could approach the human brain in complexity, its introspective experience would be much more rudimentary. Yet it would still exist. If

we consider all open systems as biperspectival, analyzable to physical as well as mental sets of events, then, as Laszlo argues,

> The consequent proposition, that transient social organiza-
> tions, as well as artificially created machines, have mental
> events, must be accepted . . . using the differentiation and
> functional level of integration of subsystems as the criterion of
> the mentality of the systems. . . . The alternatives [to this
> view] are either an arbitrary cut-off point for mind, or the log-
> ically consistent, but unfruitful tenet of solipsism.[28]

In consequence, systems philosophy sees mind as co-extensive with
the physical universe. Although it does not speculate on the nature
of the mind whose observable counterpart is manifest in systems
other than the human, it acknowledges, by the logic of biperspectivism, its existence.

The Ubiquity and Particularity of Mind

Buddhist thought also recognizes in the natural world an extension of mentality beyond the human realm. Ven. Sangharakshita,
an English-born monk and scholar, emphasizes that in the Buddhist
world view, in contrast to the Semitic religions, humans are not
seen as unique in their possession of soul or mind, nor does this
possession constitute a gulf between them and other forms of life.
The human is but "one manifestation of a current of psycho-
physical energy, manifesting now as god, now as animal, etc."[29]
This belief in psychic continuity underlies, he points out, the compassion for other creatures, the "boundless heart" which the Buddha manifested and enjoined.

In the early Buddhist view, the consciousness endemic in life
forms is not unitary and undifferentiated, because it does not derive from a supraphenomenal source. Arising in interdependence
with physicality, it is in each instance distinctive. Such a notion contrasts with Hindu perceptions of the consciousness inherent in life
whether it is seen as the omnipresence of Brahman, the pervasiveness of Vishnu or the ubiquity of *puruṣa*. Changeless and eternal
behind the screen of *māyā*, such consciousness is cloaked by matter
and becomes evident to the extent that life forms are divested of
their materiality and particularity. By the logic of dependent co-
arising, however, the consciousness manifest throughout the worlds

and planes of existence is in every instance particular, characterized not by sameness but by "thatness" or "suchness" *(tathatā)*.

While in the Buddhist view all the worlds and planes of existence teem with consciousness, human mentality presents, in contrast to other realms of life, a distinctive feature: the capacity to choose. Only the human possesses the power to choose and change—hence the rare and priceless privilege of a human life; hard to win, it brings both responsibility and the possibility of enlightenment. Such a notion is analogous to the perception of general systems theory, which sees the self-reflexive consciousness of the natural cognitive system as evolving from, and consisting in, its evaluative, decision-making functions. The challenge this kind of consciousness constitutes is, for the Buddhist, repeatedly brought to mind by meditation on the rare opportunity which a human existence presents.

Beyond the Fear of Matter

The ontological relation perceived between mind and body determines the relative reality and worth assigned to them. Here the perspective of mutual causality contrasts with the axiological distinction between spirit and flesh generally characteristic of linear thought. This contrast in psychological attitude and valuation is illustrated when we set the Buddhist perspective alongside the Hindu. With the exception of the materialists, who denied an autonomous ontological status to mind altogether, the Hindu tradition accorded reality to pure consciousness as distinct from matter. From the Upaniṣadic standpoint, the world of the senses is epiphenomenal to the *ātman*, it is less real, it is *māyā*. From the Sāṃkhyan standpoint, *prakṛti* (nature or matter) is real enough, but directly opposed to *puruṣa*, (pure spirit), and tending to delusion.

This dichotomy between consciousness and nature tends to lead, as both Sāṃkhyan and Vedantic thought testify, to a vision of spirit as struggling to be free from the toils of matter. Matter comes to be seen as polluting and binding, its fertile nature that of an arbitrary, lavish, and cruel mother. Consequently, there is a deep ambivalence on the part of the mind, a love-hate relationship with matter. As creature, one is dependent on the very element from which one seeks release; that dependence breeds resentment and an exaggerated sense of that element's power. Such a relationship to matter and body is reflected in extremes of asceticism, the yogic austerities from which Gotama turned away. In reference to those who practiced them, the Buddha said,

> Because of fear of the existing body [or own-body *sakkāya*], because of disgust with the existing body, they keep running round, keep circling round, that same existing body. Just as a dog tethered by a leash and anchored to a stout pole or post, keeps running round, keeps circling round, so too these worldly recluses and Brahmins, because of fear of the existing body, because of disgust with the existing body, keep running round, keep circling round, that same existing body.[29]

As the Buddha taught, it is our point of view, not this body of flesh and blood, that trips or traps us into bondage. In that point of view, ego, or *attādiṭṭhi*, that obsessive, tendentious trick of the mind, sets itself apart from its own physical experience. Perverting perception and inflaming appetite, it clings to the objects and ideas that feed it. Because ego is, in the last analysis, unreal, its demands and needs can never be met, and the material world itself appears as increasingly and maddeningly unsatisfactory. The world comes to be seen as an opponent, something to be tamed and conquered. But such efforts, as the Buddha pointed out, are doomed to defeat.

> Monks, as a man might come along, bringing a shovel and basket, and might speak thus: 'I will make this great earth not-earth'; so he digs here and there, tosses it here and there, spits here and there, stakes here and there, thinking 'you are becoming not-earth, you are becoming not-earth.' What do you think about this, monks? Could that man make this earth not-earth? No, Lord. What is the reason? It is that this great earth, Lord, is deep, it is immeasurable, it is not easy to make it not-earth before that man be worn out and defeated.[31]

Interestingly, Buddhist scholar I. B. Horner notes that a more literal translation of the last phrase would read, "he would be a partaker of exhaustion and slaying." This suggests that violence is, reciprocally, bred in us by that which we inflict on nature and body. We assault ourselves.

The perspective of mutual causality has, then, psychological and ethical implications for the posture we adopt in regard to nature and body. It undercuts the tendency to see them as inimical and to exploit them with fear and contempt. Respect for the phenomenal world is integral to the Buddhist notion of *tathatā* (such-ness), to the cardinal importance of right livelihood, and to the heart of boundless compassion, as we shall see in more detail in Chapter 10. Such respect is also implicit in the systems view, where body and nature appear as self-organizing open systems of awesome complexity and balance. Reverence, according to von Bertalanffy and Laszlo, is the appropriate response to such a systemic world.

The systems-cybernetic view can clarify, as Bateson attests, the way our values have been warped by dualistic perceptions of mind and body. These create, he says, an adversarial relationship between ego and nonego, engendering myopic pride and a kind of moral blindness we can no longer afford.

> If we continue to operate in terms of a Cartesian dualism of mind versus matter, we shall probably also continue to see the world in terms of God versus man; elite versus people; chosen race versus others; nation versus nation; and man versus environment. It is doubtful whether a species having *both* an advanced technology *and* this strange way of looking at its world can endure.[32]

This "versus" mentality, which turns things and people into objects for manipulation, is eroded, Bateson suggests, by the recognition that mind extends beyond personal consciousness and "is immanent in the larger system—man *plus* environment."[33]

"Minding"

If mind and matter are interdependent, what then is the distinctive domain of mind? Are our efforts toward an increase of consciousness, toward detachment from material seductions, irrelevant and pointless? Hardly. Liberation, according to the Buddhists, is liberation of mind, for it is mind that is enslaved. It is liberated, not through setting itself apart from phenomenality, but increasing its awareness of it. This rigorous attention brings insight into the dependent co-arising of phenomena, a process in which mind itself participates. Its capacity to perceive is enlisted to perceive itself, to see that its very movements and constructions are but passing dharmas. Harnessing its powers and releasing its pretensions, it presides, so to speak, at its own funeral as a separate and self-existent entity. Thereby the sequestering walls, the barriers that protected and isolated it, fall down, disappear, and a vaster panorama of life emerges in vividness and compassion. That which holds us in bondage, mind, becomes that by which release is won.

The role of mind vis-à-vis materiality would be differently expressed in the systems-cybernetic view. Everett reflects that mind, or more precisely "minding," represents the ultimate goal of the open system and the nature of its continuity.[34] The material components of the system arise and pass away, consumed in the flame of metabolic events, in the transformation of energy and information. The codes and values by which they are processed constitute the system's ongoing, evolving pattern. These intangibles both map the world and are projected upon it. They transform perceptions of the physical world into mental symbols and constructs, and in turn incarnate these in the stuff of the world.

In this process the system's survival does not depend on the material or conceptual stuff, of which its pattern at any given point is constructed, so much as on its very capacity to process information. This minding represents, as Everett suggests, both the nature and purpose of the cognitive system.

> "What" survives, then, is sheerly the action of being autonomous and self-directing. To survive means to be in some sense self-controlling. In cybernetics this means to maintain the operation of information processing—in short of minding. Body, that is material structure, is taken up into mind, that is the process of being autonomous.[35]

This "taking up into mind" is a process made possible by the interdependent nature of mind and body. In such a view consciousness is engaged in an alchemical act, transforming that on which it is dependent, transmuting the givens of life, however lowly, into patterns both insubstantial and enduring.

Rilke, in his ninth Duino Elegy, gives expression to this kind of act, this alchemical work of consciousness.

> . . . Are we *here* perhaps just to say:
> house, bridge, well, gate, jug, fruit tree, window—
> at most column, tower . . . but to *say*, understand this,
>   to say it
> as the Things themselves never fervently thought to be.
> . . . And these things that live,
> slipping away, understand that you praise them;

transitory themselves, they trust us for rescue,
us, the most transient of all. They wish us to transmute
them in our invisible heart—oh, infinitely into us!
    Whoever we are.
Earth, isn't this what you want?
. . . What, if not transformation, is your insistent
commission?[36]

Such a work is not enhanced where the self-reflective mind
sets itself apart, in pride and fear, from the body and the things it
beholds. Rather it brings meaning where and when, set free from
contempt and shame, it regards them with loving attention.
    Such a love toward things "that have form" is the stance of the
true monk, as the Buddha said.

Just, Vasettha, as a mighty trumpeter makes himself heard—
and that without difficulty—in all four directions; even so of
all things that have form or life, there is not one that he passes
by or leaves aside; he regards them all with mind set free and
filled with deep-felt love.[37]

Indeed, the particularity of matter, the thingness of things, is
helpful to the mind in returning it to the immediacy of experience.
For it is not through its fancies, delusory as they can be, nor
through the concepts to which it tenaciously clings, that mind is
illumined, but through attention to the here and now. It is in the
immediacy of experiencing what eludes its fabrications that mind
can overleap its old self-enclosing constructs and perceive the living
process of which it is a part.

Notes

1. *Saṃyutta Nikāya*, III.142; *Dhammapada*, 170.

2. *Dīgha Nikāya*, II.293.

3. *Saṃyutta Nikāya*, II.103, 113.

4. Ñāṇananda, *Magic of Mind*, p. 25.

5. *Ibid.*, p. 32.

6. *Majjhima Nikāya*, I.258.

7. *Dīgha Nikāya*, II.76.

8. *Ibid.*, II.76.

9. *Ibid.*, II.1.

10. *Saṃyutta Nikāya*, II.94–97.

11. *Ibid.*, II.61.

12. *Majjhima Nikāya*, I.247.

13. *Vinaya, Mahāvagga*, I.6.10.

14. *Dīgha Nikāya*, II.73.

15. *Ibid.*, II.74–75.

16. *Dīgha Nikāya*, I.78f; *Majjhima Nikāya*, I.69; *Saṃyutta Nikāya*, II.217, 222.

17. *Dīgha Nikāya*, I.76.

18. Kalupahana, *Causality*, 107.

19. The later Abhidharmist text, the *Paṭṭhana*, unequivocally reiterates this early teaching. "That physical basis in dependence on which the category of mental experience (manodhatu) and the category of cognitive experience (manoviññānadhatu) function, this physical basis is to the category of mental and cognitive experience and to phenomena associated with them, a condition by way of dependence" (quoted in Jayatilleke, *Survival and Karma*, p. 47.)

20. Rosenblueth, *Mind and Brain*, Chapters 7, 10; Laszlo, *Introduction to Systems Philosophy*, pp. 151f.

21. Rothschuh, "The Mind-Body Problem," p. 876.

22. Laszlo, *Introduction to Systems Philosophy*, p. 171.

23. *Ibid.*, 43.

24. Everett, "Cybernetics," p. 100.

25. Laszlo, *Introduction to Systems Philosophy*, p. 171.

26. *Ibid.*, p. 293.

27. *Ibid.*, p. 170.

28. *Ibid.*, p. 174.

29. Sangharakshita, "Centrality of Man," pp. 31f.

30. *Majjhima Nikāya*, II.232f.

31. *Ibid.*, I.127.

32. Bateson, *Steps to Ecology of Mind*, p. 337.

33. *Ibid.*, p. 317.

34. Everett, *Cybernetics*, p. 106.

35. *Ibid.*, p. 106.

36. Rilke, *Duino Elegies*.

37. *Dīgha Nikāya*, II.443.

9

The Co-Arising of Doer and Deed

Each day I walk in is made slyly one
By symmetries whose names I never seek.

—Mark Van Doren[1]

Identity and Accountability

The self, if causality is mutual, is not the knower and actor we conventionally posit, so much as a series of events, occurrences of knowing and acting. It has been likened, by both systems thinkers and early Buddhists, to a stream and to a flame, constantly flowing and undergoing transformation. If that is the case, we confront then the problem of identity and, beyond that, the question of responsibility. If I am but a succession of happenings, who am I at a given point, and in what does my continuity reside? If there is in my internal organization no separable and continuous agent that decides, can I be accountable for my acts? Does it matter what I do?

The basic issue, then, is the connection between what we do and what we are. Or, if we understand our being as our conscious participation in reality, the question is whether our acts affect that participation—that is, our capacity to know, choose, and enjoy. If not, then notions of responsibility are tangential to one's life, noble but inconsequential. If they do, then distinctions between the pragmatic and the moral dissolve. In the perspective of mutual causality, this is the case.

In this view of causal process, as we will see in both systems and early Buddhist thought, deeds and doer appear as reciprocally conditioned, and a notion is affirmed that is central to the Buddha's teaching of karma: What we do not only matters, it molds us. In this view questions of both identity and responsibility are resolved.

The Question of Rebirth

The notion of karma is associated with belief in rebirth or re-incarnation, a widespread belief in Indian thought. Yet the Buddha's concept of karma, or the determinacy of deeds (meaning "all acts, physical, mental, and verbal"), can be approached and understood apart from metempsychosis. And as I explain below it is within the spirit of the Buddha's teachings to do so. This setting aside of the question of rebirth is not meant to judge its validity, but to assert that it is not central to the concerns of this book.

Our examination of the teaching of karma relies on the early texts of the Pali Canon. Here *paticca samuppāda*, as the co-arising of conditioned factors, or *nidānas*, was not set forth in terms of successive lives. As I pointed out in Chapter 3, that interpretation arose later with the Abhidharma. While belief in rebirth, endemic to Indian culture, appears accepted throughout the early scriptures, their teaching of causality is not presented as derived from it or dependent upon it.

Belief in the cycle of rebirth was almost universally accepted in the culture of the Buddha's time. Views of survival after death were manifold; these ranged from a single after-life to an astronomical series of incarnations, and for the most part presupposed a trans-migrating psychic substance.[2] Within this context of belief many questions were addressed to the Buddha concerning the course of the spiritual life, and particularly the nature of personal continuity and the moral effect of deeds. Not only did the Buddha respond in terms of rebirth, or more precisely re-becoming (*punabhava*), he is also reported as having acquired on the night of his enlightenment personal recall of former lives.[3] This recall (*pubbenivāsanussatiñāna*) or retrocognition, as Kalupahana terms it, represents one of the "higher knowledges" (*abhiññā*) which the scriptures recognize, along with such powers as clairvoyance and telepathy.[4] It was said to have enabled the Buddha, and subsequent *arahants* who developed this ability, to perceive the consequences of behavior directly.

The Buddhist approach to re-becoming differed radically from other beliefs in survival by virtue of the doctrine of *anattā*. In its view there is no soul to survive, only a bundle of latent energies (*suddha-saṇkhārā-puñja*).[5] The conceptual difficulty of accommodating *anattā* to the notion of recall of past lives has provided a continuing source of subsequent philosophical speculation. If the self is transient how can it survive from one life to the next? Paul Demiéville, who studied relevant passages in the early texts, notes and deplores the absence of a consistent theory about memory of previous lives.[6] The Nikāyas merely state that it is a faculty that can be developed through concentration. Since, as the *Brahmajāla Sutta* says, retrocognition can dupe a yogi into eternalist views, bolstering belief in an enduring soul, care should be taken in how this experience is interpreted.[7]

The Buddha did not consider it relevant or useful to reflect on the possibility or character of other existences. He said that when the disciple rightly sees the nature of causal arising, it never happens that he "will run back to the past, thinking

'Did I live in times gone by? Or did I not? What was I in times gone by? How was I then? Or free from being what did I become what?' Or [it never happens] that he will run toward the times to come, thinking, 'Shall I be reborn in a future time, or shall I not? What shall I become in the future? . . . ' Or that he will now become perplexed within himself as to the present day, thinking, 'Am I indeed? Or am I not indeed? What indeed am I? How indeed am I? This person that is I, whence came he, whither will he go?' Why does this never arise? In that the disciple, brethren, has by right insight well seen even as they really are both this causal happening and things as having causally happened.[8]

Likewise, we will decline from musing on other births and see what the teaching of karma in the Nikāyas can tell us about the effects of acts upon the actor within the context of experience familiar and knowable to us.

Kāya and Karma

When the Buddha was queried by Kassapa and Timbaruka as to who is responsible for the suffering and pleasure we experience, he declined to answer that it is wrought by someone else, a past actor with whom we have no more connection. One cannot categorically separate the "I" who experiences the result from the "I" who set it in motion. They are not discontinuous. Yet the Buddha also refused to identify them. One cannot say that "one and the same person both acts and experiences the result," for they are different, altered.[9] He declined, as Pande has pointed out, either to identify the agent of an action with the experiencer of the result, or to separate him from it.[10] There *is* a continuity, but it is not that of an agent as a distinct and enduring being. The continuity resides in the acts themselves, which condition consciousness and feelings in dependent co-origination. It inheres in the reflexive dynamics of action, shaping that which brought it forth.

For action the term *karma* (Pali: *kamma*) is used. Originally in pre-Buddhist literature the word denoted ritual acts, and then by extension religiously ordained social duties. In the Buddhist texts, it is broadened to include all volitional behavior, and appears under three aspects: *kāya-*, *vacī-*, and *mano-kamma*, or bodily, verbal, and mental deeds. Within the philosophic context of early Buddhist teachings, this is what we "are." Given the doctrine of *anattā*, it is karma that constitutes our identity and continuity. Orlan Lee writes of the early Buddhist view, "one's salvation lies on his works, and these *are* indeed his own 'soul'—if there is one."[11] Similarly, T. W. Rhys Davids points out that "where others said 'soul', Gotama said usually 'action'."[12]

This action, rather than a continuous "I" or an external fate, shapes the experiences we register and the structure we manifest. Our own behavior molds us, as Gotama perceived in the middle watch of the night of his enlightenment. It was then he comprehended that the distinctive character we display at a given point is neither eternal, nor illusory, nor adventitious, but "that beings are mean, excellent, comely, ugly, well-going, ill-going according to the consequence of deeds."[13]

Our present psycho-physical structure is not that of a continuing self-identical entity, nor is it discontinuous from our past selves.

> This body (*kāya*), brethren, is not your own, neither is it that of any others. It should be regarded as brought about by action of the past, by plans, by volitions, by feelings.[14]

It is relevant to note that *kāya*, frequently translated as "body," is understood to derive from the verb *ci*, to "heap up," and literally means "assemblage, collection, an aggregate of a multiplicity of elements." It is frequently used to refer to groups and crowds, as well as to a corpus of teachings. In reference to the person, it often appears as one of a triad with speech (*vacī*) and thought (*manas*). It also serves as a collective expression for all three functions.

Hence, in looking at this and similar passages, two points can be made about its meaning as a product of karma. One, *kāya* represents here all three modes by which character is manifest, including speech and thought. The other point to be emphasized is its "assembled" nature. Given its etymology and the connotations of its other usages, it conveys the notion of person as a complex or organization, not unlike the systems idea of the self as a composite structure.

This structure, or *kāya*, appears then as a consequence of karma. This consequence is inescapable, for we bear it within ourselves. It is written in the Dhammapada:

> Not in the sky, not in the midst of the sea, not if we enter into the clefts of the mountains, is there known a spot in the whole world where a man might be free from an evil deed.[15]

The effect is inescapable, not because God watches and tallies, or an angel marks our acts in a ledger, but because in dependent co-origination, our acts co-determine what we become.

They do so through the formation and operation of the *saṇkhārās*. These subconscious drives and tendencies condition the ways in which we interpret and react to phenomena. Like *kāya*, they too are composite, the term meaning "put together," compounded, organized. They are accrued and constellated by previous volitional acts of interpretation and response. I. B. Horner, in qualifying them, employs the term "potential energy."[16] Their potency shapes not only consciousness, but perceptions and feelings. Their reciprocal relation to psycho-physical behavior leads Oldenberg to wish to identify them directly with action itself. "We might translate *saṇkhārā* directly by actions," he writes, "if we understand this word in the wide sense in which it includes also at the same time the internal 'actions', the will and the wish."[17] More precisely, *saṇkhārā*, both as a *khaṇḍa* and as a factor in the *nidāna* series, represents the reflexive or recoil effects of actions: the tendencies they create, the habits they form and perpetuate, the latent energies they bear.

Because the character of a person's experience is affected by these formations, his identity is indistinct from what he does and thinks, has done and thought. He is neither aloof from these acts, nor their victim. Therein are his identity and continuity, both his resource and his fate. Past and future reside therein, and only there, as the *Aṇguttara Nikāya* declares:

> My action is my possession,
> my action is my inheritance,
> my action is the womb which bears me,
> my action is my refuge.[18]

Structure and Function

The interplay between karma and *kāya*, therefore, presents a mutual causal relationship between our behavior and the psychophysical structure we present at a given point. This reciprocal relationship finds a parallel expression in general systems theory.

As Laszlo has pointed out, there are two ways of looking at order: one is spatial and is grasped as "structure," the other temporal and comprehended as a sequence of events, or "function."[19] In an organism, structure is seen as its "morphology," how it is built, and function as its "physiology," how it acts. Anatomists and historians usually study structure in dead or fixed material, as something separable from function. Indeed, where an organism is conceived as static, like a machine with a fixed arrangement of parts that can be at rest as well as in motion, structure appears distinct from function and unmodified by it.

In an open, self-organizing system, however, such a distinction is problematic, for the structure is not preestablished prior to function but co-arises with it. An example is the form of the heart, which evolved by both shaping and being shaped by its function of rhythmical contraction. Structure, then, represents not something fixed, but a slice in time, the system's spatial order or organization at a given moment. As von Bertalanffy puts it, "What is described in morphology as organic forms and structures, is in reality a momentary cross-section through a spatio-temporal pattern."[20]

From this perspective, structure and function appear as expressive of each other—different manifestations of the organism's pattern in space and time. To stress the distinctiveness of its view from the mechanistic model of reality, general systems theory has emphasized the temporal, functional, process aspect, as von Bertalanffy acknowledges; but it hardly denies the specificity of structure and its role in the arising of phenomena.[21] For morphology and physiology are seen as "complementary ways of studying the same integrated object," and indeed this complementarity represents to von Bertalanffy "a dialectical unity of structure and function."[22]

This dialectical complementarity extends beyond biology to characterize all open systems, as von Bertalanffy maintains.

The contrast between structure and process breaks down in the atom as well as in the living organism whose structure is at the same time the expression and the bearer of a continuous flow of matter and energy.[23]

In the last resort, structure (i.e. order of parts) and function (order of process) may be the very same thing: in the physical world matter dissolves into a play of energies, and in the biological world structures are the expression of a flow of process.[24]

Laszlo describes the relation between structure and function in a way that permits us to see with particular clarity its relevance to the Buddhist idea of karma.

Structure is the record of past functions and the source of new ones. Function in turn is the behavior of the structure and the pathway leading to the formulation of new structures. . . . Not what a thing is, what it is made of, or for what purpose it exists, defines it, but how it is organized.[25]

We recall the Buddhist concepts of *saṅkhārā* and *kāya* and the emphasis they place on our organized or compounded nature, dynamically "put together" by experience, volitions, and acts. We also recall, as we examined in Chapter 5 that this recognition of inner organization is basic to the systems divergence from behaviorist, stimulus-response theories. Influences or input from the environment do not determine behavior directly, in simple linear causation, because the system transforms these inputs in terms of its internal organization. External signals, be they Pavlovian bells and meat powder, or the carrot in front of the donkey and the stick behind, only partially modify acts, for these signals are processed and interpreted within the context of the system's inner structure, codes, and goals. As Laszlo says, "what systems do, is determined more by their own organization than by messages introduced into them."[26]

This organized structure is not only the source or basis of our responses and deeds but is also the record of previous acts or functions. These past functions are recorded in the gestalts and symbolic constructs, the habits and goals, which the system by feedback has evolved to render experience intelligible and maneuverable.

From the physical perspective, previous performance is internalized in neural formations. The system's activity reacts on its cerebral structures, affects its perceptual, motor, and intracortical organization, and creates new cell assemblies, pathways, and loops.[27] This complexification of the system, as it interacts with its own performance in the environment, tends to increase its autonomy. As structures for coding inputs are elaborated, its response becomes more varied, less predictable. In the process, the effect of the environment upon the system's behavior "progressively loses," as Laszlo puts it, "any semblance of linear causality."[28]

Past and Present

By virtue of feedback, past experience is accumulated, transformed, and internalized in the system's mental constructs and neural nets. Its structure at any given moment, expresses its history, as systems theorist James G. Miller affirms.

> History, then, is more than the passage of time. It involves also accumulation in the system of residues or effects of past events (structural changes, memories, learned habits). A living system carries its history with it in the form of altered structure, and consequently of altered function also.[29]

Memory becomes an active, reorganizational process, rather than a safe deposit box where the past lies unaltered and eternally immured. As we interact with the present in terms of the past, past itself appears in new patterns, guises, and vistas. It becomes freshly assembled, as Everett, applying cybernetic concepts, argues.

> Mind is a process of memory . . . . The memory breaks down complex units into their separate components and then can imagine a great variety of possible novel recombinations of these units. Thus arise proposals for new kinds of actions, responses and goals. Memory is not a graveyard of the past but a process of assembly—a beehive of continuously interacting information units.[30]

The fresh guises in which the past can appear, the new interpretations we place on it as we reassemble memory, indicate to systems-oriented psychiatrists that a patient's reported history is in reality a metaphor about the present. In the unidirectional causal paradigm, the past appears as safely behind us and hence can yield objective data for examination; unaltered by the present it can serve to explain the present. As Don Jackson put it, "the linear, cause and effect train goes by only once," and, once past, can be thought to reveal the sources of present distress. But in actuality,

Self- or patient-reported histories are notoriously unreliable, filtering the past through the present as well as through the selective vagaries of human memory. Whatever an individual says about this past is also a comment on, or way of handling, the interviewer; that is, the "history" is a metaphor about the present relationship.[31]

The present and the memory of the past modify each other because the mutually causative relation between structure and function is continual. The effects of previous acts are not cast in cement, but can be altered in the present as they are perceived in new ways.

The Dharma and Determinism

The recognition of the interaction or interdependence between past and present is central to the major divergence between the Buddha's view of karma and the more deterministic, linear notions of karma current in his time.

According to the contemporaneous Jain theory, each and every former act, regardless of its motivation or circumstance, inexorably bears its fruit; and the subject cannot develop morally or spiritually without personally undergoing all the consequences. Set in motion by the physical effects of deeds, karma represents a kind of substance, an obscuring accumulation that only through expiation can be worn away. This process of wearing away can be hastened by mortification of the flesh. The Ājīvika view, also taught in the Buddha's time, is even more deterministic. Considering *every* aspect of present experience, mental and physical, to be the result of past action, it sees any human effort whatever as fruitless.[32]

The grim fatalism of these notions of karma, where the past rules the present with a heavy mechanical hand, is evoked vividly by Lama Govinda.

The idea that the consequence of all deeds, whether of a mental or corporeal kind, must be tasted to the very last morsel, and that through every most trivial action, through the slightest motion of the heart, one is further involved in the inextricable net of fate, is assuredly the most frightful spectre that the human heart, or more correctly, the human intellect, has ever conjured up.[33]

Govinda sees such determinism as applicable only to "inert things," and not to living, growing organisms. By contrast, the Buddha's doctrine of *paṭicca samuppāda* represents to him a dynamic process of interdependent factors.

> And precisely on this account the entire chain at every moment and from every phase of it, is removable, and is neither tied to "causes lying in an unreachable distant past," nor yet referred to a future beyond the limits of vision in which, perhaps, some time, the effects of these causes will be exhausted.[34]

By virtue of the interdependence of the factors of existence, as we examined in Chapter 3, and particularly by virtue of the conditioned nature of the *saṇkhārās, paṭicca samuppāda* represents release from karmic fatalism. Perhaps because deterministic views were so strong in his day, the Buddha did not leave his position implicit in the causal doctrine, but repeatedly and specifically countered these views with his own arguments. Presented in a variety of ways, appealing both to reason and experience, they are tantamount to an attack on the unidirectionality of the determinist position.

The effect of actions cannot be traced in linear causal chains. Their interweavings are too complex to be so easily comprehended.[35] Inferences drawn from a one-to-one correlation between past and present events can be misleading; therefore, we cannot pinpoint single causes in the past for every present event and condition.[36] It even defies common sense to try, because, as we are aware, we are subject as well to other events: attacks of bile, social vicissitudes and accidents, winds, humors, and seasons.[37] Among these many causal factors, karma, deeds, is just one. In other words, behavior is not the sole determiner of experience; other events condition it also.

The effect of a deed upon a person, furthermore, depends upon the person's character as shaped by other deeds. In the *Mahākammavibhaṅga Sutta,* the Buddha points out that the same kind of act performed by different people can yield diverse results, and that different behaviors can produce similar results.[38] An apparent miscreant may end up in bliss, or a reputedly pious person in misery. This observation is analogous to those of von Bertalanffy and Maruyama in general systems theory. There, as we saw in Chapter 5, the recognition that similar conditions can lead to different results and diverse events to the same result—a contradiction of linear causality—is understood in terms of the dynamic nature of the open system, which processes inputs according to its internal orga-

nization. The Buddhist texts present such a notion in simple parables: the growth of a seed depends not just on its own nature
but also on the soil into which it is dropped. If a man puts salt into
a small cup, the water becomes undrinkable, says the *Loṇakap-
palavagga;* but,

> Suppose that a man, monks, would throw a grain of salt into
> the river Ganges. . . . Would this river Ganges also become
> salty and undrinkable because of this grain of salt? . . . In the
> same way, monks, a man could perform here even a slight sin-
> ful action the result of which would lead him to hell. But,
> again, monks, a man could perform an equally slight sinful
> action the result of which would be experienced in this very
> life, and would not appear to be even light, much less
> grievous.[39]

Previous behavior, then, molds the subject by shaping habits
and inclinations (*saṇkhārā*), patterns affecting perception, thought
and feeling. Therefore, as Jayatilleke says, "karmic laws state tendencies rather than inevitable consequences."[40]

Finally, in rejecting determinism, the Buddha repeatedly emphasized that the effects of the past can be modified by present action. As stressed, it is integral to the teaching of *paṭicca samuppāda*
that the *saṇkhārās* themselves can be altered; therefore, change in
human motivation can destroy the noxious effects of karma (*kam-
makkhaya*). In confrontation with the Jains on this issue, in the *Devadaha Sutta,* Gotama pointed out that their own present experience is
freely chosen, not sentenced by their past. He asked the *niganṭhas*
(Jains) whether they thought one could alter the outcome of karma
by effort. When they in reply denied the possibility of changing
karma in any way, the Buddha responds with obvious irony.[41] In
referring to the rigorous and painful ascetic pursuits of the Jains, he
comments,

> If the pleasure and pain that living beings experience is caused
> by previous deeds, then, monks, the *niganṭhas* must have been
> in previous lives doers of evil deeds, for they now undergo
> such sharp, severe and painful sensations.[42]

Both Jains and Buddhists held themselves to be *kriyāvādins* (or
karmavādins), believing in the consequences of human action, or the
causal connection between behavior and being, in contrast to those

who did not—the *akriyāvādinas*, who saw human acts as ineffective. But the Jains, in view of the Buddha's belief that karma can be changed, considered him and his followers to be *akriyāvādin*.[43] They recognized, in this fashion, his departure from the determinism which a linear view, holding to the preexistence of effect in cause, logically dictates. The Buddha openly acknowledged and emphasized this departure, for, if you cannot change karma, as he said in the *Devadaha Sutta*, "all effort is fruitless".[44] This he would not allow. He rejected the alternative views of karma because, in his view, they provided

> neither the desire to do, nor the effort to do, nor the necessity to do this deed or abstain from that deed. So then, the necessity for action or inaction [is] not found to exist in truth or verity.[45]

The Determinacy of Choice

This "desire to do, effort to do"—in other words, will, volition—affect both the determinacy of past action and the scope for present endeavor. It is in this emphasis on will that the Buddhist concept of karma is most distinctive. Gotama took care to qualify that the acts whose consequences are subsequently experienced, are those that are chosen. "Where there have been deeds, Ananda, personal weal and woe are in consequence of the will there was in the deeds."[46] It is will, *cetanā*, that is determinative.[47]

> That which we will, brethren, and that which we intend to do and that wherewithal we are occupied: this becomes a condition for the persistence of consciousness.[48]

Hence the *saṇkhāras*, which condition our cognitions and perceptions, are understood as "volitional" formations constellated by intentions and bearing, in the form of impulse, the energy of the will. Oldenberg, as we have quoted him, sees them as "internal actions, the will and the wish."[49] By the same token, Jayatilleke qualifies karma as "volitional action."[50] Therefore, we can say that the determinative aspect of past acts resides in the choices that produced them.

Choice, as I use it here, does not mean the object or behavior chosen, but the selection of it, the decision to do it, the motivation. According to the texts, karma is qualified by the nature of such choice.[51] Harmful consequences devolve from *akusala* (unskilled) acts, which are motivated by any of the three roots of suffering: greed, hatred, and delusion (*lobha, dosa, moha*). Their opposites, nonattachment, loving-kindness, and wisdom (*alobha, adosa, amoha*) motivate *kusala* (skillful) acts and provide the conditions for beneficial and pleasurable results. There are also those acts, called *avyakata*, which are unmotivated by any of the above and are effectively neutral.[52]

Indeed because intention is seen as so important, and choice so determinative, the opportunity provided by human existence is considered in the Buddhist view to be incomparably precious. As noted in the last chapter, animals, ghosts, and gods experience pain and pleasure, but only the human being can affect her experience through choice. The power to determine one's fate is the prerogative of the human realm; and given the astronomical number of other forms of life, this human opportunity is extraordinarily rare and valuable.[53]

Since will determines the effect of acts, for good or for grief, it must be cleansed and exercised—an undertaking requiring exertion. The early scriptures abound in exhortations to vigorous effort. Those who would "rise up from what is unskilled and establish [themselves] in what is skilled," are summoned repeatedly to be "intent on vigilance," "of stirred up energy, self-resolute, with mindfulness aroused," full of striving and zeal.[54] A cardinal failing, miring one in unskilled ways, is *thīnamiddham*, sloth or lethargy.[55] By the same token, *viriya*, energy, resolution, vigor, is seen as essential to the Path and a cardinal virtue in its own right. Its summons presents a vivid contrast to the passivity and fatalism popularly associated with the notion of karma.[56] In the Buddhist view of karma, will is primary, and it can be trained.

> Wherefore, brethren, thus must ye train yourselves: liberation of the will through love we will develop, we will often practice it, we will make it a vehicle and a base, take our stand upon it, store it up, thoroughly set it going.[57]

In the early Buddhist view, then, a person's identity resides not in any enduring substance or self (*attā*) but in his acts (*kamma*)—that is in the choices which shape these acts, which in turn through the conditioning effect of the *saṅkhārās*, shape him. Because this causal process is reciprocal—the dispositions formed by previous choices modified in turn by the present acts they influence—this identity as choice-maker is fluid, its experience alterable. While it is affected by the past, it can also break free of the past.

The Cognitive System as Decision Center

In general systems theory as well, given the mutual causality between structure and function, choice emerges as decisive in determining the effect of action upon agent. Indeed, action appears as choice and identity appears as the decision-making process itself.

Because the open system is self-organizing, its behavior cannot be dictated or directly modified from without. External pressures or circumstances can only operate in interaction with internal organization. Past experience, as recorded in the system, is fed back into the making of present decision. As organization increases, the system becomes less determined by the environment, more autonomous. In the systems philosophical view, self-reflexive consciousness emerges when the degree of complexity has evolved to the point that monitoring requires evaluation and selection between alternate courses of action. Freedom enters. As Laszlo puts it,

> When a man acts on the basis of his empirical and meta-level reflective cognitions he could always have acted otherwise than he did, for his constructions and cognitions of his environment are not dictated by his environment, but by his present cognitive (= cortical) organization.[58]

Because this organization represents the record of past functions, the scope of choice available to the system is limited by the past. For, "the system can only choose that which his past interactions with the environment made available to him."[59] Stored within and providing modes by which reality can be interpreted and results envisaged, the past both makes options available and limits them. This past does not mold or predestine actions, because it functions in mutual interaction with the present. Because it is dynamically self-organizing, the cognitive system, as Karl Deutsch says, "is changing and remaking with each decision in the present."

> Thanks to what it has learned in the past, it is not wholly subject to the present. Thanks to what it still can learn, it is not wholly subject to the past. Its internal rearrangements in response to each new challenge are made by the interplay between its present and its past.[60]

To our capacity to take distance on past decisions, in order to evaluate them and broaden present choice, Deutsch offers the analogy of an internal "circuit breaker."[61] This circuit breaker is also a "habit breaker," opening the cognitive system to new data and facilitating the inflow of new information. Such an operation is evident in the exploratory self-organization of gestalts and constructs in positive feedback, as we examined in Chapter 7 in relation to learning. Old patterns of perceiving, knowing, and responding are disrupted, permitting new options to appear, fresh alternatives to emerge.

Whether we opt for old ways of doing or new, choice remains integral to the processing of information and the making of responses; for by virtue of the very existence of metalevel reflective cognitions, the individual "could always have acted otherwise than he did." Such a recognition, intrinsic to the systems-cybernetic view, leads Deutsch to say,

> Each of us is responsible for what he is now, for the personality he himself has acquired by his past action. . . . Nor are we wholly prisoners of any one decision or any one experience. Ordinarily, it takes many repetitions so to stock a mind with memories and habits that at long last lead to the same city, whether it be taken, in religious language, as the City of Destruction, or the City of Salvation.[62]

The parallels to the Buddhist idea of karma are obvious, as also to that of the *saṇkhārās*, the memories and habits that "stock the mind" and impel us onward.

In this cybernetic view, as in the Buddhist one, we are not victims of our past, hapless pawns of forces and times beyond our reach; rather, as Deutsch continues,

> It sees in the actual moment of decision only a *dénouement* in which we reveal to ourselves and to others what we have already become thus far. This view has parallels to that of St. Augustine, and more recently perhaps to Karl Jaspers and other existentialists, but it does not involve outside predestination. For each step on the road to "heaven" or to "hell," to harmonious autonomy or to disintegration, was marked by a free decision. . . . The determinate part of our behavior is the stored result of our past free decisions.[63]

Excluding the factors which limit the intake of information through impairments resulting from heredity or disease, Deutsch sees manifest in this process of free and determining decisions, our "moral responsibility."

So fundamental to the systems view is this notion of choice and its mutual causal relation to the chooser, that it appears as the definitions of person. Constantly opting, ranking values, "the self is a decision-center," as Everett puts it.[64] To systems-psychologist O. H. Mowrer, choice defines consciousness itself. In the context of pointing out the conceptual weakness of behaviorist theory, where consciousness appears as the passive recipient of conditioning, Mowrer says,

> I will venture the guess that consciousness is, essentially, a *continuous-computing* device or process. The eternal question is, "What to do? How to act?" And consciousness, as I conceive it, is the operation whereby information is continuously received, evaluated and summarized in the form of "decisions," "choices," "intentions."[65]

The cybernetic view is of assistance in resolving problems that can puzzle the Buddhist scholar in dealing with the doctrine of karma. Gomez, at the conclusion of his paper on free will in the Nikāyas, demonstrates the difficulty of conceiving of determinacy without a determiner, of control without a controller.

> The basic dilemma could be stated thus: "if there is control, then there must be a controlling power which must be 'self-existing' or 'independent' (self-acting)," but this to the Buddhist seems too close to the self to be acceptable. On the other hand, if there can be no control, since no-control implies total dependence on external conditions, then there is determinism.[66]

Gomez seeks to solve the problem he perceives by suggesting that Buddhists, by causation, mean "weak," rather than "total conditioning."[67] This misses the point and confuses the issue. The apparent logic behind his "dilemma," a logic by which causal efficacy requires an independent doer, is not necessary or appropriate to mutual causation. For in the interdependence of doer and deed, neither determinacy nor choice requires an agent external to the decision-making process itself. This is so, because karma is, essentially, the operation by which choices are embodied, and the individual *is* that embodiment, or rather that operation.

Process theologian Bernard Loomer puts such a view succinctly and vividly.

> His [the individual's] concrete life is constituted by a process of deciding what he will make out of what he has received. This is his emergent selfhood. What he makes out of what he has received is who he is. This is also his emergent freedom because he is his decision. His subjective life is his process of deciding who he is.[68]

Returning to the questions posed at the start of this chapter, we see, then, that identity, from the perspective of mutual causality, is just that: the process of decision making. By virtue of the reciprocity of function and structure, deed and doer, that is also the basis of our continuity as persons. In that causal flow lies our consistency as characters, bearing the stamp of repeated choice, and in it also is our freedom, for that flow is altered by each present act of will. Implicit in this is the answer to the other question, "does it matter what we do?" It matters to the extent that *we* matter. For our acts incarnate *in* us, they make us what we are.

The interdependence of doer and deed spells both grief and promise for that self we tend to posit and on whose behalf we generally act. Because it is constantly changing and altered by each act, wise or foolish, fearful or brave, it is, even as "decision-maker," doomed as an enduring entity, ever dying and passing away. Yet in that very evanescence lie hope and promise. For in the flow of decisions and deeds choices can be made that open broader vistas to perceive and know, wider opportunities to love and act.

Notes

1. Van Doren, "Undersong," p. 25.

2. Jayatilleke, *Survival and Karma*, pp. 3–5.

3. *Dīgha Nikāya*, I.82.

4. *Ibid.*, p. 104f.

5. Jayatilleke, *Survival and Karma*, p. 32.

6. Demiéville, "Le Mémoire," pp. 283–98.

7. *Dīgha Nikāya*, I.17–8.

8. *Saṃyutta Nikāya*, II.26.

9. *Ibid.*, II.19.

10. Pande, *Studies in Origins of Buddhism*, p. 420.

11. Lee, "From Acts—to Acts."

12. Rhys Davids, T. W., *Dialogues of Buddha*, II, p. 189.

13. *Majjhima Nikāya*, I.22.

14. *Saṃyutta Nikāya*, II.62.

15. *Dhammapada*, p. 139.

16. Horner, *Middle Length Sayings*, I, p. 67 n.4.

17. Oldenberg, *Buddha: Life, Doctrine, Order*, p. 242.

18. Quoted in Oldenberg, *Ibid.*, p. 243.

19. Laszlo, *Introduction to Systems Philosophy*, p. 70f.

20. Quoted in Laszlo, *Ibid.*, p. 71.

21. von Bertalanffy, "General Systems Theory—Critical Review," p. 21.

22. *Ibid.*

23. von Bertalanffy, *General Systems Theory*, pp. 247–48.

24. *Ibid.*, p. 27.

25. Laszlo, *Strategy for the Future*, p. 17.

26. Laszlo, *Introduction to Systems Philosophy*, p. 252.

27. *Ibid.*, pp. 181–82.

28. *Ibid.*, p. 252.

29. Miller, "Living Systems," p. 84.

30. Everett, "Cybernetics," p. 101.

31. Jackson, *Individual and Larger Contexts*, pp. 319–20.

32. Jayatilleke, *Survival and Karma*, pp. 26–27; Kalupahana, *Causality*, pp. 38–40; Gomez, "Some Aspects of Free-will," pp. 81f.

33. Govinda, *Psychological Attitude*, pp. 56–57.

34. *Ibid.*, p. 57.

35. *Aṇguttara Nikāya*, II.80.

36. *Majjhima Nikāya*, III.207–15.

37. *Saṃyutta Nikāya*, IV.228–30; Jayatilleke, *Survival and Karma*, p. 29.

38. *Majjhima Nikāya*, III.207–15.

39. Quoted in Gomez, "Some Aspects of Free-will," p. 83.

40. Jayatilleke, *Survival and Karma*, p. 40.

41. This view, incidentally, does not seem to correspond to classical Jain teachings, as Gomez points out ("Some Aspects of Free-will," p. 84).

42. *Majjhima Nikāya*, II.214f.

43. Gomez, "Some Aspects of Free-will," p. 183.

44. *Majjhima Nikāya*, II.214.

45. *Aṇguttara Nikāya*, I.174.

46. Samyutta Nikāya, II.38.

47. While there is no term in Pali which corresponds in a precise and exclusive fashion to our word "will," *cetanā* comes close. In the verb *cinteti* from which it derives, and which means "to reflect and be of opinion," the notion of choice is implicit. As such, *cetanā* is defined as "thinking as active thought, intention, purpose, will" (Rhys Davids and Stede, *Pali-English Dictionary*). The related terms *citta* and *cetas*, also from *cinteti*, similarly include the connotations of intention and volition. The thinking or thought these terms represent are acts expressive of will and bearing the stamp of choice. In mutual causality, as we have stressed, knowing and thinking do not consist in a passive registering of data, but are a transactional process and hence, as discussed further in Chapter 11, involve our moral responsibility.

48. *Saṃyutta Nikāya*, II.64.

49. Oldenberg, *Buddha: Life, Doctrine, Order*, p. 242.

50. Jayatilleke, *Survival and Karma*, p. 17.

51. *Aṇguttara Nikāya*, I.188.

52. The qualifying terms *kusala* and *akusala*, literally "skillful" and "unskillful," rather than "good" or "bad," stress the inherent efficacy of the motives in question, more than the moral evaluation of them.

53. Sangharakshita, "Centrality of Man," p. 31.

54. *Majjhima Nikāya*, I.32.

55. *Ibid.*, I.19.

56. C. Rhys Davids observes that an indiscriminate use of the word *desire* in some translations of the texts, and its wholesale application to such Pali terms as *tanhā* (craving), *trṣna* (thirst), *kāmā* (passion), and *upādāna* (grasping), contribute to a misconstruction of the positive role of desire, and encourage the notion of Buddhist passivity and abnegation ("On Will in Buddhism"). She says,

> If there be one feature in Buddhist ethics eminent for the emphasis attached to it, it is not only that will as such, desire as such, are not to be repressed, but that the culture and development of them are absolutely indispensable to any advance toward the attainment of its ideals.

57. *Saṃyutta Nikāya*, II.264.

58. Laszlo, *Introduction to Systems Philosophy*, p. 249.

59. *Ibid.*, p. 239.

60. Deutsch, "Toward a Cybernetic Model," p. 397.

61. *Ibid.*, p. 397.

62. *Ibid.*, p. 398.

63. *Ibid.*, p. 398–99.

64. Everett, "Cybernetics," p. 108.

65. Mowrer, "Ego Psychology," p. 338.

66. Gomez, "Some Aspects of Free-will," p. 88.

67. A. B. Keith also had difficulty in squaring the doctrines of *anattā* and *paṭicca samuppāda* with the Buddha's emphasis on free will, and concluded that it represents an inconsistency in regard to determinism which the Buddha "simply ignored."

> Moreover, man has the power to act . . . the Buddha has no doubt whatever that the determinism of Makkhali Gosala is the most detestable of heresies. The position is the more remarkable because one of the arguments in the Canon and later against the existence of the self is that such a thing must be autonomous, while all in the world is conditional and causally determined. But the issue is solved by the simple process of ignoring it and Buddhism rejoices in being freed

from any error of determinism to menace moral responsibility. (Keith, *Buddhist Philosophy*, p. 116.)

In the contempt Keith expresses for such apparent contradictions, it is evident he assumes that choice requires an independent and unconditioned self.

68. Loomer, "Two Conceptions of Power."

10

The Co-Arising of Self and Society

No man is an Island, intire to its selfe, every man is a piece of the Continent, a part of the maine; if a Clod bee washed away by the sea, Europe is the less as well as if a Promontorie were, as well as if a Mannor of thy friends or of thine own were. Any man's death diminishes me, because I am involved in Mankind. And therefore never send to know for whom the bell tolls. It tolls for thee.

—John Donne[1]

The opening words of this passage have become a commonplace saying, woven into the fabric of our language, because they reflect a truth about our existence. Our separate lives are grounded in a social reality. Social systems impinge on our lives and relate us to our fellow beings, as a continent connects its promontories, a landscape its trees. Even when we set ourselves apart, they condition our private pursuits and reflect them in turn.

Is our imbeddedness in society inherently oppressive, entailing unavoidable opposition of interests and the curtailment of freedom? Or does it, on the contrary, promote our fulfillment and provide scope for choice? Will allegiance to the welfare of society erode our individuality or enhance it? Our responses to these questions depend on our understanding of the causal dynamics that give rise to social systems.

To explore them let me begin by pointing out that, from the perspective of mutual causality, the individual self is both unique and inseparable from its natural and social matrix. A fleeting meeting-ground of intricately woven relations, its nature is profoundly participatory, but is, for that, no less endowed with distinctiveness, particularity.

Participation and Particularity

The individual self, as we examined in Chapter 6 and subsequently, appears as a process, a pattern of psycho-physical events. Because it is formed through sensory, affective, and cognitive interaction with its environment, it cannot be abstracted from its context in nature and society. In the Buddha Dharma this view is integral to the teachings of the *khaṇḍas,* the causal relation of the *nidānas,* and the doctrine of *anattā.* In general systems theory it is basic to the concept of the open system. As the person processes and transforms food from the natural world, so also does the person self-organize by processing and transforming and exchanging information derived from the community.

As systems thinkers have recognized, such a view makes it impossible categorically to distinguish self from nonself, and any definitive delineations between "I" and "other" are arbitrary. The feelings, sensations, and cognitions we identify with our "I" are not intrinsic or exclusive properties of that "I", so much as the coming to awareness of processes that extend beyond our conventional identity. To be a person, therefore, is to participate, at every level of our being, in a reality wider than that enclosed by our skin or identified with our name.

As a social and linguistic convention, the notion of an "I" is useful, but, if taken to represent a fixed or separable entity, it is a fiction. In systems terms it is a construct which is dysfunctional to the extent that it distorts the system's perception of its own relation to the external world. To the Buddhist, the belief in a permanent, separate self represents a fundamental error: engendering greed, anxiety, and aggression, it is an illusion basic to the suffering we experience and which we inflict on others. Our liberation, by whatever techniques or circumstances it is attended, involves a shattering of such preconceptions, a breakthrough to the release-bringing realization that there is, in actuality, no separate "I" to defend or enhance, or to whose service we need bind our efforts.

This is not to say, however, that the distinctiveness of our experience is illusory. From the mutual causal point of view, where mind and matter are seen as interdependent, reality cannot be apprehended or consciousness experienced apart from particularity of form. Release from the confines of ego, or from an atomistic view of the self, does not mean immersion in an undifferentiated whole, where all distinctions are erased or seen as unreal, invalid, irrelevant.

Between the alternatives of atomism and holism, mutual causality presents a third—that of articulated integration, where diversity and unity are seen as equally integral to the play of reality. As we saw in Chapter 8 mind is viewed as correlative to matter, as inside is to outside. Mind is the interior, lived dimension of systems that, externally observed, are physical. So, while we as conscious, cognitive selves participate in a psychic continuum that extends far beyond us, it is interdependent with and inseparable from the diversity of forms we sensorially apprehend. Hence, regard for the particular is integral to the mutual causal view.

This regard for the particular is evident in Buddhist teachings. Co-arising with body, consciousness is seen as endemic to life, extending beyond the realm of the human in a psychic continuity that relates the human being to other creatures and summons him to live in nonviolence, concord, and compassion. This Buddhist recognition of other forms of consciousness is distinct from the Hindu belief in the pervasiveness of *Brahman* or the ubiquity of the *Puruṣa*. There, in the Hindu perspective, materiality represents a cloak or covering of that which becomes progressively more evident and worthy of reverence as it is divested of particularity and physicality. In contrast, the Buddha Dharma, seeing consciousness and matter as co-arising, features no ontological or axiological gradation of the mentality inherent in life forms. These are revered, held in *metta* and viewed with a "boundless heart" not for their underlying sameness, but for their suchness, *tathatā*.

General systems theory offers fresh ways of understanding and imaging this particular and participatory nature of personhood. Through the process termed feedback, the words and acts by which a person would modify her world shape her in turn. Furthermore, her very existence is constituted by networks of biological and social relationships, in which she, like other open systems, is a "holon"— both an integral whole and a part within a larger whole. As open systems interact, be they atom or organism, they form larger self-sustaining patterns, which in turn relate to build yet more inclusive and more varied forms. Each level is irreducible, and each whole is a holon—comprising subsystems, it is itself a subsystem in a larger system, each level revealing greater diversity and improbability or, to use Wiener's term, greater negentropy. As Koestler put it, "no man is an island, he is a holon."[2]

As a holon, the person's existence is intimately, intricately and inextricably interwoven with other forms of life. No free-wheeling monad, his life is a tapestry of biological and socio-cultural relationships, from the organic subsystems which shape his body to the larger social and natural systems in which he functions. He can abuse neither subsystems nor suprasystems, neither body or society, without personal cost, for they comprise the raw material of his existence.

The self, then, in mutual causality has no independent position, no Archimedean point, from which to decide whether or when it will participate in the lives of other beings. It does so already, by its nature. Let us turn now to the dynamics involved, and particularly the reciprocally creative interaction between self and society.

The Interdependence of Person and Community

From the mutual causal point of view, then, the pains, pleasures, and projects of the self are formed in interaction; they are not private. Where minds interact, they mutually create. Only the autistic is independent. A Helen Keller needs communication with others to gain access to the wealth of her own spirit. A Messiah needs people looking for a Messiah. Even a criminal monomaniac, a Hitler or an Idi Amin, requires others to act out his dreams and shapes his fantasies to give utterance to theirs. Let us see how this mutuality is imaged, both in general systems theory and the Buddha Dharma.

According to general systems theory, the natural open system maintains itself by processing energy and information, and transforming these inputs according to previously established codes. When the codes are inadequate to permit response to persistent changes in the environment, they alter if the system is to survive. The system self-organizes in order to adapt, becomes more complex, differentiated. Self-awareness evolves when the system becomes so complex that self-monitoring and decision making are required for its successful adaptation. The cognitive system which emerges, and which we recognize in persons and some higher mammals, sustains and organizes itself in the same manner. It processes and transforms data, extracting meanings derived from previous experience. In such fashion, it maps its environment and manipulates and modifies its world by projecting its constructs upon it. It can thus continue to interpret its perceptions in the accustomed ways. When new data are anomalous to its preconceptions and these anomalies persist, the constructs by which experience is interpreted are themselves changed. They complexify, make new connections and broaden in relevance in order to make new experience meaningful.

Survival and the flowering of intelligence, then, involve both differentiation and functional integration. As the system becomes internally more complex, with circuits and constructs evolving to process a greater variety of data, so its interactions with the environment become richer, more manifold and more open. Its connections with the world around it multiply, as it evolves the capacity to take more into account. It becomes structurally less stable and in behavior less predictable as its flexibility and responsiveness increase. A cell is more unstable, unpredictable, improbable, and flexible than a molecule, a person more than a cell. This represents a movement toward what systems thinkers term cybernetic stability.

While cybernetic stability entails a greater vulnerability on the part of the system, it permits it to adapt with greater flexibility. The system maintains its balance, that fine metabolic equilibrium between the building up and the breaking down of its components, by becoming ever more open, more susceptible. In that process of interaction, where intangible webs of relationship are spun, new forms, new ideas, new realities emerge. Highly varied and improbable, these constitute, as the course of evolution attests, a movement away from entropy.

In this view differentiation and integration go hand in hand; they abet and give rise to each other. I emphasize this because we often assume that organization implies uniformity, that order requires sameness. In the systems view, the reverse is true. In our own lives we frequently experience how relationships can summon what is distinctive in ourselves, how intercourse can reveal latent gifts and call into play greater variety in our behavior. The dynamics of mutual causality are such that the interaction of open systems leads not only to cohesion, but also variety—to distinctiveness as well as adaptive integration.

This notion is at variance with the idea that there is an inherent conflict between instinct and culture. Freud's thinking suggests that the individual's drives for self-expression, epitomized in sexuality and aggression, are inevitably at loggerheads with society's need for order. This opposition gives rise to tragic conflict within the individual, who then must trade off, weighing gratifications and autonomy against security and acceptance.

Instead of a break and a conflict here, the systems view perceives a continuum in the flowering of integrated heterogeneity. From its perspective, the notion that self-realization is at odds with harmonious interaction is a misconception; for it is in relationship, not in isolation, that beings give expression to diversity and distinctiveness. It would seem that Freud's view, so influential in our culture, stems from a polarization of the notions of order and variety—as if order, sacred or secular, were some preset master plan we can only follow by inhibiting novelty, by being good children obedient to an autocratic father.

When we dichotomize nature and society, it seems we can only serve the latter by doing violence to the former. Seeing them, however, as manifestations of a continuous thrust toward self-organization, the systems view would suggest that there is no ineradicable conflict here. Harmonious social integration is as deep an instinct as sex or aggression, and indeed takes precedence when the cognitive system breaks out of its arbitrary dichotomies of "self" and "other" and experiences its own drive for larger identification.

Such a drive is evident in countless acts of love and heroism, not explicable in terms of Freud's polarity. The persistent labors of many on behalf of the public weal, as well as the simpler, more mundane acts whereby pleasure is found in giving pleasure, testify to a widespread intuition that we are, by nature, part of each other. From such a perspective, even the violence of war and the passions it can evoke can be seen, not just as an eruption of hostility, but also as an expression, however tragic, of our drive to band together more solidly, to surmount our separate lonelinesses and experience the heightened vitality we find in cohesive interaction.

The Dharma of Social Systems

The interdependence of person and community finds expression in early Buddhist teachings as well, pervaded as they are by the notion of *paṭicca samuppāda*, dependent co-arising. Here also the self is seen as a changing complex process formed by its physical, cognitive, and conative interactions with the world. As the teachings emphasize, it is not a static or isolable entity that can be viewed apart from such interactions nor is its social context fixed or preordained. Self and society condition each other, are mutually creative. This assumption is reflected in the institution of the Sangha, the community the Buddha founded, and in its symbolic value as a model for social, political, and economic ideals. The assumption of interdependence between person and community is also reflected in the social teachings of the Buddha embodied in the *suttas* and *vinaya*, teachings dealing with the institutions of caste and private property, with employment and political process. For basic to the ideals of social equality, economic sharing, and political participation, which the teachings present, is the notion that the human being arises interdependently with its natural and social environment.

The kind of dynamic which the Buddhists see operative here, and which shows remarkable parallels to the systems view of mutual causality is illustrated in the *Aggañña Sutta*. A popular teaching found in the *Dīgha Nikāya* and the *Jātaka* and recurring in the *Mahāvastu*, the *Visuddhimagga* and other postcanonical writings, this is the Buddha's fanciful genesis story, his tongue-in-cheek recounting of the beginnings of things and origins of institutions. It was told pursuant to a discussion of caste, when some Brahmins asked the Buddha whether caste as a social institution was not divinely ordained, a worthy and permanent fixture in the order of reality. Illustrating the dynamic or law (*dhamma*) by which things co-arise, this story could serve as allegory for the systems concepts we reviewed above, for it presents self, society and world as evolving by interaction and progressive differentiation. Remember, as you read this summary that in the very pretense to know the beginnings of things, the Buddha was poking fun at such metaphysical speculations.

In the beginning of a world cycle neither beings nor their world have solid form or distinctive features. Weightless, luminous, and identical, the beings waft about over a dark and watery expanse. When a frothy substance appears on the waters, they taste it. It is delicious, and for its sweet, honey flavor a craving arises. As the beings consume more and more, both they and their world change, become more distinct. The beings begin to lose to the world their identical luminosity: sun and moon and stars appear, and the alternation of day and night. The beings begin to solidify and vary in appearance. Pride and vanity arise as they compare themselves in beauty . . . and the savory froth vanishes. The beings bewail its loss: "Ah, the savor of it!"[4] In its place, on earth that is now firmer, mushroomlike growths appear of comparable tastiness—only to disappear as the creatures fatten on them and change. The mushrooms are replaced by vines and these, in turn, by rice. With every new growth the beings crave, eat, grow more solid and diverse. At each stage their use of the environment modifies it, gives rise to more solidity and new forms of vegetation, and with such usage they themselves alter, developing more distinctive features. In this interaction both creatures and world progressively differentiate, each gaining in solidity and variety.

When it first grew, the rice was without husk or powder and, when gathered, would grow again in a day. A lazy one, to save effort, decided to harvest two meals at once. Soon beings are harvesting for two days at a time, then for four days, then eight. With this hoarding the rice changes: a husk appears around the grain and the cut stem does not grow again but stands as stubble. So the people divide and fence the land, set boundaries to ensure their source of food. Soon a greedy one takes rice from a neighboring plot. Admonished by the others, he promises to refrain, but he takes again, repeatedly. Since admonishment is of no avail, he is beaten. In such fashion, with the institution of private property, arise theft and lying and abuse and violence.

Soon such acts are so rampant, the scene so chaotic, that the people decide to select one of their own to act on their behalf—"to be wrathful when indignation is right and to censure what rightly should be censured"—and to receive in return for this service a portion of their rice.[5] So arises the *Mahāsammata*, the great elected one, and with his rule order prevails. Such is the origin of kingship and the Kshatriya class (Pali: *khattiya*), and so also evolve, by the assumption and differentiation of roles, the other major divisions of society: the Brahmin, Vaisya (Pali: *vessa*) and Sudra (Pali: *sudda*) castes.

Caste or class is not established by divine fiat, but arises, as the text stresses, from the actions of beings like ourselves, and according to *dhamma*, the law of dependent co-arising.[6] These social institutions are circumstantial in origin. Misguided and without foundation, therefore, is "the copious and characteristic abuse" with which the Brahmins revile those of their rank who go over to the Sangha, and with which they denigrate that company of the Buddha for including "the vulgar rich, the swarthy skinned and the menials."[7] While social ranking conditions the lives, skills and hopes of persons, it does not, the scripture affirms, predetermine or foreclose their capacity to live nobly and achieve enlightenment.[8]

The causal dynamics which this story metaphorically expresses underlie the social, economic, and political teachings and practices we find in scripture: the Buddha's rejection of caste discrimination and the egalitarian composition of the Sangha; his distrust of private property and the institution in the Sangha of voluntary poverty, sharing, and alms-begging; his advocacy of government by open assembly and consensus, and the Sangha's rules for debate, ballot, and the settlement of differences. These ideals and practices have been well described in Buddhist scholarship.

My interest here is to stress their profound connection with the doctrine of dependent co-arising. Within that mutual causal perception of reality one is not a self-existent being nor are the institutions of society eternally fixed. They are mutable and they mirror our greeds, as does indeed the face of nature itself. Co-arising with our actions, they, like us, can be changed by our actions. As our own dynamic processes can be transformed, so can they.

This story in the *Aggañña Sutta*, so often repeated in Buddhist writings, has been recognized as the first expression in Indian political thought of a theory of social contract.[9] The beings banded together to make their own government; the *Mahāsammata* was not divinely appointed and anointed but was chosen by his peers to act in their stead and for their purposes. The causality which the story portrays would indicate a difference between the Buddhist view and the Western, Rousseauian notion of social contract. In dependent co-arising, self, society, and world are reciprocally modified by their interaction, as they form relationships and are in turn conditioned by them. The Western idea contrasts with such a view to the extent that it assumes a free association between individuals who remain basically distinct and unaltered by such association.

In this chapter we have seen that societies display the same systemic properties as biological and cognitive systems, co-arising with them according to the same Dharma. The dynamics of this interdependence reveal that diversity is as important as unity. Let us now consider the ethical norms that emerge from this dependent co-arising.

Notes

1. Donne, *Complete Poetry*, p. 441.

2. Koestler, *Beyond Reductionism*, p. 209.

3. *Dīgha Nikāya*, II.80f.

4. *Ibid.*, III.86.

5. *Ibid.*, II.93.

6. *Ibid.*, III.95.

7. *Ibid.*, III.82.

8. *Ibid.*, III.82.

9. Ghoshal, *History of Indian Political Ideas*, pp. 66f; Ling, p. 53.

11

Mutual Morality

Our own pulse beats in every stranger's throat.

—Barbara Deming[1]

In the perspective of mutual causality the self appears as a fluid, changing structure, formed through interaction between the world it experiences and the codes by which it interprets this experience. From such a perspective values emerge as formative. Values are not only formative in constituting the criteria by which the self measures and guides its behavior—that is, in the descriptive sense—but also in the normative sense. For the very dynamics of mutual causality suggest that certain moral values are woven into the fabric of life, intrinsic to its harmony and continuity. These dynamics present a reality so structured as to require, for our conscious participation in it, that we live in certain ways.

These norms presuppose, of course, a positive valuation of reality—whether the goal of conscious participation in it is envisaged in terms of enjoyment, as in "the pursuit of happiness," or in terms of knowing, as in "enlightenment." There is no logic to prove that such participation is desirable, but our experience disposes us to grant that assumption. Our strivings and even our conflicts manifest a thrust from ignorance to knowing, from separateness to connection, from powerlessness to efficacy and a wider share in being. The recognition of that thrust and its positive valuation is evident in the religions of humankind. It is also evident to the systems thinker, who sees how life-forms self-organize, increasing their capacity to survive, adapt, and interconnect. Maintaining themselves against great odds and in states of enormous improbability, these open natural systems, as Laszlo observes, are programmed on the premise that life is valuable.[2]

If that much is granted, then on the basis of mutual causality as it appears in general systems theory and early Buddhist teachings, certain normative values become evident. Ways in which life should be lived appear as intrinsic to such an order of things. These have been intimated in the foregoing chapters, but I want now to view them more directly—in terms of the kind of morality which a mutual causal view of reality appears to enjoin.

Concern for Other Beings

If self is a pattern of *khaṇḍas,* or transformations of energy and information arising in interaction with the surrounding world, its nature is profoundly participatory in that of other beings. This would be true, then, on two levels: Not only are our raw materials, the food and fancies from which we construct our "I," derived from a shared environment, but the very patterns we make of them are woven and textured by relationship. In such a state of affairs we are, quite literally, part of each other—free neither from indebtedness to our fellow-beings nor responsibility for them.

We can, of course, choose to ignore our involvement in their lives and block our perceptions of their needs and hopes. To the extent we do so, however, we cripple ourselves. We screen out data that is relevant not only to our adaptation as individuals and as species, but also to our conscious participation in reality, whether that goal is apprised in terms of bliss or knowledge.

Such goals require an ever-increasing openness. In systems terms this means processing data from wider sources, evolving subtler, more inclusive constructs by which the information is made meaningful, and relinquishing constructs that are no longer valid—a dying, so to speak, to old habits and self-definitions. The cognitive system's movement toward cybernetic stability entails, as we have seen, increasing conscious interaction with other systems and levels of the systemic hierarchy. In the maintenance of the delicate balance on which life depends, this involves an extension of constructs of self-interest, in which the needs of others begin to emerge as covalent with one's own.

Cybernetic stability requires, therefore, a broadening of the sense of self and its responsibility: an identification with others which includes both respect and self-restraint. In periods of simpler technology, this requirement could be ignored at the cost of personal maturity, not planetary survival. But now it becomes evident that the very viability of our societies and ecosystems necessitates such a shift in identification. It is questionable whether the human cognitive system, possessed of both free will and technological capacity, will choose to make the shift, but the nature of systemic invariances indicate that it will not survive unless it does so.

We are called, then, to recognize that our relationship with other systems and levels of the systemic hierarchy is collaborative and not competitive. To further such a recognition, Laszlo offers as an operative ideal "reverence for natural systems."[3] As open systems, forms of life, both mental and physical, manifest an awesome complexity and balance. In beholding them we can sense a grandeur in the orderly processes they reveal and a profound kinship, for our own subjectivity is an expression of them. We are summoned, then, as a part of this order, to act with appreciation and self-restraint, rather than with the utilitarian, exploitative attitudes that have dominated Western culture since the rise of the industrial era.

In the Buddha Dharma, concern for other beings, which is integral to the perception of the dependently co-arising nature of reality, finds purest expression in *metta*, "loving-kindness." It represents the extension to all other forms of existence of the love one feels for one's own life. As with Laszlo's "reverence for natural systems," it is not only directed to other humans, but to all beings. This universality is evident throughout the scriptures, from the early *jātakas*, where many of the former births of the Buddha took animal form, to the Mahayana, where the *bodhisattva* (enlightened being) vows to remain in *saṃsāra* until the last blade of grass is enlightened.

> As a mother even at the risk of her own life watches over her only child, so let everyone cultivate a boundless love for all beings. Let him cultivate toward the whole world—above, below, around—a heart of love unstinted. . . . Standing, walking, or sitting, or lying, let him devote himself to this mind: [for it] is the best in the world.[4]

Correlative to this loving-kindness, as aspects of it, are the capacities for compassion, joy in the joy of others, and impartiality. Together all four represent the abodes of the Buddha, also known as the *Brahmāvihāras*, which are to be cultivated through specific meditative exercises. They open the heart to the pain and pleasure all beings experience and, in so doing, break down the walls of ego, leading to both service and enlightenment.

Tolerance and Iconoclasm

The mutual causal paradigm presents an epistemology in which knower and known are interdependent, as we examined in Chapter 7. Our consciousness, co-arising with sensory data, is modified by them, and the world we perceive is modified in turn by our projections and manipulations. Hence perception is a highly interpretive process and the thinking mind itself a factor in the arising of phenomena. This causal interplay renders it impossible, as we saw, to claim or to prove an ultimate truth. Any statement we make is relative to our position and perspective, our project and purpose.

The ethical import of such an epistemology is fairly evident. It indicates the moral character of knowing itself. Data gathering and interpretation are not value-free, but freighted with emotional predispositions and cognitive preconceptions. We are, at all levels of our being, accomplices to the assertions we make, and accountable for them. By the same token, such a view summons us to live with ambiguity, an ambiguity in which we are both tolerant of differences and skeptical of certitudes. Final answers, absolutist dogmas and ideologies—whether those of others or our own—are unhinged and revealed as presumptuous, for all interpretation is partial at best. Such iconoclasm we find built in to both general systems theory and early Buddhist teachings.

Even in the eyes of its founder, von Bertalanffy, systems theory makes no claim to finality, for "any statement holds from a certain viewpoint only, has only relative validity."[5] The last word has yet to be spoken, and, given the limits of cognition, never can be. To subsequent systems thinkers, this recognition is taken as a value.

> We must underline the value of general systems theory in terms of its perspectivist qualities—that is, its insistence that no world view, its own included, is ultimate truth or ultimate reality.[6]

The relativism of the systems-cybernetic epistemology does not mean that the true cannot be known or that all statements have equal claim to accuracy, but that the true includes us, as knowers, and that no statement is exempt from the particularity of experience. As co-creators of our worlds we cannot extricate ourselves to claim a vision of its workings that is aloof from our own participation in it. Where their perspectivist and participatory qualities are acknowledged, our knowings can reveal informative patterns, significant insights. Where they are not so acknowledged, they can be misleading and dangerous, as von Glasersfeld and Varela stress, in pointing out epistemology's moral implications.

> We are now beginning to see that the age-old dichotomy between the knower and an ontological reality-to-be-known was a rather dangerous illusion. It has led both philosophy and science into the attitude that has persistently kept man, the constructor of philosophies and sciences, out of his own construction, fostering the belief that, in the last analysis, man was not responsible for the world he came to know and manipulate.[7]

The Buddha rejected dogmatic assertions about the nature of things for two reasons: 1) because these are by nature partial and 2) because they become objects of attachment. To the disappointment of many followers, he refused to offer ultimate definitions of objective reality. To these questions requiring some Olympian viewpoint external to human experience, he remained silent or dismissed them as presumptuous and perilous. For all knowing derives from dependently co-arising perception, feelings and cognitions, and dogmatic statements claiming a certitude beyond that which human experience can afford are both dangerous and divisive. Claims to ultimate truth whereby one would say, "This alone is true, all else is false," are seen by the Buddha as so many barbs on which mankind is impaled.[8]

While the reader might argue that the Buddha's own teachings represent such final affirmations about reality, the difference is that *paṭicca samuppāda* and the four Noble Truths do not seek to define a reality external to the observer. They focus not on the ultimate "what" of things, but on the "how"—such as how they arise in the mind and how suffering is conditioned. They present all statements as relative to experience. Indeed, the Buddha instructed his followers to accept nothing on his authority, but to determine the validity of his teachings for themselves, out of their own attentive awareness. The recognition of the limits of knowing and the dangers of certitude underlies both the tolerance characteristic of the Buddhist ethical stance, and the barely disguised contempt Gotama showed for dogmatism.

In mutual causality, therefore, the domain of morality is extended beyond action to interpretation, beyond deeds to ideology.

Our theorizing is neither objective nor value-free but is based on relative constructs which bear our moral responsibility.

Political Engagement

In the mutual causal paradigm, person and society appear as interdependent processes. Political structures are not fixed, preordained structures to which the person must accommodate his being (and in the context of Brahmanical society the Buddha stresses this), nor are they adventitious and disconnected to personal pursuits. Rather they are fluid, systemic patterns in whose unfolding we participate and by which in turn our lives are conditioned. It is incumbent on us to act so as to ensure their health, not only because they condition our lives, but also because they serve as vehicles for our concern for other beings. So doing, we withhold total allegiance, for no entity can claim final truth or wisdom; indeed, active participation is not surrender to political institutions so much as contribution to their creative change.

Interdependent with the state then, we bear responsibility for its health, and this health in turn is reflected in the extent to which the state facilitates the exercise of that responsibility. Where the state's interest diverges from the adaptive well-being of its citizens, distorting their perceptions of need and the communication of information, it becomes pathological. Its health requires wide public participation in decision making, the diversity such participation entails, and the measure of decentralization it necessitates. That such political values are implicit in mutual causality is evident both in early Buddhist teachings and general systems theory.

In contrast to other wandering religious teachers of his period, the Buddha spent much of his career in and around cities, in the company of rulers, on the periphery of political power. And in contrast to the Brahmanical notion of a divinely ordained and eternally valid social order, his teachings presented political institutions as man-made and transient, subject to the law of dependent co-arising (as in *Aggañña Sutta*). Gotama had grown up to the north of the monarchies in which he taught, in a tribal republic ruled by council or assembly (*sangha*). The Order he instituted, and called by the same name (*Sangha*), represented at the outset less a retreat from the world than an alternative community. A vehicle for the transmission of teachings and a locus for the restructuring of consciousness through meditation, it represented as well an embodiment of certain social ideals. As such it served as a model for social equality, cutting across class and caste lines, and also of economic sharing and democratic process.

The Sangha accepted persons regardless of caste and was, on that account, the object of some scorn and ridicule. Not only did Brahmins—who had a socially recognized religious vocation—join the Buddha, but merchants as well, and not only the well-born, but Untouchables and runaway slaves.[9] As Jesus did also, the Buddha saw pride in social rank as perilous to the spirit, a kind of bondage. He is quoted in the *Ambattha Sutta:*

> Whosoever. . . . are in bondage to the notions of birth or of lineage, or to the pride of social position, or of connection by marriage, they are far from the best wisdom and righteousness.[10]

In political organization as well as social complexion, the Sangha represented a contrast to Brahmanical notions. Admittance to the Order involved responsibility, for in its governance, emulating the ancient confederate tribal councils, decisions were to be made by consensus, "in concord." Scriptural passages such as the following represent the first references in Indian thought to rule by assembly.[11]

> So long, O Bhikkhus, as the brethren foregather oft, and frequent the formal meetings of their Order—so long as they meet together in concord, and rise in concord, and carry out in concord the duties of the Order . . . so long may the brethren be expected not to decline, but to prosper.[12]

Since unanimity could hardly be expected to prevail, and since the repression of beliefs was not to be tolerated, a rule of schism, or *Sanghabheda*, was instituted, by which dissenting groups formed new settlements within the Order.[13] Within each settlement, select groups or committees, each having its own jurisdiction and procedural rules (*adhikarana-samathas*), were established to deal with matters administrative and doctrinal. The expression of varying opinions in the *Sanghakammas*, or assemblies for decision making, was facilitated by the taking of ballots (*salākā*), the first recorded use of such procedure in Indian political history.[14]

While, on the one hand, the value of integration was stressed in frequency of assembly and rule of consensus, on the other, differentiation was facilitated by the allowance of minority views,

which no preordained structure of organization or belief was to silence. To that end ideological solidarity and centralized authority
were sacrificed. While internecine wars of religion, such as have
characterized other faiths, were avoided, the Sangha itself split into
many sects and schools. Given the energy and relative amicability of
their intercourse, however, this proliferation of forms testifies more
to strength than weakness. And given the endurance of the Buddha
Dharma over two and a half millenia, it would appear that it hardly
required the centralized authority so often deemed necessary for
the preservation of religious teachings and practice. While hierarchical structures of authority in the Sangha grew up in different
times, these reflected the norms of different cultures; and at no
time did one single center emerge to claim organizational supremacy or doctrinal control. Without a Rome or Jerusalem, the Buddhist
presence lost some cohesiveness, but it flowered in diversity of
forms, while repeatedly renewing, through study of scripture and
meditative practice, its roots in the teachings of the Buddha.

The value of heterogeneity for the health of the body politic,
and the kind of participation and integration it can enable, can be
clarified in terms of systems-cybernetics. The evolution of a system,
its adaptiveness and movement toward cybernetic stability, require
both differentiation and functional integration. The latter represents
the subsystems' engagement in goal-oriented interaction; without
it, there is no entity to self-organize. But this self-organization is not
gained through uniformity. Sameness impoverishes the system,
limits both its perceptions of the world and the scope of its responses. The health of a social system, that is, its flexibility and
adaptiveness, is enriched by heterogeneity and, by the same token,
threatened by regimentation which restricts its variety and internal communications. For a system to adapt effectively, as Karl
Deutsch has stressed, the free and voluntary flow of information is
essential.[15] While bureaucratic mechanisms may be necessary for
coordinating data and decisions at differing levels of priority, decentralization is also requisite to the system's perceptions of its own
needs and the maintenance of flexibility. In pluralistic and decen-
tralized integration the capacities of all components can be enlisted,
so that, in mutual causal interaction, they can enhance the adaptability and intelligence of the system. As Magoroh Maruyama argues, this kind of interaction is symbiotic, and heterogeneity
increases a collective's capacity for "symbiotization."[16]

A totalitarian society might seem to be more unified and coherent than a free one, and seem to display in its apparent disci-

pline an ideological "group head." Yet, to the extent that it discourages differentiation between its subsystems and hampers the voluntary flow of information, its mentality, from the cybernetic standpoint, is on a more primitive level than that of a free one. At the other extreme, a society where individuals and groups are not ready to assume transpersonal loyalties and responsibilities is not integrated enough effectively to self-organize. Fractured and incoherent, it remains on a low level of adaptability and awareness.

The notion of "holon"—the interface between systemic levels—can clarify the kind of participation and responsibility that is incumbent on the individual in relation to her political institutions. Her existence arises within a systemic hierarchy. Sustained by this hierarchy, she shapes it in turn, for she is not so much a connecting link in a preestablished chain as a transformer of energies, creating new syntheses. As a system within systems, she is related to all other forms of life, and is summoned to enhance their symbiotic interaction. She can choose to do so—or she can refuse, and in so doing restrict the intelligence and flexibility of the larger system.

This responsibility includes the readiness to intervene with corrective measures when and where the social system becomes dysfunctional. Given our discussion of the prerequisites for its health, it follows that a social system is maladaptive where, through external force or the incapacitation of its members, it hampers diversification and the processing of information. It is also dysfunctional within the larger systemic hierarchy when it cannot integrate its members to exist in harmony with other societies or with the ecosphere. If it is alienated from surrounding realities, it imposes this alienation on its members. "To 'adapt' to such a social system is," as Laszlo puts it, "just as desirable as to 'adapt' to a tumor on the brain."[17] Rather, corrective measures are needed in such cases, if the social body is to retrieve the flexibility necessary to survive.

The nature of the intervention, whether reform or revolution, depends on the responsiveness of the institutions. If they are too rigid to be amended by gradual therapy, then radical restructuring may be necessary if the subsystems they comprise are to be readapted to the larger systemic hierarchy.[18]

Within this hierarchy the individual's consciousness represents that systemic interface where biological and social systems meet. Cognitive capacity entails an enormously high degree of both integration and differentiation, and these attributes merge in the human who stands as link between organic and social world—or at that point where they appear as such. On one side he includes biological systems, cells, glands, organs, that are not in themselves differentiated enough for self-reflexivity, and on the other, he participates in social complexes not sufficiently integrated for such consciousness yet to appear. Given the kinds of crises we face, we seem to be approaching the point where social forms of consciousness must emerge if this planetary experiment is to continue.

Our political and economic interdependence may have progressed to a degree where collective self-awareness must manifest itself for the world as we know it to survive. Lively interest and explorations into forms of transpersonal consciousness indicate a widespread sense that this is so. In any case, our responsibility to the political institutions we live with involves an extension of concern, a broadening of identity. From the viewpoint of mutual causality, the evolution of a viable social order cannot be achieved through the balancing of separate private interests. Rather it entails the realization by the participant that life is rooted in an area broader than that defined by the body or identified with individual needs.

By the same token, from the systems view, our adaptation and survival require higher allegiances than those we accord nation-states. A "world system" in which we all inhere is emerging. Charles Dechert, a systems-oriented political scientist, says, "The relational web tying the world into a single international system is growing in intensity . . . built on organic interrelations among territories, nations and functional organizations."[19] Given the systems view of heterogeneity as requisite to organization, Dechert argues that such an evolution does not entail regimentation or uniformity. In fact it is hindered by attempts to impose them.

> Perhaps the greatest enemy of this organic complexification in liberty would be a premature effort to impose oversimplified, formalistic, or centralized bureaucratic structures for which we have today the technical capacity.

The relational web on which our and our children's lives depend can emerge organically as we open to metalevel allegiances.

Right Livelihood and Economic Sharing

This recognition extends to economic institutions and activities as well. As we saw in Chapter 8, mutual causality perceives an interdependent relationship between mind and matter, for consciousness and body represent correlative, or dependently coarising, aspects of existence.

The moral values that impinge on our economic considerations arise, then, from two kinds of interdependence. One is that which exists between persons and is social and transactional in nature. The other is psycho-physical, representing the interconnection between mind and matter. Together these types of invariant reciprocity are such that the satisfaction of material needs and the ways in which we produce, consume, and distribute goods, are integral to our conscious existence, both reflecting and shaping the kinds of persons we are.

Such a vision differs from the preconceptions that have molded the dominant economic strategies of our time. Colored by dualistic apprehensions of mind and matter, these have tended to see economic processes either as the rightful exercise of man's dominance over nature and dumb matter, or as the sole determining source of his being. Whether the individual is understood to labor for the greater glory of God, for a classless society, or for his own status and well-being, his value has been largely measured in terms of the production or consumption of goods. Considerations of short-term economic profitability are so paramount as to have become largely axiomatic in policy determinations. That these considerations are gradually beginning to be questioned is chiefly due to increasing evidence of the ecological destruction and social dislocations they have engendered.

In contrast to this economic view, the Buddhist and cybernetic perspectives on mutual causality place economic activity within the larger context of systemic interdependence. As we saw above, this frame of reference is twofold: on one hand, the intricate, unbroken web which interconnects our lives with the natural environment and with other beings, and, on the other, the reciprocal impact on consciousness of our physical condition and activities. In mutual causality these are givens, more determinative of our adaptability and survival than questions of economic return. As individuals as well as a society, what we do to serve our material needs reflects and conditions our conscious participation in reality. Whether that participation is envisaged as a kind of knowing or a kind of enjoying, it is hindered by want, warped by stultifying, meaningless employment, and obstructed by the denial of the needs of others. The walls we erect to block our perception of the needs of others wall us in also, stifling our capacities to comprehend and adapt.

The economic practices and teaching we find in early Buddhist scripture illustrate the kind of ethics which express these mutual causal assumptions. Central here are the values of nonattachment, economic sharing, and right livelihood.

The Buddha's teaching that suffering stems from craving (the second Noble Truth) places a high value on self-restraint and low consumption. The traditionally mendicant way of the *bhikkhu* (monk), modelled after the Buddha, underscores the conviction that freedom derives not from wealth or the satisfaction of appetite, but resides in nonattachment, in liberation from the restless greed to possess and consume, and from the objects, thoughts, and habits that stimulate that wanting. Private acquisitions, furthermore, are dangerous to the extent they express and exacerbate the notion of "mineness" (*mamattā*), and thus encourage the assumption of an "I," a permanent, personal self who possesses. In the *Aggañña Sutta* the institution of private property is presented as the occasion for the arising of theft, mendacity, and violence. From this Buddhist perspective, the goal of modern advertising to induce the sensation of need and the desire to acquire is immoral, as, for that matter, is an economic system dependent on an ever-widening public consumption of nonessential commodities and artifacts.

As an antidote to attachment and the delusion it engenders, the Buddha preached generosity (*dāna*) and organized a community in which private property was renounced, all goods shared in common. The Sangha comprised as its members *bhikkhus* and *bhikkhunis*, terms which literally mean, not "monk" and "nun," but "sharesman" and "shareswoman," one who receives a share of something. Their alms-begging was not just a handy means of subsistence, but sacramental in nature, betokening their relinquishment of personal wealth and their dependence instead on the public resources of society.[20] The *bhikkhus'* relation to lay society was viewed as reciprocal and symbiotic, since, in return for material support, they provided counsel, delivered teachings, and modeled moral behavior. They also offered the public the opportunity to exercise and experience its own generosity. In later centuries the Sangha's reciprocity included social services, such as hospitals and orphanages maintained by the *bhikkhus*, as well as the erection of monuments, libraries and universities, whereby the Sangha, from the gifts it received, created a rich heritage of art and learning.

In the Buddha's teachings, economic sharing was held out as an ideal for the relations between lay persons as well as *bhikkhus*, and as a prerequisite of a healthy society. While restraint in consumption is seen as salutary, the condition of poverty is not. We recall that the Buddha rejected mortification of the flesh, and affirmed the rightful claims of this body "born of the great elements." Indeed, poverty increases attachment; as the Buddha pointed out, a person cannot listen to the Dharma on an empty stomach.[21]

The responsibility given to the individual in working out his own salvation requires an economics of sufficiency, as Emmanuel Sarkisyanz points out in his work on *The Buddhist Roots of the Burmese Revolution*.[22] Because the restructuring of consciousness is essential to the Path, and because no vicarious means of salvation is offered, the ideal social order as presented in the Pali Canon would allow each person the necessary economic base. Reflecting this assumption, an array of *suttas* and *jātaka* tales portray the wise ruler as engaging in broad public works and providing jobs, food, and shelter to the needy.

These scriptures express the economic interdependence that exists between the state and its citizenry, and the extent to which its health and security is a function of the well-being of all its people. When the king, in the *Kūtadanta Sutta*, desires to offer a great royal ritual sacrifice to ensure his future welfare, he is reminded that crime harries his realm, pillaging towns and making roads unsafe. His chaplain, who is identified as the Buddha himself in a former life, argues that neither fresh taxation nor arrest and punishment of the miscreants will end the disorder. The one way to stop it is to create productive employment opportunities: to give food and seed-corn to the farmers, capital to those who would engage in trade, and food and wages to those who would enter government service. Then "those men, following each his own business, will no longer harass the realm."[23] And, according to the Buddha's story, not only did that happen, but, with the advent of peace and security, the state's revenues went up.

In the *Mahāsudassana Sutta*, the king "of greatest glory" is described, and his magnificence is reflected in the facilities he establishes for the comfort of his people.

> Then, Ānanda, [he] established a perpetual grant by the banks of those lotus-ponds—to wit, food for the hungry, drink for the thirsty, raiment for the naked, means of conveyance for those who needed it, couches for the tired, wives for those who wanted wives, gold for the poor, and money for those who were in want.[24]

Many a *jātaka* tale presents the wise ruler as ministering to his realm in similar fashion, offering resources that serve not only humans, but beasts and birds as well, "so as to extend the benefits down to dumb creation."[25] For all hangs together, and when the king is un-righteous that unrighteousness seeps through society, through of-ficers and Brahmins and townspeople, and then even the sun, moon, and stars go wrong in their course.[26]

This ideal of concern for the common weal was most notably demonstrated in the reign of the Buddhist king Aśoka. As his pillar and rock edicts witness, public works were instituted, roads, wells, hostels, hospitals—the first social welfare services on historical record.

> Moreover I have had banyan trees planted on the roads to give shade to man and beast; I have planted mango groves, and I have had ponds dug and shelters erected along the roads at every eight kos. Everywhere I have had wells dug for the ben-efit of man and beast. . . . What I have done has been done that man may conform to the Dhamma. (Seventh Pillar Edict of Aśoka)[27]

The inherent right to worthwhile work is suggested by the concept of "right livelihood," and by the fact that this features as a requirement of the Buddha's Eightfold Path. The Buddhist view of causality recognizes that the character of a person is both expressed in the work he performs and modified by it, and that therefore high value must be placed on the character of this work. Instead of being considered as a necessary evil to which one is condemned, or as a "disutility," as in the eyes of classical economists, work is a vehicle for the organization and expression of that pattern we call the self. Meaningful employment is more important than the goods it pro-duces, as the *Kūṭadanta Sutta* suggests. Unlike consumption, it links the person to her fellow-beings in reciprocal relationship, and ex-presses the interdependence which underlies her existence. The value of her work, then, is beyond monetary measure. Labor poli-cies and production plans that view this work in terms of pay or profit alone degrade it and rob it of meaning. High wages, high div-idends, high production, or high unemployment payments cannot compensate for the human loss that occurs when assembly-line techniques or joblessness deprive a worker of acquiring and enjoy-ing her skills.

The ethical implications of mutual causality for our economic existence can be seen in cybernetic terms as well, but the utility of general systems theory in this regard has been obscured by its far more extensive application to microeconomic objectives than to macroeconomic concerns. In systems analysis and management, it has been employed as a corporate tool for purposes of efficiency, with little questioning of the values and goals of this "efficiency" within the larger bio-social systemic hierarchy. Yet when the systems paradigm is applied to an understanding of the underlying causes of our economic disorders by such thinkers as Kenneth Boulding, Herman Daly, Hazel Henderson, E. F. Schumacher, and Gunnar Myrdal, it reveals the need to reevaluate the basic assumptions on which industrial society has been built—a reevaluation which emphasizes the concerns for low consumption, equitable sharing and the dignity of work that are found in Buddhist teachings.

When economic patterns and enterprises are viewed within the larger systemic context of the ecological and social costs they inflict, the premises of John Maynard Keynes and Milton Friedman appear as outmoded and dysfunctional. Assuming an unlimited availability of material resources, a stable birth rate, and a nondisruptive technology, their premises measure economic health in terms of productivity, and continue to induce statesmen and classical economists to call for unrestricted growth in production and consumption. The price such policies inflict, in terms of inflation, unemployment, depredations on the environment, and depletion of reserves, are not computed in cost-benefit analyses, but they do appear dramatically when systems thinking broadens the concept of what is "economic."

As Henderson documents, a widespread disaffection with these inappropriate economic assumptions is evident in the sector she terms the "counter-economy."[28] In the revitalization of the cooperative movement, the spread of worker self-management experiments, and a plethora of small-scale alternative economic ventures, new patterns of production, ownership, and consumption are emerging. They stress the moral right to meaningful work, low consumption and broader redistribution of income—values which we have perceived as consistent with the perspective of mutual causality. The articulation and demonstration of these values tend to be limited still to scattered grass-roots efforts on the fringes of our politico-industrial complex, and largely invisible to it. Yet, as the notion of mutual causality implies, radical innovations cannot be imposed from above, but must also be tested and found practical in individual lives, if they are to take root—and that is beginning to happen.

Ends and Means

As has been repeatedly affirmed throughout human history, moral considerations pertain not only to the goals we try to achieve but also to the manner in which we go about trying to achieve them. Frequently these appear at odds with each other, like the "war to end all wars." We all are familiar with the moral anguish that arises when worthy objectives seem only attainable by acts which appear, by their nature, to compromise them.

Within the linear causal paradigm the problem of ends and means has tended to be precisely that—a problem. It stems from an epistemological dichotomy between form (or idea) and matter (or action), a dichotomy which assumes that the goal "out there" has an existence independent of ourselves or the methods we employ. In his concept of final cause (*telos*), Aristotle recognized the determinacy of intention, for *telos* is that "for the sake of" which one acts. Yet this determinacy appears as unidirectional, because *telos*, having the nature of form, immaterial and immutable, operates solely through attraction. It "produces movement or change in other things without itself being affected.[29]

The goal, then, appears more real and more valuable than the activities its existence engenders. "Wherever there are certain ends over and above the actions themselves, it is [their] nature . . . to be better than the activities," says Aristotle in the Nicomachean Ethics.[30] In this gradation of value, each successive stage of activity in art and nature "is for the sake of the one that follows."[31] Acts themselves are, therefore, instrumental to an end whose nature is more final and complete (*teleios*). By the same reasoning the goal, say happiness, "is never chosen" as a means, according to Aristotle, for means by his definition are instrumental and subordinate.[32]

Such presuppositions, harbored in heads less noble than Aristotle's, lead into instrumentalist ways of thinking, where concern for ends overrides considerations of the ethical appropriateness of the means. Such considerations come to appear as moral niceties, welcome where they can be accommodated but, "when push comes to shove," irrelevant to the goal in view—whose attainment may dictate more "pragmatic" and "realistic" choices.

Mutual causality turns this kind of thinking inside out, and does so by virtue of its epistemology. It asserts, as indeed have many saints and teachers over the ages, that the goal is not something "out there," aloof from our machinations, but rather a function of the way itself, interdependent with our acts. As doer is interdeterminate with deed, modified by his own responses in thought and action, so are his objectives modified. For however he articulates these objectives, they reflect his present perceptions and interpretations of reality—perceptions and interpretations which are altered, however slightly, by every cognitive event. Such a view breaches the instrumentalist dichotomy between the pragmatic and the moral, for here means are not subordinate to ends so much as creative of them—they are ends-in-the-making.

In cybernetic terms this interdependence of ends and means is a function of feedback. We saw how the idea of feedback, arising with the discovery that open systems are self-guiding, affirmed the significance of purpose, a notion earlier banished from science as nonempirical and "subjective." To the systems theorist purpose emerges as an inherent characteristic of open systems in their self-maintenance and self-organization.

> There can be no rational explanation of behavior that overlooks the overriding influence of an organism's present structure of goals . . . and there can be no non-trivial description of responses that leaves out purposes.[33]

While goals shape behavior, the operation of feedback is such that they are in turn shaped by it, modified or refined by the flow of information and the events in the system. There is, as Rosenblueth and Wiener put it, a "two-way relationship" between goal and behavior, or ends and means. Hence in general systems theory purpose is seen as emergent, rather than preexisting or supratemporal in nature. Stressing this distinction, Laszlo qualifies it as telenomic or "telic" rather than teleological.[34]

If goals are emergent, co-arising with the system's dynamic interaction with its environment, they are never completely realizable. As the context within which the system operates is itself dynamic, the goal of complete adaptation and intelligibility is always just out of reach. As von Bertalanffy recognized in condemning the notion of stasis or rest-equilibrium, it appears that the system itself is geared to and enjoys this out-of-reachness. Systems theorists Ackoff and Emery acknowledge this by qualifying the cognitive system as "ideal-setting": pursuing objectives which it may know it can never fully attain, but from the pursuit of which it derives satisfaction.[35] This satisfaction in incomplete satisfaction or out-of-reachness would be anathema to behaviorist psychologists, who assume that the organism seeks tension reduction. It is expressed rather neatly by novelist Edith Wharton when she writes of the good things she has savored in life: "I shall go away grateful—if not satisfied. Satisfied! What a beggarly state! Who would be satisfied with being satisfied?"[36]

From the cybernetic perspective, then, ends are open-ended. Their value for us is not as states we much achieve, come what may, or blueprints by virtue of which we manipulate persons and objects, but as ever-unfolding visions of what is valuable. The means we employ to realize the vision are steps taken in consequence of it. And each step expands or alters this vision, for what is realized, made real, are our acts themselves.

In the path of salvation the Buddha sets forth, the Dharma is offered not as a goal to be reached so much as a way, *magga*. Each step on this way is of intrinsic value, the Dharma being "glorious in the beginning, glorious in the middle, glorious at the end."[37] Value is intrinsic to each act because action (karma) represents, in the last analysis, what we are and what we become. Although we are summoned to strive, to transform our lives and our consciousness, we do so with the paradoxical knowledge that, though we may feel very far from where we want to be, there is no place to get to, for we are already there, or, as Jesus put it, "the kingdom of God is within you." This religious paradox, manifest in many faiths, overturns the problem of ends and means in much the same way as does the cybernetic perspective. For in mutual causality, whether viewed religiously or scientifically, the views we hold are not distant from us in time or space, but present realities, unfolding out of the core of our existence and capable of transforming it in the present moment.

Like Lao-Tzu and Confucius, and to a large extent like Jesus also, the Buddha presented moral conduct as self-validating, and not deriving its worth from any standard external to it. Acts characterized by loving-kindness, mindfulness, and self-restraint are seen as good in their own right rather than as means to another end, even that of *nirvāna*. As the Buddhist scholar Bastow expresses it, "accounts of the Way in the Suttas are never introduced as method to achieve freedom from rebirth, rather as the proper way to live the higher life, as an account of true righteousness and true wisdom." The Buddha and his early followers understood "the Way as a progressive revelation of the possibilities of self-restraint and the freedom resulting therefrom."[38] The absence, in Buddhist moral teachings, of any transcendental referent for the sake of which one acts has rendered it difficult to define the metaphysical basis of Buddhist ethics in traditional Western terms. For here no supernatural sanctions operate. There is neither an absolute entity nor even an enduring self, in whose terms the good is measured or for whose pleasure the good is done.

Taking issue with these assertions, a reader might argue that Buddhist ethics are indeed goal oriented, the goal being *nirvāna* or enlightenment or the cessation of suffering. But, let us remember, these do not represent an external objective which the self can attain, nor a body of information the self can acquire. Rather they represent the very eclipse of self: the radical transformation that occurs when the illusions of separate egohood are relinquished. And this alters the idea itself of a goal. For there is nothing the self we now experience is going to get and no place it is going to go—except, perhaps, "out" like a blown candle. Though we are summoned to endeavor, to make progress on the path, such exertions of will are not in order to grasp a desired goal so much as to loosen the grip of the desiring ego itself.

While moral conduct (*śila*) is not instrumental to a superordinate goal, neither is it irrelevant, for deeds shape the doer. By their own momentum they carry us on the way, just as the practice of *metta*, for example, relaxes the bonds of ego. *Śila* is equivalent in value to wisdom itself, the very insight into the nature of reality. As declared in the *Sutta,* they are as equal and necessary to each other as our two hands.

> From morality comes wisdom and from wisdom morality. . . .
> Like washing one hand with the other . . . so is morality
> washed round with wisdom and wisdom with morality.[39]

This interplay between act and insight is comparable to that between means and ends. The Pali term for means is *upāya,* and in the early texts the skillful use of means (*upāya-kosalla*) in presenting the Dharma is recognized as a mark of the good teacher.[40] In the Mahayana skillful means (Sanskrit:*upāya-kausalya*) is a characteristic of the *bodhisattva,* covalent with wisdom and essential to enlightenment.[41] It is seen as a manifestation of compassion and necessary for its expression. Later, in Buddhist tantric symbolism, *upāya* appears as wisdom's consort. Their connubial embrace symbolizes the interplay of thought and act, the interdependence of insight and its manifestation in the world. No mere instrumentality, *upāya* is wisdom in action—the action that both reveals insight and deepens it in turn, in reciprocal relation.

In considering the kind of morality that mutual causality entails, we have seen that extension of self-interest in lively concern for the welfare of other beings is central. The acknowledgement of reciprocal relationship provides the context for our politics and economics. The goals we set and our attitudes toward them are not dogmatic, but characterized by both tolerance of other views and readiness to question our own. The effective pursuit of these goals entails the awareness that they are not separate from our acts, but conditioned by them in the continual co-arising of ends and means.

The ethical norms we have examined do not issue from the command nor require the sanction of an absolute being. Nor do they derive from it their authority. They are grounded in the very relativity that, in the mutual causal view, conditions all existence. These norms and values reveal that the liberation of the individual and the health of her society are inseparable. Indeed, they point to a profound mutuality between personal and social transformation.

Notes

1. Deming, and Meyerding, *We Are All Part of One Another.*

2. Laszlo, *Introduction to Systems Philosophy,* pp. 277, 8.

3. *Ibid.,* pp. 282–90.

4. *Sutta Nipata,* I, 8, 149–50.

5. von Bertalanffy, *General Systems Theory,* p. 248.

6. Gray, *et al. General Systems Theory and Psychiatry,* p. 33.

7. von Glasersfeld and Varela, "Problems of Knowledge," p. 22.

8. *Anguttara Nikāya,* II.24.

9. The Buddha's defiance of social strictures is especially meaningful today to the "new Buddhists" of India, the millions of ex-Untouchables who, in the last decades, have followed their leader Ambedkar into the Buddhist faith.

10. *Dīgha Nikāya,* I.99.

11. Ghosal, *History of Political Ideas,* Chapter IV.

12. *Dīgha Nikāya,* II.77.

13. *Vinaya,* Cullavagga IV, XII.

14. Dutt, *Buddhist Monks*, pp. 74–121.

15. Deutsch, "Toward a Cybernetic Model," pp. 398–99.

16. Maruyama, "Symbiotization," pp. 127f.

17. Laszlo, *Introduction to Systems Philosophy*, p. 273.

18. *Ibid.*, p. 274.

19. Dechert, "Integration and Change," pp. 136f.

20. Ling, *The Buddha*, p. 123.

21. *Anguttara Nikāya*, VI.45.

22. Sarkisyanz, *Buddhist Background*, pp. 56f.

23. *Dīgha Nikāya*, I.135.

24. *Ibid.*, II.180.

25. Jātakas 501, 540, cf. Ghoshal, *History of Indian Politics*, pp. 70f.

26. *Anguttara Nikāya*, II.74–76; Jātaka 334, cf. Ghoshal, *History of Indian Politics*, p. 72.

27. Stryk, *World of the Buddha*, p. 245.

28. Henderson, *Creating Alternative Futures*, pp. 381–99.

29. *Aristotle: Natural Science*, p. 35.

30. *Ibid.*, p. 109.

31. *Ibid.*, p. 38.

32. *Ibid.*, p. 119.

33. Powers, "Feedback," p. 352.

34. Laszlo, *Introduction to Systems Philosophy*, p. 176.

35. Ackoff and Emery, "Ideal-Setting Systems."

36. Wolff, *Feast of Words*.

37. Vinaya, I.113.

38. Bastow, "Buddhist Ethics," pp. 195–206.

39. *Dīgha Nikāya*, I.124.

40. *Ibid.*, III.220.

41. Conze, *Perfection of Wisdom*.

12

The Dialectics of Personal
and Social Transformation

Go forth on your journey, for the benefit of the many, for the joy of
the many, out of compassion for the welfare, for the benefit and joy of
all beings.

—The Buddha[1]

Moral values are not acquired by intellectual assent alone, as
many religious teachers have affirmed, but involve a reorganization
of personality. By the same token, they do not transform society unless they transform the doer himself. Otherwise institutional reform
or revolution is "turning over the dung heap," the dispossessed taking power with the same ignorance and self-serving as their oppres-
sors. So tenaciously do we cling to our notions of self-interest that
even the noblest of ideals and ideologies can be subverted to our
private purposes.

The need to break the bonds of self-centeredness, both for social equity and the cessation of our own pain, has been a central
message of the world's religions, expressed through story and
creed. What do we do with this clamoring ego, this posturing "I"
that distorts our perceptions, warps our endeavors? Religious faiths
offer means of transcending it by setting it into larger perspectives.
Whether the overcoming of the ego is imaged in terms of sacrifice
or crucifixion or becoming one with the Father, the common element is the transformation that occurs as consciousness encounters
and opens to wider dimensions of reality.

The perspective of mutual causality suggests that, while such
images have efficacy and depth, there is, in the last analysis, no
abiding self to be sacrificed or crucified. This is because it is not a
self-existent entity, but a fluid and changing pattern, a process in-

terlinked and co-arising with the entire universe. What is to be overcome, or rather "seen through," is not this stream of events, this fountain of thoughts and feelings, but the construct of "I" we impose upon it and the assumption that it is separate from other beings.

Free to Reconnect

Open systems go through stages of "positive disintegration" before reorganizing into more inclusive and adaptable wholes. This ongoing self-organization requires an ever increasing openness on the part of the cognitive system, and the relinquishing of constructs that are no longer valid. Since the pattern or personality is organized by virtue of these codes, this movement represents a kind of dying—or at least a readiness to die, in letting go of old habits and self-definitions. As open systems we are in constant metamorphosis, and if with our free will we support the system's capacity for adaptation and survival, this metamorphosis involves a progressive dying to our own separateness and an increasing internalization of the needs and joys of others. This process, a function of positive feedback, is evident in evolution, where new life emerges with the letting go of outgrown modes. For the cognitive system such an outgrown mode is the illusion of separate selfhood, because the pursuit of this self's own claims, certitudes, and possessions is dysfunctional both to the cognitive system itself and to the larger systemic hierarchy.

We have seen how such a perspective is presented in Buddhist terms. The four Noble Truths, the teaching of the *khaṇḍas* and of *anattā* and, at the root of these, the doctrine of *paticca samuppāda*, all proclaim that the ego to which we are in bondage is a fiction. As we are urged to experience for ourselves in meditative practice, there is in reality no self separate from our experiencing, no self we need to protect, punish, improve, or even sacrifice. Being illusory, its appetites for security can never be quenched. This realization offers release from that squirrel cage where ego runs in circles of pain and futility.

Such a realization, however, is so counter to our ingrown operating assumptions that it requires diligent practice to unhinge them, to defuse the defenses that trigger our cravings and angers. Ego reactions and claims are not to be suppressed so much as dissolved in the clear strong light of meditative awareness. While it can be frightening to encounter a void where we thought a substantial self resided, this initially scary emptiness, if passed through like a door, opens into a greater connectedness with the phenomenal world of beings.[2] The sense of intrinsic relatedness, into which one then moves, becomes both the occasion and means of love.

Meditative practice that makes this possible is not, therefore, at odds with the imperatives for social action. Nor are efforts for institutional change antithetical to the search for enlightenment. Spiritual development in its contemplative mode has often been seen as an escape from social engagement and responsibility. Sometimes it is—when the inner objects of contemplation are considered more valuable or more real than the world outside. But skillful meditation, that journey into the wilderness where we confront our own tricks and delusions, can empower social action, freeing us to respond in simplicity and immediacy to our fellow beings. There is no sequential chronology here, no question of having *first* to get saved or enlightened—or even get our "heads straight"—before being ready or worthy to act, for doing and knowing are interdependent.

The grip of ego is weakened not only in meditation, but also in acting on behalf of others. The risk-taking and courage which moral action often requires can catapult us beyond constructs of individual self-interest. We are shot into a larger space where the old boundaries of self dissolve and the interdependence of all life-forms is brought into vivid focus. This dialectic between act and insight is represented by the Buddhist tantric figures we mentioned above, by the embrace of wisdom with her consort, compassionate and skillful means. Different as they are, she aloof and serene, he vigorous and dynamic, neither stands alone; each empowers the other. Mutually causative, they symbolize the dance of polarities at the heart of this dependently co-arising universe.

The Tree and the Flame

Two images appear in both general systems theory and early Buddhist teachings, as these two bodies of thought convey their vision of mutual causality. These are the tree and the flame.

We encountered the tree image in general systems theory. Symbolic of the manner in which systems and subsystems hierarchically structure themselves, growing out of and into each other like trunk and branches and limbs, the tree represents relationship. It images the multiformity and unity of our interconnectedness as holons, from atom to person to community and ecosystem.

Tree is also a dominant feature in early Buddhist imagery. There it appears both as *bodhi* tree, under which Gotama sat and gained enlightenment, and as the wishing tree which, laden with the good things of life, bestows the answers to our hearts' desires.

Originating as a motif in early Indian tree-worship, it came then to symbolize for the Buddhist world both wisdom and plenty, consciousness *and* nature. Carved on stone gates, pillars, and railings, the tree abounds: sometimes as *bodhi* tree representing the Buddha's enlightenment, sometimes as wishing tree, with jugs, cakes, even lovely human forms, issuing from its fruitful branches. Sometimes, as at Sanchi, it is shown aflame, with fire at its roots or branches blazing.

And that is our second image, flame. It appeared at the outset of general systems theory, as noted in Chapter 6. Von Bertalanffy, Brillouin, Wiener and others used this image to convey how the open system endures in shape while constantly altered by metabolic events. As the open system consumes the matter that passes through it, burning it, so metaphorically does it process information—ever breaking down and building up, renewed. Like fire, it both transforms and is transformed by that on which it feeds. Flame then represents the metabolic nature of life, and the nature of our identity as selves.

This metaphor features in the Buddha Dharma as well, from the first teaching the Buddha gave at Gaya, the fire sermon. "Everything, O bhikkhus, is burning. . . . "[3] Later when he explained the arising of consciousness the image of flame was also employed, the mind igniting and feeding on sensory perceptions like a fire burning from grass or sticks.[4] And when selfhood is extinguished, it is like a candle blown out—that blowing-out serving etymologically as the source of the word *nibbāna*. While fire in the Buddhist texts appears generally to be accorded negative valence, in contrast to the coolness of *nibbāna* which quenches the burning of ego-striving, that is not always the case. Our nature is such that even our perceptions of bliss and peace and *nibbāna* arise in us like flame, as Śariputra said. "Just as, friend, when a faggot fire is blazing one flame arises and other flame fades out, even so one perception arises in me, 'cessation of becoming is nibbāna,' and another perception fades out, 'cessation of becoming is nibbāna'."[5] Whether negatively or positively valued, our co-arising with the world is an igniting, as transient as flame and as dependent on that which feeds it.

Tree and flame are images central in other faiths as well. They are seen by many scholars and depth psychologists as archetypal to the human spirit. As Iggdrasil and *arbor vitae*, tree of knowledge and tree on which the Christ was nailed, the tree transects and interconnects the levels of our world; it is a symbol of the Axis Mundi. That the essence of this interconnected world is like fire is also affirmed by many who have known it in the raw immediacy of mystical experience. When in the *Bhagavad Gita* Krishna reveals his true nature as the god Vishnu, he turns to flame; mouths and eyes ablaze, his irradiating splendor fills the world and into him as into a living furnace all beings are drawn. As burning bush and pillar of fire did Jahweh appear to the Jews, and to the Christians at Pentecost the holy spirit poured out in tongues of flame. On the night of the vision that changed his life, all that Pascal could write to describe it was the word "FIRE." "FIRE . . . God of Abraham, God of Isaac, God of Jacob . . . Certitude . . . Joy."[6]

What have tree and flame to do with the ethics of mutual causality? Significant to both general systems theory and early Buddhist teachings, these images serve to convey the interdependence of our lives and also the process by which transformation takes place. Or, to put it another way, they symbolize the reciprocal interplay of structure and process. Like roots, trunk, and branches, we beings are interconnected and part of each other. Our griefs and hopes are not separate, nor can our fulfillments be private, for we are as organically linked as a tree. To act with this knowledge, and shape our lives and institutions to reflect it, requires transformations that threaten our comfort and security. It requires a dying to old ways. This is easier to accept and face when we realize that, like a flame, we are ever dying and renewing, for that is the nature of things.

The black preacher in Albany, Georgia, who called his congregation on a civil rights march to jail, did so by using such an image. He said, "Everything shines by perishing." He warned his people of the police dogs waiting, but summoned them anyway, saying, "The sun uses up its energy at a fantastic rate of speed and so does a candle perish as it shines. And so do you and me. We all shine by perishing."[7]

To close we let these two images merge. Arthur Koestler, in describing the structure and process of open systems, puts them together. In a paper entitled "The Tree and the Candle," honoring the work of von Bertalanffy, Koestler suggests that they represent our nature as natural cognitive systems. The holonic structure, reticulating into subsystems and merging in larger branches, is that of a tree, while the process by which it happens in the transformation of energy and information is like that of a flame.[8]

Such is the perspective on existence which mutual causality presents. As ephemeral as flame, we are also as interrelated as parts of a tree—out of whose interweaving relationships we cannot fall, for we are they. By virtue of our very incandescence, we can sense our interconnections and let the knowing and the caring they permit take root and branch through us. As the Buddha's teachings attest, the realization of both transiency and relationship breaks down the walls of ego; freeing us from that anxious cell, it releases the heart to loving-kindness, the will to self-restraint and sharing. And the mind, that conditioned and co-arising flame, seeks then not to flee its interdependence with all phenomena, but rather opens in awareness and joy to that of which it is indissolubly a part.

Notes

1. *Vinaya*, I,21.

2. The recognition that encounter with emptiness of own-being can be alarming is implicit in the gesture of *abhaya*, "fear not," that is found in graphic portrayals of the Buddha, and later on in those of Prajñāpāramitā, who represents the wisdom of seeing into emptiness.

3. *Vinaya*, I,21.

4. *Majjhima Nikāya*, I,259–60.

5. *Aṅguttara Nikāya*, V.9f.

6. Pascal, *Pensees*, pp. 309–310.

7. SNCC, *Freedom in the Air.*

8. Koestler, "Tree and Candle," pp. 287f.

Bibliography

Ackoff, R. L. and F. E. Emery. "Ideal-Setting Systems," *General Systems* XVII, SGSR, 1972.

Allport, Gordon. "The Open System in Personality Theory," in Buckley, Walter, editor. *Modern Systems Research for the Behavioral Scientist*. Chicago: Aldine Publishing Co., 1968.

Anguttara Nikāya, edited by Morris and Hardy, PTS 1885–1900. Translated as *Gradual Sayings* by F. L. Woodward, PTS. London: Luzac & Co., 1960.

Areiti, Silvano. "Toward a Unifying Theory of Cognition," in Gray, William, *et al. General Systems Theory and Psychiatry*. Boston: Little, Brown & Co., 1969.

Aristotle: Natural Science, Psychology and Nicomachean Ethics, edited and translated by P. Wheelwright. New York: Odyssey Press, 1935.

Ashby, W. Ross. "Principles of the Self-Organizing System." in Buckley, Walter, ed. *Modern Systems Research for the Behavioral Scientist*. Chicago: Aldine Publishing, 1968.

———. "Variety, Constraint, and the Law of Requisite Variety," in Buckley, Walter, editor. *Modern Systems Research for the Behavioral Scientist*. Chicago: Aldine Publishing, 1968.

Bastow, David. "Buddhist Ethics." *Religious Studies* V.

Bardwell, Stephen. "Nonlinearity and the Biological Sciences." *Fusion Energy Foundation Newsletter* II/4 (May 1977).

Barks, Coleman, and John Moynes. *Open Secrets, Versions of Rumi*. Putney, Vermont: Threshold Books. 1984.

Bateson, Gregory. *Steps to an Ecology of Mind*. New York: Ballantine Books, 1972.

Berne, Eric. *Games People Play*. New York: Grove Press, 1964.

von Bertalanffy, Ludwig. *General Systems Theory*. New York: George Braziller, 1968.

———. "General Systems Theory—A Critical Review," in Buckley, Walter, editor. *Modern Systems Research for the Behavioral Scientist*. Chicago: Aldine Publishing, 1968.

————. "General Systems Theory—An Overview," in Gray, William, *et al.* *General Systems Theory and Psychiatry.* Boston: Little, Brown & Co., 1969.

————. *Perspectives on General Systems Theory.* New York: George Braziller, 1975.

————. *Robots, Men and Minds.* New York: George Braziller, 1967.

The Bhagavad Gita, Franklin Edgerton tr., N.Y.: Harper Torchbooks, 1964, Chapter XI, pp. 55ff.

Boulding, Kenneth. "Business and Economic Systems," in Milsum, John H. *Positive Feedback.* London: Pergamon Press, 1968.

————. "Economics and General Systems," in Laszlo, Ervin. *The Relevance of General Systems Theory.* New York: George Braziller, 1972.

————. "General Systems Theory—the Skeleton of Science." *General Systems I,* SGSR, 1956.

Brand, Stewart. *II Cybernetic Frontiers.* New York: Random House, 1974.

Brillouin, Leon. "Life, Thermodynamics and Cybernetics," in Buckley, Walter, editor. *Modern Systems Research for the Behavioral Scientist.* Chicago: Aldine Publishing, 1968.

Brown, George Spencer. *The Laws of Form.* New York: Julian Press, 1972.

Buckley, Walter, editor. *Modern Systems Research for the Behavioral Scientist.* Chicago: Aldine Publishing, 1968.

Buddhaghosa, *Visuddhimagga.* Translated by Ñanamoli: as *The Path of Purification.* Colombo: R. Semage, 1956.

Bunge, Mario. *Causality: The Place of the Causal Principle in Modern Science.* Cambridge: Harvard Univ. Press, 1959.

Burhoe, Ralph W. "Civilization of the Future." *Philosophy Forum,* 1973.

Burnouf, Eugene. *Introduction à l'histoire du bouddhisme indien.* Paris: Imprimerie Royale, 1844.

Capra, Fritjof. *The Turning Point.* New York: Simon & Schuster, 1982.

Conze, Edward. *Buddhist Thought in India.* Ann Arbor: Univ. of Michigan Press, 1970.

————. *The Perfection of Wisdom in Eight Thousand Lines and Its Verse Summary (Aṣṭasāhasrikāprajñāpāramitā).* Berkeley: Bookpeople, 1973.

————. *Thirty Years of Buddhist Studies.* Columbia, S.C.: Univ. of South Carolina Press, 1968.

Coomaraswamy, A. K. *Buddha and the Gospel of Buddhism*. London: George C. Harrap, 1928.

Copleston, Frederick, S. J. *A History of Philosophy*. New York: Doubleday, 1946.

Corrigan, Theresa and Hoppe, Stephanie, editors. *With a Fly's Eye, A Whale's Wit and a Woman's Heart*. San Francisco: Cleis Press, 1989.

Dechert, Charles R. "Integration and Change in Political and International Systems," in Milsum, John H. *Positive Feedback*. London: Pergamon Press, 1968.

Demiéville, Paul. "Le Mémoire des vies anterieures." BEFEO, XXVII, 1927.

Deming, Barbara, and Jane Meyerding. *We Are All Part of One Another*. Philadelphia: New Society Publishers, 1984.

Deutsch, Karl. "Toward a Cybernetic Model of Man and Society," in Buckley, Walter, editor. *Modern Systems Research for the Behavioral Scientist*. Chicago: Aldine Publishing, 1968.

Dīgha Nikāya, or *Dialogues of the Buddha*. Part I: translated by T. W. Rhys Davids, London, PTS 1899, reprinted 1977. Parts II & III: translated by T. W. and C. A. F. Rhys Davids, London PTS 1910, 1921, reprinted 1977.

Dhammapada and Khuddakapatha, edited and translated by C. Rhys Davids, SBB VII. London: Oxford Univ. Press, 1931.

Dhammasaṇgani, edited by J. Kashyapa. Nalanda-Devanagari Pali Ganthamalaya, 1960. Translated by C. Rhys Davids as *Buddhist Manual of Psychological Ethics*. London: Royal Asiatic Society, 1923.

Donne, John. *The Complete Poetry and Selected Prose of John Donne*. Edited by Charles M. Coffin. New York: Random House, 1952.

Van Doren, Mark. "Undersong," in *Poet's Choice*, edited by Paul Engle and Joseph Langland. New York: Time-Life Books, 1962.

Dubin, Robert. "Causality and Social Systems Analysis." IJGS, II, 1975.

Dudley, Guilford, III. "Mircea Eliade as Anti-Historian of Religion." *Journal American Academy of Religion*, XLIV, June 1976.

Dutt, Nalinaksha. *Early Monastic Buddhism*. Calcutta: Calcutta Oriental Book Agency, 1960.

Dutt, Sukumar. *The Buddha and the Five After-Centuries*. London: Luzac & Co., 1957.

————. *Buddhist Monks and Monasteries of India*. London: George Allen & Unwin Ltd., 1962.

Engle, Paul, and Joseph Langland, editors. *Poet's Choice*, New York: Time-Life Books, 1962, p. 25.

Everett, William W. "Cybernetics and the Symbolic Body Model." *Zygon* VII (1972).

Fischer, Roland. "A Cartography of the Ecstatic and Meditative States." *Science* 174, No. 4012, 1971.

Frankl, Viktor E. "Beyond Pluralism and Determinism," in Buckley, Walter, editor. *Modern Systems Research for the Behavioral Scientist*. Chicago: Aldine Publishing, 1968.

————. "Reductionism and Nihilism," in Koestler, Arthur, editor. *Beyond Reductionism: New Perspectives in the Life Sciences*. The Alpbach Symposium. London: Hutchinson & Co., 1969.

Fuller, R. Buckminster. *I Seem to be a Verb*. New York: Bantam Books, 1970.

————. *Synergetics*. New York: Macmillan Publishing Co., 1975.

Ghoshal, U. N. *A History of Indian Political Ideas*. London: Oxford Univ. Press, 1959.

von Glasersfeld, Ernst, and F. Varela. "Problems of Knowledge and Cognizing Organisms." *SGSR/AAAS Proceedings*. Denver 1977.

Gomez, L. O. "Some Aspects of Free-will in the Nikāyas." *Philosophy East and West* XXV/i.

Govinda, Anagarika. *The Psychological Attitude of Early Buddhist Philosophy*. New York: Samuel Weiser, Inc., 1971.

Gray, William. "Bertalanffian Principles as a Basis for Humanistic Psychiatry," in Laszlo, Ervin. *Relevance of General Systems Theory*. New York: George Braziller, 1972.

————., F. Duhl, and N. Rizzo. *General Systems Theory and Psychiatry*. Boston: Little, Brown & Co., 1969.

————and N. Rizzo. *Unity in Diversity*. New York: Gordon and Breach, 1973.

Griffin, Susan. *Woman and Nature: The Roaring Inside Her*. New York: Harper & Row, 1978.

Guenther, Herbert. *Buddhist Philosophy in Theory and Practice*. Baltimore: Penguin Books, 1972.

Hartshorne, Charles. *Philosophers Speak of God*. Chicago: Univ. of Chicago Press, 1953.

Henderson, Hazel. *Creating Alternative Futures: The End of Economics*. New York: Berkley Publishing Co., 1978.

Horner, I. B., editor and translator. *Middle Length Sayings (Majjhima Nikāya)*, PTS. London: Luzac & Co., 1954–59.

Hume, Robert E., translator. *The Thirteen Principal Upanishads*. London: Oxford Univ. Press, 1877.

Jackson, Don D. "The Individual and the Larger Contexts," in Gray *et al. General Systems Theory and Psychiatry*. Boston: Little, Brown & Co., 1969.

Jātakas or Stories of the Buddha's Former Births, edited by E. B. Cowell & translated by various scholars. Cambridge 1895–1907, reprinted PTS, London 1957.

Jayatilleke, K. N. *Early Buddhist Theory of Knowledge*. London: George Allen & Unwin, 1963.

———. *Survival and Karma in Buddhist Perspective*. Kandy: Buddhist Publication Society, 1969.

Kalupahana, D. J. *Buddhist Philosophy: A Historical Analysis*. Honolulu: Univ. of Hawaii Press, 1976.

———. *Causality: The Central Philosophy of Buddhism*. Honolulu: Univ. of Hawaii Press, 1975.

Karunaratne, T. B. *The Buddhist Wheel Symbol*. Kandy: Buddhist Publication Society, 1969.

Katthāvatthu, translated by C. Rhys Davids and S. Z. Aung as *Points of Controversy* PTS. London: Luzac & Co., 1960.

Keith, A. B. *Buddhist Philosophy in India and Ceylon*. Varanasi, Chowkhamba Sanskrit Series, 1963.

Koestler, Arthur. *The Ghost in the Machine*. London: Hutchinson, 1967.

———. "The Tree and the Candle," in Gray *et al. General Systems Theory and Psychiatry*. Boston: Little, Brown & Co., 1973.

———, editor. *Beyond Reductionism: New Perspectives in the Life Sciences*, The Alpbach Symposium. London: Hutchinson & Co., 1969.

Kramer, Ernest. "Man's Behavior Patterns," in Milsum, John H. *Positive Feedback*. London: Pergamon Press, 1968.

Kuhn, T. S. *The Structure of Scientific Revolutions.* Chicago: University of Chicago Press, 1970.

Lamotte, Étienne. *Histoire du bouddhisme indien.* Louvain: Museon, 1958.

Land, T. George Lock. *Grow or Die, the Unifying Principle of Transformation.* New York: Random House, 1973.

Laszlo, Ervin. *Essential Society: An Ontological Reconstruction.* The Hague: Nijhoff, 1963.

———. *Introduction to Systems Philosophy.* New York: Harper Torchbook, 1973.

———. *Strategy for the Future.* New York: George Braziller, 1974.

———. *System, Structure and Experience.* New York: Gordon and Breach, 1969.

———. *Systems View of the World.* New York: George Braziller, 1972.

———, editor. *The Relevance of General Systems Theory.* New York: George Braziller, 1972.

Lee, Orlan. "From Acts—to Non-Action—to Acts." *History of Religions* VI/4 (May 1967).

Ling, Trevor. *The Buddha: Buddhist Civilization in India and Ceylon.* New York: Charles Scriber's Sons, 1973.

Loomer, Bernard. "Two Conceptions of Power." *Process Studies,* Spring 1977.

Macy, Joanna. *Despair and Personal Power in the Nuclear Age.* Philadelphia: New Society Publishers, 1983.

———. *Dharma and Development.* West Hartford, Connecticut: Kumarian Press, 1983.

Majjhima Nikāya, edited by Trenckner & Chalmers, PTS. Oxford Univ. Press, Geoffrey Cumberlege, 1948–51. Translated by I. B. Horner as *Middle Length Sayings,* PTS. London: Luzac & Co., 1954–59.

Makridakis, Spyros. "The Second Law of Systems." *International Journal of General Systems* IV/1 (Sept. 1977).

Maruyama, Magoroh. "Mutual Causality in General Systems," in Milsum, John H. *Positive Feedback.* London: Pergamon Press, 1968.

———. "Paradigmatology and its Application to Cross-Disciplinary, Cross-Professional and Cross-Cultural Communication." *Cybernetics* XVII (1974).

————. "The Second Cybernetics: Deviation-Amplifying Mutual Causal Processes," in Buckley, Walter, editor. *Modern Systems Research for the Behavioral Scientist*. Chicago: Aldine Publishing, 1968.

————. "Symbiotization of Cultural Heterogeneity." *General Systems XVIII*, SGSR, 1973.

Maturana, Humberto, and Francisco J. Varela. *The Tree of Knowledge*. Boston: Shambhala, 1987.

Meyerding, Jane, editor. *We Are All Part of One Another*. Philadelphia, New Society Publ, 1984.

Milindapanha, edited by Trenckner. London: Royal Asiatic Society, 1928. Translated by T. W. Rhys Davids, SBE, vol. 35–6. Oxford: Clarendon Press, 1890–94.

Miller, James G. "Living Systems: Basic Concepts," in Gray, William, *et al. General Systems Theory and Psychiatry*. Boston: Little, Brown & Co., 1969.

Milsum, John H. *Positive Feedback*. London: Pergamon Press, 1968.

Mizuno, K. *Primitive Buddhism*, translated by K. Yamamoto. Ube, Japan: Karinbunko, 1969.

Mowrer, O. H. "Ego Psychology, Cybernetics and Learning Theory," in Buckley, Walter, editor. *Modern Systems Research for the Behavioral Scientist*. Chicago: Aldine Publishing, 1968.

Myrdal, Gunnar. *Economic Theory and Underdeveloped Regions*. London: Duckworth, 1957.

Ñāṇananda, Bhikkhu. *Concept and Reality in Early Buddhist Thought*. Kandy: Buddhist Publication Society, 1971.

————. *The Magic of the Mind*. Kandy: Buddhist Publication Society, 1974.

New Settler Interview, The, Willetts, California, July 1989.

Nyanatiloka, Bhikkhu. *Guide through the Abhidharma Pitaka*. Colombo: Lake House, 1938.

Oldenberg, Hermann. *Buddha: His Life, His Doctrine, His Order*. Delhi: Indological Book House, 1971.

Pande, G. C. *Studies in the Origins of Buddhism*. Allahabad: Dept. of Ancient History, Culture and Archeology, 1957.

Pascal, Blaise. *Pensées*, translated by A. J. Crailsheimer, Baltimore: Penguin Books, 1966.

Pattee, Howard, editor. *Hierarchy Theory*. New York: George Braziller, 1973.

Plotinus. *Ennead* 5.21.1 and 5.1.6, cited by William R. Inge, in *The Philosophy of Plotinus*. London: Longmans, Green & Co., 1929.

Poussin, Louis de la Vallée. *Théorie des Douze Causes*. London: Luzac & Co., 1913.

Powers, W. T. "Feedback: Beyond Behaviorism." *Science*, Vol. 179, 1973.

Rapoport, Anatol. "A Philosophic View," in Milsum, John H. *Positive Feedback*. London: Pergamon Press, 1968.

Rahula, Walpola. *What the Buddha Taught*. New York: Grove Press, 1974.

Reese, William L. *Dictionary of Philosophy and Religion: Eastern and Western Thought*. New Jersey, Humanities Press, 1980.

Rhys Davids, Caroline A. F. "On the Will in Buddhism." *Journal of the Royal Asiatic Society*, 1898.

————. "Paṭicca Samuppāda." *Hastings' Encyclopaedia of Religion and Ethics*, vol. IX. New York: Charles Scribner's Sons, 1924–27.

————, editor and translator. *Book of the Kindred Sayings (Saṃyutta Nikāya)*, PTS. London: Luzac & Co., 1917–30.

————, and S. Z. Aung, editors and translators. *Points of Controversy (Kathāvatthu)*, PTS. London: Luzac & Co., 1960.

Rhys Davids, T. W. *Buddhist India*. Delhi: Indological Book House, 1970.

————, editor and translator. *Dialogues of the Buddha (Dīgha Nikāya)*, PTS. London: Routledge & Kegan Paul Ltd., 1973–77.

————, and Wm. Stede. *Pali-English Dictionary*, PTS. London, 1947–49.

Rilke, Rainer Maria. *Duino Elegies*, translated by C. F. MacIntyre. Berkeley: Univ. of California Press, 1968.

Rosen, Robert. "Complexity as a System Property." *International Journal of General Systems* III/IV (May 1977).

Rosenblueth, Arturo. *Mind and Brain*. Cambridge: Harvard Univ. Press, 1970.

Rothschuh, K. E. "The Mind-Body Problem," in Gray, William, and N. Rizzo. *Unity in Diversity*. New York: Gordon and Breach, 1973.

Russell, Bertrand. *Our Knowledge of the External World*. Chicago: Open Court Publishing Co., 1914.

Saṃyutta Nikāya, edited by Leon Feer, PTS. London: Luzac & Co., 1960. Translated by C. A. F. Rhys Davids and F. L. Woodward as *Book of Kindred Sayings*, PTS. London: Luzac & Co., 1952.

Sangharakshita, Bhikkhu. "The Centrality of Man," in *World Buddhism*. Vesak, 1967.

Sarathchandra, E. R. *Buddhist Psychology of Perception*. Colombo: Ceylon Univ. Press, 1958.

Sarkisyanz, Emmanuel. *The Buddhist Background of the Burmese Revolution*. The Hague: Martinus Nijhoff, 1965.

Sayre, Kenneth. *Cybernetics and the Philosophy of Mind*. Atlantic Highlands, N.J.: Humanities Press, 1976.

Schumacher, E. F. *Small is Beautiful: Economics as if People Mattered*. New York: Harper & Row, 1975.

Seed, John, Pat Fleming, Joanna Macy, and Arne Naess. *Thinking Like a Mountain: Towards a Council of All Beings*. Philadelphia: New Society Publishers, 1988.

Simon, Herbert A. "The Organization of Complex Systems." Pattee, 1973.

SNCC. *Freedom in the Air*. A Documentary on Albany, Georgia 1961–1962. Student Non-Violent Coordinating Committee, 135 Auburn Ave. N.E., Atlanta, GA.

Stcherbatsky, Theodor. *Buddhist Logic*. 'S-Gravenhage: Mouton & Co., 1958.

———. *The Central Conception of Buddhism*. Calcutta: Susil Gupta Ltd., 1956.

———. *The Conception of Buddhist Nirvana*. Varanasi: Bharatiya Vidya Prakashan, 1968.

Stewart, Ian. *Does God Play Dice? The Mathematics of Chaos*. Oxford: Basil Blackwell, 1989.

Streng, Frederick. "Reflections on the Attention Given to Mental Constructions in the Indian Buddhist Analysis of Causality." *Philosophy East and West* XXV, 1 (Jan. 1975).

Stryk, Lucien. *World of the Buddha*. New York: Doubleday Anchor, 1968.

Sutta Nipāta, edited and translated by R. Chalmers as *Buddha's Teachings*, Harvard Oriental Series, vol. 37, Cambridge, Mass., Harvard Univ. Press, 1932.

Thayer, Lee. "Communication—*Sine Qua Non* of the Behavioral Sciences," in *Vistas in Science*. Univ. of New Mexico Press, 1968.

Thomas, E. F. *The History of Buddhist Thought.* New York: Barnes and Noble, 1971.

Udāna, translated by F. L. Woodward, SBB, Vol. VIII. London, 1935.

Upaniṣads, The Thirteen Principle, translated by R. E. Hume. Oxford Univ. Press, 1877.

Varela, Francisco, and Ernst von Glasersfeld. "Problems of Knowledge and Cognizing Organisms." *SGSR/AAAS Proceedings,* 1977.

———— and Joseph Goguen. "Systems and Distinctions: Duality and Complementarity." IJGS, 1978.

Vinaya, translated by I. B. Horner, SBB, Vols. 10, 11, 13, 14, 20, 25. London: H. Milford, Oxford, 1938–66.

Warder, A. K. *Indian Buddhism.* Delhi: Motilal Banarsidass, 1970.

Weiss, Paul A. "The Living System: Determinism Stratified." in Koestler, Arthur, editor. *Beyond Reductionism: New Perspectives in the Life Sciences,* The Alpbach Symposium. London: Hutchinson & Co., 1969.

Whyte, Lancelot L. "The Structural Hierarchy in Organisms," in Gray, William and N. Rizzo. *Unity in Diversity.* New York: Gordon and Breach, 1973.

Wiener, Norbert. *The Human Use of Human Beings: Cybernetics and Society.* New York: Avon Books, 1967.

Wolff, C. G. *A Feast of Words: The Triumph of Edith Wharton.* Oxford Univ. Press, 1977, quoted *New York Times,* May 7, 1977.

Yeats, W. B. *A Vision.* New York: Macmillan & Co., 1937.

Index

39456511R00145

Made in the USA
Lexington, KY
24 February 2015